# FROM HARLEM TO THE RHINE

*ARGONNE — VIENNE-la-VILLE bombardé*

6 Division                          Le 16 Mai 1918
                    Ordre nº 697

        Le Général le Gallais Cdt la 16e D I
cite à l'ordre de la Division les militaires
du 369e R.I.U.S

1º Johnson Henry nº mle 103348 soldat à la Cie C :
"Se trouvant en sentinelle double de nuit et ayant été
assailli par un groupe d'une douzaine d'allemands en a
mis un hors de combat à coups de fusil et blessé grièvement
deux autres à coups de couteau. Bien qu'ayant reçu 3 blessures
par balles de revolver et par grenades dès le début de l'action, a
été au secours de son camarade blessé qui allait être emporté
par l'ennemi et a continué la lutte jusqu'à la mise en fuite des
allemands". A donné un magnifique exemple de courage et d'énergie

2º Roberts Needham nº mle 103369, soldat à la Cie C :
        "Étant en sentinelle double de nuit, assailli et blessé
grièvement à la jambe par un groupe d'allemands, a
continué à lutter à coups de grenades bien que tombé
à terre, jusqu'à la mise en fuite de l'ennemi. Bon
et brave soldat."

        Le général a demandé que la citation du soldat
        Johnson soit transformée en citation à l'ordre de l'Armée
2A. Le Chef d'État Major,        Le général Cdt la 16e D. I
                                          le Gallais

HENRY JOHNSON                     NEEDHAM ROBERTS
HEROES OF THE BATTLE OF HENRY JOHNSON
FIRST AMERICAN PRIVATES IN THE ARMY OF FRANCE
TO RECEIVE THE CROIX DE GUERRE
FOR TRANSLATION OF CITATION SEE APPENDIX.

# FROM HARLEM TO THE RHINE

### THE STORY OF

## *New York's Colored Volunteers*

BY

## Arthur W. Little

COVICI · FRIEDE · *PUBLISHERS*

NEW YORK

TYPOGRAPHY BY ROBERT JOSEPHY
MANUFACTURED IN THE UNITED STATES OF AMERICA
BY J. J. LITTLE AND IVES COMPANY, NEW YORK

# DEDICATED

*To the 367 "Men of Bronze" who sleep today
in France the long sleep of eternity; and to
their comrades, and mine, who volunteered in
1917 for the duration of the War under oath*

TO

"PRESERVE, PROTECT AND DEFEND"

THE CONSTITUTION OF THE UNITED STATES

*It was my privilege to serve in the World War with the 15th New York Volunteer Infantry (Colored), known as Harlem's Hell Fighters.*

*In my service as Captain of a company, Adjutant of the Regiment and Major of a battalion, I saw the Regiment grow from but little more than an idea to be one of the great fighting units of a shock division of Gouraud's Fourth Army of France.*

*Naturally the experiences we went through made a deep impression; deeper undoubtedly because I was far beyond the draft age and saw it all from an angle much different from that of younger men.*

*If this story rambles and becomes emotional in spots put it down to the fact that it is the story of a man's rare privilege of living his red-blooded days through—for a second time.*

*It is all true, however, and I am glad to add it to the sagas of a race that I have learned to understand and respect.*

ARTHUR W. LITTLE

*Written between June 1919 and August 1920 from notes from my war diary.* A. W. L.

# CHRONOLOGY OF THE 15TH INFANTRY (COLORED) N. G., N. Y. 369TH U. S. INFANTRY

| | |
|---|---|
| JUNE 2, 1913 | Bill authorizing Regiment signed by Gov. Sulzer. |
| JUNE 16, 1916 | Gov. Whitman appointed William Hayward, Colonel, and ordered Regiment formed. |
| APRIL 8, 1917 | Federal recognition of Regiment as unit of National Guard. |
| JULY 15, 1917 | Responded to the call of the President. |
| JULY 25, 1917 | Mustered into United States service. |
| AUGUST 5, 1917 | Drafted with entire National Guard into United States Army. |
| NOVEMBER 12, 1917 | Sailed for France. |
| DECEMBER 27, 1917 | Landed in France (wrecked three times en route). |
| APRIL 9, 1918 | Commenced fighting (Secteur Main de Massiges, Champagne District). |
| NOVEMBER 20, 1918 | "First to the Rhine." |
| DECEMBER 13, 1918 | Collective citation for Regiment and Croix de Guerre pinned to colors. |
| FEBRUARY 12, 1919 | Home again. |
| FEBRUARY 17, 1919 | Welcome Home Parade. |
| FEBRUARY 28, 1919 | Mustered out of service. |

*The illustrations are, with the exception of ten, from the official negatives of the Signal Corps, U. S. Army. Acknowledgment is made of the material assistance of Mr. Frank H. Cole, 611 Bangs Ave., Asbury Park, N. J., in securing them.*

*The six trench pictures signed "Gouraud" are from negatives made by the French. Gen. Gouraud's letter transmitting these will be found in the Appendix.*

# FOREWORD

IN the days preceding the World War, or rather of the active participation of the United States in it, and during the early days of the war, there existed a general speculation, and there were expressed many opinions, as to the part to be played in the war by the colored men of our country—the negroes of America.

It was generally agreed that our enormous colored population must be utilized in our military establishments; but by no means was it generally agreed that it would be the part of wisdom to attempt to make of colored men soldiers of combat units.

Many so-called military experts and many leaders in the organization of public opinion expressed themselves to the effect that colored soldiers should be used exclusively as labor troops—engineer regiments, stevedore regiments, or bakery companies.

A leader of a minority of thought in this field was found in the person of a young Nebraskan-New Yorker named William Hayward. William Hayward at the time of our declaration of war with Germany, was about forty years of age. He was possessed of a vision, however, and of an imagination in matters promising of wide public interest and importance, which would have done credit to a man of half again his years. And he was possessed of these valuable elements of leadership through no mere chance of fate.

The son of U. S. Senator Monroe L. Hayward, of Nebraska, he had been Colonel of the 2nd Regiment of Infantry, Nebraska National Guard. He had been a judge. In 1908 he was in charge of Western Headquarters of the Republican National Committee. In 1910 he moved to New York and opened a law office. 1913 saw him an Assistant to District Attorney Charles S. Whitman. In 1914 and 1916 he managed the Whitman campaigns for Governor. In time he became Public Service Commissioner.

During Gov. Whitman's second term Col. Hayward was invited to organize a regiment of colored infantry for the National Guard of New York.

So the 15th Infantry began with one member only—the Colonel commanding.

In telling my story of the regiment I shall be compelled, as a faithful historian, to paint word pictures which are bound to appeal to the reader's sense of the ridiculous. By no means were all of the comic incidents attributable to the enlisted strength of the regiment, to the colored men. In some of the most grotesque situations the jokes were on the officers.

In emphasizing the humble beginning of the 15th Regiment, in recognizing frankly the military ignorance and lack of up-to-date experience of all hands, from Colonel to cook, I have no purpose of inviting any appraisement of disparagement for the organization growing out of such well-nigh impossible early days.

Upon the contrary, it is my desire to make a truthful picture of such extremes of ignorance and of knowledge, of military utter uselessness and of military efficiency, as will make my readers feel, as I feel, that the record of this regiment, valued without racial prejudice, constitutes one of the very great constructive developments of the colored group in its long and discouraging climb in worldly estate, from the day of Emancipation. Moreover, I feel that that record should find interpretations of gratitude, and of recognition of eligibility, for colored men for service in positions of responsibility, trust, and dignity hitherto denied them.

With such accomplishment, or with even a marked step towards such accomplishment, the leader, William Hayward, who fought at times almost single-handed in organizing his regiment, in getting it sent overseas among the very first of all combat units, and in securing for it its chance to fight in the front line trenches at so early a period of America's participation in the war as to win distinction for every member of the regiment, and for the colored race at large—that leader, if he never should give any other service to his country, would be entitled to a splendid place for his name in the history of his country. It is a part of my purpose, in writing of these reminiscences, to register my feeling that that place in national history should be incubated in the hearts of the men and women of the colored group of America.

It is probable that, of all the humorous anecdotes of the American Army in the World War, almost half of them are attributed to the colored soldiers. Many of the funny things told never happened; but a great number did happen. I served with the regiment almost two years. I am reporting only incidents in which I had personal participation. During all that period there was scarcely a day which did not present some incident for a good laugh. But let no man, on account of that record, put down the colored man in his mind as a comic soldier. A regiment of colored men, properly organized and properly officered, is a great regiment—for fighting or for any duty.

I have read in the statistics of our regiment that we were under fire 191 days; that we lost in battle, killed and wounded, about 1,500 men; that we lost in battle during the offensive of the Meuse-Argonne, September 25, 1918, to October 6, 1918, about 1,100 men; that we never lost a prisoner; that we never lost a foot of ground in defensive operations; that in offensive operations we took every objective but one, and in that one the fault lay with a failure of artillery support.

Of my own knowledge I can testify that the impression so frequently expressed to the effect that the colored man cannot or will not stand physical hardship, is just buncombe.

If our men believed that going without food was unavoidable, they would never complain of hunger. If our men were satisfied that new shoes were unavailable for issue they would march all day (and cheerfully) with their bare feet touching the ground through the broken soles of their old shoes.

When our men realized that their officers were doing everything possible in trying to draw new blankets for the regiment, after most of our old blankets had been lost in the Champagne (or Meuse-Argonne) offensive of September and October, the men went into the trenches of the Vosges Mountains (3,000 to 4,000 feet above the level of the sea) and did their tricks of sector guard duty in the cold of that high altitude during the months of October and November, with an average of about one blanket to each four men—and they laughed to keep warm.

Our men sang while they marched; they sang while they cooked; they sang while they washed their clothes and while they dug their ditches; and, as for sentiment, their lives were just one long, continuous, and never-ending picture of love of home and of country.

# CONTENTS

xiv

# LIST OF ILLUSTRATIONS

*The photograph on the wrapper shows our Regiment, in full French equipment, being inspected just before going into the front line. That on the inside of the covers is of our Welcome Home parade, which gave America its first view of the French phalanx formation.*

# HUMBLE BEGINNINGS

AFTER war was declared, April 6, 1917, I made strenuous efforts to get into the service. After many discouraging re-buffs, it was General O'Ryan who suggested taking advantage of my long militia service. He urged me to offer myself to Col. Hayward. This I did. On April 13 I' was officially advised I had been taken from the Reserve List, detailed for active service with the 15th Infantry, and assigned as Captain commanding Co. F of that Regiment.

I arranged by telephone to report that evening to the Commander of the 2nd Battalion, at the armory, 191 Harrison Avenue, Brooklyn. The "armory" was a dilapidated old dance hall and beer garden. Upon the ground floor was an assembly hall about thirty-five feet wide by about sixty feet long. Adjoining this room and separated from it by pillars was another hall about half as large. There was still another assembly hall about fifty feet long by about fifteen feet wide. There was an entrance hall with doors opening almost flush upon the street. There was a small room used by the armorer for stores, which served also as a passage room between the entrance hall and the office. The office was a room of about twenty feet by thirty feet, and there was adjoining a private office for the major, about five feet by ten feet. Upon the second story there were four rooms, fitted with lockers of a primitive type, used as company rooms and a small chamber used as a store room. The furniture of the office consisted of two roll top desks, half a dozen chairs, a file cabinet, a typewriting machine on a table, and two long benches. In the private office was a roll top desk for the battalion commander and a side table for the adjutant with a chair for each.

As I entered the building at about 9 P. M., I had to elbow my way through a good-natured mob of colored men and women. A few men were in olive drab uniforms. No drills were being conducted, and no formations were in progress. I worked my way into the office and was delighted to recognize in the major commanding an old schoolmate, Monson Morris.

The room was half filled with candidates for enlistment in various degrees of nudity. There was no surgeon present, and so Morris himself was examining the recruits as to their physical fitness to serve. A lieutenant was writing in upon an enlistment blank the findings which Major Morris called out in loud and unfaltering tones. I was astounded at the apparent knowledge of anatomy and physical condition being revealed by my old schoolmate:

"Eyesight—fifty-fifty!

"Hearing—normal!

"Color of eyes—brown!

"Color of hair—black!

"Complexion—dark!

"Height—sixty-six inches!

"Weight—one hundred and forty!

"Open your mouth—number three upper missing!

"Skin—clear!

"Sit down and cross your knees." (Cracks candidate with ruler)—"No reflex action!

"Feet—second degree broken arches!

"Pulse—normal!

"Heart—normal!

"Now cough!"

And so on, through a long list of items of examination.

Presently the major looked up and recognized me. Examinations were suspended. I had a greeting more than cordial, and I was introduced to a number of lieutenants—Eric Winston,

Dougal White, Whitney Kernochan, Seth MacClinton, "Buck" Waters, Frederick Frothingham, Richardson Pratt, Durant Rice, Harold Landon and Roger Whittlesey. The two last mentioned were the lieutenants of my company. We sat right down for a count of stock so to speak.

Neither Landon (who was first lieutenant) nor Whittlesey had had much experience at soldiering. I soon learned there was no property to take over; and that our records consisted merely of a bunch of duplicate enlistment blanks, a pocket roster of drill attendance, and an address book. Landon and Whittlesey had worked hard and cleverly. They had done all that could be done with the limited material and they were remarkably well acquainted with the characteristics of the sixty or so men that made up the company.

At about half past nine o'clock the company was assembled for drill. I told the lieutenants to go ahead with the drill and let me look on. I wanted to find out how much the men knew. It didn't take long. The realization of the situation aroused a sense of true appraisement of the terrific amount of work ahead of us—to turn this delightful, happy-go-lucky mob into an organization of soldiers. Also, it drove out of my heart every sense of embarrassment over my own shortcomings of professional knowledge. But the professional ignorance of the officers was overbalanced by their zeal, by their determination to master the situation. Every afternoon and every night until well past midnight that dilapidated old ramshackle of an armory was filled with these splendid young men, most of them graduates of Yale, Harvard or Princeton, and most of them also members of the Union Club, the University, the Racquet, the Knickerbocker, or the Metropolitan, young men, to whom "the easiest way" was open, but in whom there existed no spirit apart from the determination to do their bit, and without hope or expectation of reward except the fullness of their own hearts in the knowledge of a love of country faithfully served.

3

# RECRUITING

RECRUITING service enlisted the keenest interest of competition among the officers of the Brooklyn Battalion. Drilling was looked upon by almost all of the men, and by many of the officers, as a nuisance and a silly waste of time. Punctuality was honored completely in the breach. Discipline between the grades of privates, corporals, and sergeants was enforced more frequently by arguments based upon manual training than by inspiration of training based upon the manual of drill regulations.

One evening, at about eleven-thirty o'clock, I was seated before one corner of one of the two desks which served about a dozen officers, making up a report of the drill which had just been concluded. An excited sergeant rushed into the room, drew up before me and gasped:—"Oh, Suh, Cap'n, Suh! Giles is er-goin' ter kill der sentry at der do'. Day's er-farght'n wi' knarfe an' bay'net!" When I reached the corridor I found the space jammed with gesticulating and chattering humanity, all milling about a couple of central figures who stood glaring at each other, eye holding eye, and bodies poised in the stance which suggests preparation for combat. The smaller of the two men held a bayonetted rifle in the position of "charge." The other man, a giant of strength, six feet two in height, held an open knife in a position ready to thrust. The latter man was Giles.

By great activity of pushing and squirming I reached the centre of the mob before the affair had passed beyond the glaring stage. I raised my voice in command. I could scarcely hear myself. Not the slightest impression of my influence was apparent upon the mob. Then I clapped my hands vigorously between the faces of the combatants. Each man, in apparent astonishment at my action of applause, released his opponent's eyes and turned to stare at me. A hush came over the crowd assembled in the hallway.

Presently, I was enabled to make myself heard without the necessity of raising my voice above a natural tone.

"Giles, put your knife in your pocket! Sentry, unfix your bayonet! Both of you stand at attention! Every man here—*Atten*-TION!" The orders were not obeyed promptly; but they *were* obeyed. When the group was at attention I said to the sentry, "Now, tell me what was the matter."

"Well, Suh, Cap'n Suh, Ah-m on guard ter keep dese men from er-go'n' home in dare uniforms, and I dun tole Giles ter stop and he jes trared ter push bah me and he dun call me bad names."

"Now, Giles—what's your story?"

"Well, Suh, Cap'n Suh, de Major he dun guv me a pass fur ma uniform, cuz Ah brings in lots of recruits. Ah gits 'em better ef Ah has my uniform on. An' dis here li'l shrimp saiz ter me when Ah's er-go'n' out de do'—'Halt dere, ye big black so and so! Ah'se on guard here and you all cain't go out wid dat uniform.' And so I saiz ter him, Suh, Cap'n Suh, 'Ever-ting you saiz Ah am—yoo is double—even de part against yoo mudder. Now, stan' out er ma way, you li'l flea of a so-and-so—cuz Ah'm er-goin' t'roo and ef yoo saiz anyt'ing mo' ter me Ah'll cut yoo heart out.'"

By brief cross examination the version of Giles was verified by the sentry. It was admitted by Giles that he had made no tender of his pass, and that he had made no mention of it. I then proceeded to explain to the sentry and, of course, to the crowd that a sentinel on guard is the monarch of his post, answerable only to the officers and non-commissioned officers of his guard, the officer of the day, and the commanding officer of the camp or post. I advised Giles of his error in offering disobedience to the sentinel, and in failing to tender his pass, and in using con-

5

temptuous language to a sentinel on post. Also, of course, I pointed out the gross offense of threatening the sentinel with violence. I advised that the sentinel was wrong in using violent and disrespectful language in the discharge of his duty, but advised further that the regulations were clear in their instructions covering such a case—that it was the duty of every soldier to obey every legal order or command coming to him from an officer or non-commissioned officer or sentinel on post, even though the order was obviously an order issued with a purpose of personal annoyance, in a spirit of unfairness or in bad judgment of the requirements of a situation. I explained that the order must be obeyed first, and the protest or complaint made afterwards—through channels leading to the superiors of the soldier or officer to be complained of. Then I told the men that we were an organization in course of training, and that such points as I had explained were a part of the training—so, there would be no disciplinary action taken. I asked all hands present if they understood. They answered in chorus that they did. Then I asked Giles and the sentinel to shake hands and be friends. That proposition required considerable argument; but it was finally accomplished. Then I shook hands with each of the principals, and thanked them for their patriotic spirit in burying their private quarrels for the good of the service. And the giant Giles, who had in him the makings of a great outlaw, spoke to me with emotion, and told me that he would always do anything that I asked him to do, and that I could trust him.

I went home that night tired, but happy in the belief that over there in Brooklyn, in our 2nd Battalion, we were making progress. I could see the dawn of what is known in the army as the subconscious spirit of obedience—the spirit which was later to make the American doughboy the despair of the German soldier.

6

# AT THE STATE CAMP NEAR PEEKSKILL

*May 13–May 30, 1917*

IN its rumor-absorbing capacity, the 15th Infantry N. G., N. Y., achieved its full soldier estate at a very early stage in its career. Early in the second week of May, 1917, one of the rumors upon which we had been feeding took material form in the appearance of an order for the regiment to go into camp at the state reservation near Peekskill, N. Y., for two weeks. The order was hailed with delight. It would give our regiment an opportunity not only for intensive drill training and for rifle practice; but it would give it a look at itself. Getting ready for that tour of duty was one of the most exhausting bits of work that the officers of the regiment ever had to perform.

There were but a few days for preparation. During those days and nights we had to draw and distribute uniforms for about seventy-five percent of our strength. Also, we drew, or "borrowed," from the state ordnance supplies almost a thousand rifles. We had had, as I recollect, about 250 rifles for the entire regiment prior to the time of our being ordered to camp. About twenty-five percent of all the rifles had bayonets, and about the same proportion of our men were equipped with cartridge belts and bayonet scabbards. In order to keep up appearances when we paraded before the public, the men upon the flanks of squads and in the front ranks of leading platoons were given these belts to wear. The men on the interiors of formations, who didn't show so much, went without belts. In camp we had the men detailed for guard wear the belts and carry the bayonets. Trying to keep an accurate record of the daily whereabouts of belts and bayonets helped to make things pleasant for company officers.

7

When the order for camp came, soldier instinct wouldn't admit of its being interpreted according to the simple meaning of its words. The colored population of Brooklyn read into the order a mysterious mission upon which its sons, husbands, brothers and sweethearts were to embark. The armory and the streets near the armory were the scenes of great demonstrations of emotional patriotic expression, and of emotional fears. Many men who had been unmoved by the recruiting speeches of our best spellbinders responded with a rush to the rumor that the 15th Regiment was called out—that the colored Infantry was to be the first to go. The dominant agitation of this large class of citizens was—"Am Ah in tahm?" and "When kin Ah git mah uniform?" Then, too, there was the other class of patriot uncovered. They usually let their women folks do the talking.

"Dis boy is on'y fifteen y'ars ol'. He lied when he 'listed and tole yoo all he wus eighteen. Doan' take mah bebby erway ter war ter git shot!" "Mah man is mah on'y suppo't. Ef yoo all takes him erway me and mah fo' chillen will stave, cuz I cain't do no washin' now 'till after mah bebby is bone."

Then there were brave women who wanted their men to go and do their bits, but who wanted to cry a little with the captain over the farewell. And there were the ones who wanted the captain to be sure that their boys shouldn't get their feet wet because they had recently had bad colds. And there were the ones who wanted the captain to make their men be sure to send their pay home. And there were the wise old fathers with wink of eye and undertone of voice who understood, of course, all about this Peekskill Camp talk, but would the captain just tell them in confidence what steamer the regiment was sailing on, and what time of day it was to start. And there was one expectant young mother who was ready to register her vote upon marriage being a failure. This young woman was the daughter of well-to-do parents. Her husband was too good looking for her peace of mind, and he contributed nothing to her support, devoting much of his time and all of his earnings to another. This young wife made quite

8

an impression upon my mind. She betrayed no signs of hysteria, or even of excitement. She shed no tears. She introduced herself, and stood before me in the beautiful, sweet dignity of her condition and said:

"Captain Little, my husband (naming him) will try to beg off by telling you that he is my sole support and that I am soon to have a baby. I expect my baby to be born next week and I shall love it and try to bring it up to be a good man or woman; but its father, my husband, is a bad man. He is living right now with another woman. He contributes nothing to my support. My father is rich and I am well provided for by my father. My husband is afraid to go. Don't let him off upon the grounds of dependency. All these people crowding about you here are asking favors of you. I have a favor to ask, too. I ask you to try to make this man of mine into a good soldier; and when you go into battle put him in the front line. Then perhaps he will win fame or death, and my baby, in either case, will be able to speak with pride of its father."

On Sunday morning May 13th, we started for Peekskill. Our 2nd Battalion left the Brooklyn armory at about half past eight. We travelled by elevated railroad train across the Brooklyn Bridge and up Third Avenue. At Forty-Second Street we detrained, and marched to Park Avenue where we formed in line between Forty-Fifth and Fiftieth Streets. There we waited to be joined by the 1st and 3rd Battalions, the Machine Gun Company and the Band, which had to come down from the Harlem armory at 132nd Street and Seventh Avenue. There was delay and confusion.

At about half past twelve, midday, we marched up Fifth Avenue. The march was made in the simplest of formations. Many of our men had had no drilling at all; none had had much drilling. We took no more chances of disaster, by passing from one formation to another, than were absolutely unavoidable. Our men, however, were natural born marchers and cadence observers. With a band playing, or with spectators cheering, they just

9

couldn't be held from keeping step. That bright, sunny, Sunday morning we had both—the playing band and the cheering spectators. The churches had just concluded their services; and the crowds, inspired by sermons of patriotic appeal, were strolling along New York's wonderful promenade avenue as our picturesque organization swung up the line, to the brass toned expression of *Onward Christian Soldiers.*

As I heard those roars of applause, trying to drown out Jim Europe's bandsmen at the head of the column, I forgot all about the mis-fit and incomplete uniforms hidden through the ranks of my company, I forgot all about the ignorance and other weaknesses of our command, I forgot that we were merely going to a state training camp for drill and for rifle practice, forgot that we were, as some newspaper cynic had said, merely a glorified organization of *Mulligan Guards,* and I felt, as I am sure twelve hundred other men of that column felt that morning, that *we were* Christian and American soldiers marching on to war.

At Fifty-Seventh Street we turned West, and made our way by the most favorable route to the New York Central freight yards running along the river front. At about Sixtieth Street we found our special trains waiting. But here, also, we found waiting a wonderful band of ladies, armed with baskets and pots, filled with sandwiches and steaming coffee and packages of chocolate and cigarettes. We had had very early and very sketchy breakfasts. No train ration had been provided. Our first meal at Peekskill was (as we were later to discover) to be served between ten thirty that evening and midnight. If it had not been for those angels in Red Cross Canteen Service uniform, the first day in the field of the 15th Heavy Foot would have developed some pretty bad cases of faintness. We hadn't learned as much about roughing it up to that time as we learned later.

It was during the march up Fifth Avenue, that morning, that Major Dayton's horse won his name. The horse was restive, and, upon the slippery pavement, difficult to control. So a couple of orderlies laid quieting hands upon the bridle and marched, one

10

upon either side of the horse's head. Our men, ever ready to see a joke or to make one, and being well versed in the language of the Bible and the hymnal, promptly named Major Dayton's horse *"Kindly Light."* The Major, being blessed with a sense of humor of that delightful quality that admits of appreciation of a joke even when upon oneself, was the first to accept the name for his steed, and for months one of the favorite stories the regiment told to visitors was the story of how the Major rode in safety up the Avenue at the head of his Battalion, with two of his faithful attendants detailed to *"Lead Kindly Light."*

Arrived, at about three o'clock in the afternoon, at the great camping plain upon a bluff overlooking the Hudson River two miles north of the city of Peekskill, we worked, under conditions of confusion and imperfect organization, all through the afternoon and evening, making camp. Only a small percentage of our men had ever made a military camp. Most of our officers had had experience as enlisted men but not as officers. There is considerable difference between driving a peg, digging a hole, or pulling on a rope when told to do so and planning for seventy-five or eighty men to drive pegs, dig holes and pull on ropes, all at the same time, and in such a manner as to create a village of tentage and drains along lines of symmetry.

We had no regimental or company equipment for messing. The state authorities met the emergency by sending to Peekskill a lot of tin dishes and other utensils and turning over to our use the great messing pavilion and permanent kitchen built many years ago when soldiers at the state camp of instruction were fed by a caterer under contract.

A special kitchen detail was put to work in these pavilions to provide for a regimental mess for the entire command of some twelve hundred officers and men. If the organization of this special unit had been perfected so quickly, and if the kitchen ranges, long unused, had been gotten into working order so promptly as to have admitted of an orderly, served cooked meal that first night in camp, it seems to me that the accomplishment would have ranked as a miracle. No miracle occurred. In fact, not much of anything occurred in the messing line, until after half past ten in the evening. About that time everybody seemed to feel that the work of getting up shelters had reached a proper resting point, and a rumor was passed along to the effect that supper was served in the mess hall. It is possible, even, that an order to that effect was published. And it is not impossible that a bugler may have sounded "mess call." It would have made no difference. Ninety percent of the men wouldn't have known *Mess Call* from *Retreat* or from *Reveille;* but an aching void under the belt (or under the place where belts would have been worn had we had belts) made every man ready to accept the rumor as official.

A stampede occurred and the mess hall was filled in a twinkling with a pushing, shouting, hungry mob. There were no regular lights. A few officers carried lanterns, and a very few candles had been found and placed upon the tables.

An attempt to create order and to seat the men by companies, died at birth. A small quantity of cooked food disappeared quickly under the rule of first come first served; and then, with the advertised knowledge that there was no more food ready to serve, pandemonium broke loose.

The officers formed patrols like those of police reserves, which appear suddenly upon the scenes of popular demonstrations upon Fifth Avenue and Broadway, to bring order out of disorder. Presently we got two great lines formed, and in blessed comparative silence the men passed along in front of a counter and received an issue of cold canned salmon, beans, and bread, which, while not exactly a hot supper, was, as Sam Weller said, "Wery cheap and wery filling for the price."

Colonel Hayward stood behind that counter, and, almost with his own hands, issued the twelve hundred rations that sent our men to bed well and happy.

For eighteen days our men worked as few soldiers had ever before had to work in a mere camp of instruction. Every hour of

au 369ᵉ National Guard et à son chef
le Général Little en souvenir des jours
héroïques de 1918, où nous avons combattu
ensemble, et comment !

18 février 1923        Gouraud

TO THE 369TH NATIONAL GUARD, AND TO ITS CHIEF GENERAL LITTLE, IN
MEMORY OF THE HEROIC DAYS WHEN WE FOUGHT TOGETHER AND WON.

COL. HAYWARD

JAMES MONTGOMERY FLAGG

COL. WILLIAM HAYWARD
COMMANDING OFFICER OF THE REGIMENT
"FOR THE DURATION OF THE WAR"

daylight was devoted to drill and to rifle practice. We drilled and shot, rain or shine. As soon as darkness interfered with formation work of troops the officers assembled for a so-called "school." This school consisted of a roll call by company when each captain was invited to express his opinion as to how the men were enjoying the routine. Each captain made a point of reporting his company in the highest possible condition of morale. Each field officer was invited at these evening meetings to "say something." Also, each inspector-instructor from other organizations of the National Guard was given an opportunity to speak. All of this preliminary work was, ordinarily, covered within a half hour.

The officers of the 15th New York did wonderful things during those eighteen days at Peekskill. Our men, by the time we returned to our city, could drill in close order formations; and they could drill as well as any regiment in the New York Guard. They knew the important names of the many parts of the service rifle. They knew the functions of those parts. They could take their rifles apart and put them together again. They knew the duty of a sentinel on post upon Interior Guard duty, and could perform such duty in most exacting fashion. Every man had shot for the standard qualification score of the U. S. Rifle Association, over every range from 100 yards to 600 yards, including both deliberate and rapid fire. More than half of the men of the regiment and, I believe, all of the officers, had passed the preliminary qualification.

Captain Fish, known all over the United States and a good part of Europe as "Ham Fish," was our best advertised officer. As Harvard's great football leader for two years, his name and picture had been published in every great newspaper in the country. He was the son of Hamilton Fish, formerly Speaker of the Assembly of New York State, a nephew of Nicholas Fish and of Stuyvesant Fish, the latter for years President of the Illinois Central Railroad and husband of Mrs. Stuyvesant Fish, one of the most brilliant leaders of Society ever known to New York

13

City. He was a cousin of the celebrated "Ham Fish" of Roosevelt's Rough Riders, who gave his life for his country in the first land battle of our war with Spain, in Las Guasimas in June, 1898. He was a great-grandson of Secretary of State Hamilton Fish, one of the most distinguished ministers of President Grant's cabinet.

It was at the Peekskill Camp that I first met First Lieutenant James Reese Europe, the colored man who became famous on two continents as a band leader of first quality.

At Peekskill our regiment achieved its first nick-name. It was dubbed *The Saluting Fifteenth*. This name was intended as a compliment, and it came from three very experienced officers of the Twelfth who were sent to our regiment to serve as Inspector-Instructors during our Peekskill encampment. Our men accepted the principle of a salute to officers more readily than any other principle of a soldier's training. They seemed to love to salute. They would walk out of their way to approach officers so as to find an excuse for a salute; and for an officer to walk down the main avenue of camp became a pilgrimage of positive arm exhaustion, through the necessity of returning the salutes of the many men always to be found at the heads of company streets ready to render honors. A large proportion of our men were Pullman porters and waiters, hotel waiters, railroad red caps, and apartment house and theatre doormen. These men, through force of habit, adopted a style of military salute all their own. They would first raise the right hand smartly to the visor of the cap over the right eye, as provided by regulations, but then they would bow very low in the most approved style of cordiality of a Saratoga Springs hotel head waiter, and murmur, "Mawnin' Suh—mawnin'!"

One of our officers was so impressed with this style of salute that he invited his best girl to come and see him upon the afternoon that he was to be Officer of the Day. When the young lady arrived, the officer suggested that they take a walk through the camp, and he anticipated with delight the impression to be made by the many salutes to be rendered in his honor. The first man approached was one of the officer's own men—a member of the guard, and to the disgust of the officer, no salute of any kind was rendered.

"Well," demanded the Officer of the Day, "don't you salute officers in this regiment any longer?"

"Whah yassuh, Cap'n suh," answered the sentinel, "Ah salutes ev'ry officer in dis regiment."

"Well, you didn't salute me!"

"Whah, Suh Cap'n Suh, how kin yoo all say dat, Suh? Doan' yoo remember, Suh? Ah saluted yoo dis mawnin'!"

Our first evening parade presented some most astonishing features. It was functioned upon the evening of our second day at Peekskill. The field and staff officers paraded on foot. Probably no greater proportion of all officers than twenty percent had ever before commanded troops in a ceremony; and of that experienced twenty percent group most of us were far from up to date. The band labored and brought forth noise. At times it brought forth forty-two noises; and between times, when the forty-two musicians stopped playing, the imprecations of Jim Europe could be heard from one end of the field to the other, striving by fantastic forms of speech to prevent his musicians from acquiring the malady known as swelled head.

On Sunday afternoon, May 20, I assumed my first responsibilities as Officer of the Day. It was a most fatiguing tour of service. Complete ignorance of guard duty was the professional equipment of every member of that guard.

At about two o'clock in the morning of May 21st during the progress of my rounds of inspection of the guard, I approached the so-called "Outpost," down upon the river bank at the boat landing, and at the foot of a long, steep flight of steps leading to the bluff and plain upon which the camp is built. A sentinel, walking his post along the road, made no challenge upon my approach. He met me in a fine spirit of democratic friendliness, and offered no objection to my coming close to him. After considerable instruction upon my part the sentinel called for the corporal of the guard. There was no response to the call. Several times the call was repeated without effect, and then I relieved the man from his post, and told him to go inside the guard tent and bring the corporal to me. Presently a very sleepy, much undressed man stood before me, and reported that he was the corporal. I instructed him to turn out the guard for inspection. That meant nothing in his life. Then I directed him to call the officer of the guard. After some delay a young lieutenant stumbled out of a small tent in the rear of the guard tent. The officer was hatless, coatless, and leggingless. His shoes were unlaced, and he was clutching his breeches with one hand while striving with the other hand to fasten buttons and belt. He carried no side arms. I directed him to turn out the guard for inspection. The officer and the corporal disappeared inside the big tent, from which there soon came sounds of sincere sleepers being aroused unwillingly. One by one the men lurched down the two or three steps from the platform upon which the tent was pitched and, in the vernacular of the soldier—"Fell in."

There was a beam, either of moonlight or of a road electric light, imperfectly illuminating one strip of an otherwise very dark area. In that strip the guard had formed. I stood back in the darkness of a deep shadow from the trees overhanging the road, and laughed quietly while watching the performance.

The little group looked for all the world like one of Frederick Remington's pictures of Cuban Reconcentradoes, published in *Harper's Weekly* during the years 1896 and 1898.

After a delay of more than twenty minutes, when the lieutenant had reported the guard as formed, I inspected it solemnly, and noted the irregularities of dress and equipment.

No man was completely dressed. Some were stripped right down to drawers and undershirt. A few were in bare feet, and most of the men were in stocking feet. After the inspection, I took the young officer for a walk down the road, and talked to him in a fatherly manner upon the subject of the seriousness of the offense.

As I continued my rounds, and stopped to test each sentinel upon his knowledge of the duties of a sentinel on post, I experienced many amusing incidents. One man was walking a post with the great broad drill plain in front of him. This man appeared to be afraid of the sound of his own voice. I worked hard, and after several trials I succeeded in getting the man to challenge in a loud tone of voice—"HALT! WHO IS THERE?" I explained that the object of challenging loudly was to make sure of the approaching party's halting at a safe distance, so as to admit of no rushing of the post.

The sentinel said "Yassuh" to all that I had to say. Then I instructed the man that, in the event of a party of more than one approaching the post, he should order one and one only to come forward for recognition. "Yassuh," was still the answer to my explanations. Then I said that we would try it. I pointed out over the plain, and said, "Now, just make believe that you see a little group of men scrambling up over the bluff!"

"Yassuh," said the soldier in the hoarse whisper of suppressed emotion.

"Well, aren't you going to challenge them?" I inquired.

"Yassuh."

"Well, go on and challenge, then!" I ordered.

Out ripped the challenge, in good loud tones, as the sentinel had just been taught:—"HALT! WHO'S DAR?"

"That's fine," I said. "Now the answer comes back,—'Friends with the countersign.'"

There was a long silence during which the soldier, in the rigid poise of "Charge," peered out into the darkness.

"Well," I said, "don't you understand?"

"Yassuh."

"Then what do you say?"

No answer.

"Don't you remember what I just told you that you must do

17

in a case like this? When the answer comes back, 'Friends,' or 'Friends with the countersign,' or 'Officers of the post,' you must call to the party again and say, 'Advance one to be recognized,' or 'Advance one with the countersign.' Can't you remember that?"

"Yassuh."

"Do you understand—can you say it?"

"Yassuh."

"Then why don't you say it?" I exclaimed, having no desire to go all through my lesson again.

"Well, Suh, Cap'n Suh," said the man, peering out towards the bluff, in most approved form of watchfulness, "well, Suh Cap'n, Suh, yoo all kin see dose men per'aps, an' sometahmes Ah t'nks Ah see dem and sometahmes Ah'm sure Ah doan'; but Ah kin tel' yoo one t'ing sho'. No matter wha'h dey calls back ter me when Ah stops 'em, no matter wha'h dey saiz—dey jes' ain't no frens er mahn."

One day at about noon, a young second lieutenant of our Brooklyn Battalion came to me and asked me if I would give him some advice. I nodded, and he told me, in a low tone of voice, that he had been junior officer of the guard two days before, and that he had finished his tour of duty and had been relieved the previous afternoon.

"That's thrilling," I said, "but quite customary. Why all the mystery, and what do you want to be advised about?"

"Well," the lieutenant said, "we were told to put out a special guard on the bridge over Annsville Creek, about a mile or more down the road, and I posted them down there yesterday morning, quite early, three men and a corporal."

"Well, what of it?" I inquired.

"Well, Sir, you see when it came time yesterday afternoon for our relief, I turned out the old guard without that special squad down at the bridge. I forgot them. The guard was dismissed, and I never thought a thing about those men on the bridge until a few minutes ago; and I guess they've been there

18

for about thirty hours, and I don't believe they've had anything to eat since noon yesterday. Now, the Officer of the Day doesn't know anything about it, and I'm afraid to tell him. As you're not officially concerned in this, and as you're so experienced in all these things, I thought I'd just ask your advice as to what I'd better do."

"I advise you to go out and bring your men in, as quickly as you can," was my answer.

"Oh, how splendid!" exclaimed the young man, "I never thought of that."

The stories of all these military absurdities are told, not with a view to holding either the individuals concerned or the organization up to ridicule, but with a purpose of making complete the development picture of this famous American volunteer regiment. The reader should bear in mind that about sixteen months after that Peekskill encampment, the regiment, so humbly born and so amateurishly nursed through its early stages, won a citation of a great General of France which took expression in the pinning of the *Croix de Guerre* to its colors. Also, more than a hundred and fifty individual or personal *Croix de Guerres* had been won during those intervening sixteen months; and fifteen or sixteen decorations of higher grade.

The 15th Heavy Foot was the self-made regiment of the American Army. It started without traditions, without education, and without friends. In all its career it never had even one thoroughly equipped first class officer as a member of the regiment. It never had an American Army instructor come from the outside to try to teach it anything, until about two months after the armistice had been signed, when, while waiting for a ship to take us home, in a preparatory embarkation camp at *Le Mons*, a young officer from a military school, who had never heard a hostile shot, lectured to the regiment upon the subject of the open sight in battle.

During the Peekskill encampment the soldier Giles, introduced in a former chapter, won his corporal's chevrons—and lost them again.

We were on our last week, when the check roll call at Taps, one night, informed me that six or eight of my men were out of camp.

In the morning they were lined up in front of me for company discipline; and on the extreme left of the line, with shamefaced mien, stood—Corporal Giles.

The men in turn mumbled their silly excuses, striving by ingenious stories to deceive me into believing them innocent of wrong-doing or at least of the intent of wrong-doing. At last came Giles's turn.

"Well Giles?" I said, and I looked at him with disappointment written all over my face.

"Suh Cap'n Suh," said Giles, "Ah dun et, an' ah knowed it wuz wrong w'en Ah dun et, and Ah wants ter git et. Ah'd lahk ter tel' yoo dat Ah'm sorry, but ef Ah doo Ah'm afeard yoo'll all t'ink Ah'm er-tryin' ter git orf; an' Ah'm not. Ah wants ter git et. Ah wants yoo ter take mah Co'p'al's strahpes erway, cuz Ah dun et, an' Ah knowed it wuz wrong. But Suh Cap'n Suh, Ah'd lahk ter git er chance ter git 'em back ergin, after Ah've behaved mahse'f some mo'."

A day or two later Giles stood before me again. This time his face was cheerful and bright with eagerness.

"Suh Cap'n Suh, der Furst Sargen' guv me purmission ter speak ter der Cap'n."

I asked Giles what he wanted to say; and he answered that he'd like to be detailed to the provost squad. He explained that he knew all the places where the men could get out of camp in running the guard. He explained that it had cost him his corporal's stripes to learn these fine points, and that, as he had determined not to use his knowledge any more in illicit pleasures, he would like to turn his knowledge to orderly account by putting a stop to other men's running of the guard. Giles got his appointment; and he made good.

The day before we left Peekskill the men received their State pay in individual checks. Colonel Hayward had gone to considerable pains to provide enough currency to admit of cashing these checks for the men. To some readers the difference between $22.50 in cash and $22.50 in a check may not mean much by way of convenience or inconvenience; but to many of our men it meant the difference between hunger and food. In the early days of the building of the regiment, Colonel Hayward scarcely ever overlooked a little proof of thoughtfulness of that kind for the comfort of his men.

# MEMORIAL DAY, 1917

ON Memorial Day, May 30th, 1917, we broke camp very early and took train to New York. At nine o'clock we joined the column of National Guard organizations to parade up Riverside Drive. Our eighteen days of camp life had hardened us, and given us the snap of experienced soldiers; or, so it had made us appear, in contrast to the other regiments parading that day, with large percentages of new recruits swelling their ranks. Our uniform was that of field service with olive drab shirts and blanket rolls slung from left shoulder to right thigh.

New York gave us a wild reception that morning, and our men marched beautifully. All through our days in France, some days of great discouragement, of hardship, of hunger, cold, and fatigue, and some days of great danger, our men would spur themselves to efficiency by talking about the march up Fifth Avenue and Lenox Avenue when we should get home after the war.

It was our Decoration Day parade of 1917, and the generous reception given us by the citizens of New York on that day, that enabled our men to visualize in some degree the greater parade to come. At last the Fifteenth had a tradition to support. To the majority of its members, officers and men, it had a reputation to maintain in the face of the enemy more precious than the lives to be given or risked in its service.

# V

## THE CALL OF THE PRESIDENT
### *July 15, 1917*

U P to this time I was serving with the 15th on assignment from the Reserve List. To be mustered in to the U. S. Army I must be an actual, active member of the National Guard. That meant re-enlistment. Colonel Hayward agreed to nominate me for captain if I would enlist in the ranks. So I enlisted as a private in the 7th Regiment. July 13th I received my commission and took the oath.

Upon Sunday morning July 15th, 1917, at 8 o'clock, the officers and men of the 2nd Battalion, 15th N. Y. Infantry N. G., were ordered to report—to be mustered in to the U. S. Army.

What a hectic, mussy day it was!

Of course the men did not report on time. That is, not many of them. The eight o'clock roll call was nothing but an idea. By noon, however, we had better than 80 percent present. Lists of absentees were made up and arranged according to districts; and provost squads were sent out under officers, to get the delinquents. For out of town absentees we used the telephone and the police of the respective localities.

I was Officer of the Day—in addition to my other duties.

Our armory was overcrowded. In addition to housing nearly six hundred men equipped for heavy marching order, we were trying to run a mess, with improvised cook-stoves. Our army field ranges were to be delivered to us upon our arrival at Camp Whitman the following day.

The streets about the armory were crowded with relatives and friends of the men and with sightseers. We had sentinels at the doors of the armory and at the corners of the streets bounding

23

the armory block. The men who could be trusted to behave themselves were permitted the freedom of the street directly in front of the armory, but within the line of outer sentinels. Relatives of the men were permitted inside the lines—to visit with the soldier men of their families. Men of well established reliability were given passes for a few hours—to go to their homes or the homes of their sweethearts.

The battalion was now, however, more than twice as large as it had been in May, and the spirit of war excitement was two months further advanced. The lot of company commanders, that day, was no sinecure. During the afternoon and evening, drunkenness commenced to make itself known. The cases were not numerous in respect to a proportion related to the whole strength of the command; but some of the cases were of marked degree. We had established a small inner room upon the upper story of the armory as a guard house, and there prisoners were put, temporarily, for safe keeping. The police station was a couple of blocks away; and the captain of the precinct gave us permission to use some of his cells for our very disorderly cases, without the necessity of subjecting the men to the formality of civil arrest, with Police Court trials to follow. The police patrol wagon ran a fairly regular route between the armory and the station house.

At about three o'clock in the afternoon my attention was drawn to a scene of violence near the door of the armory farthest from the office. There had been some altercation between one man and a group of men and women. I did not take the trouble to look into the merits of the respective causes, as the one man was highly inebriate—and violent, both of language and of fists. I believe he had, at the outset of the affray, drawn his knife; but that had been knocked out of his grasp. The man was by no means a giant. In fact, he was not even a large man. But, in the ferociousness of his alcoholic state, he exhibited the strength of a giant, and an active one, too. I signaled for some of the men of the guard to rush him from behind, and hold his arms. Then his

24

legs had to be held. Finally, a blanket was thrown over his head, and—kicking and writhing and biting and snarling and screaming —the man was borne upstairs, and locked in the prison room.

Half an hour later I went upstairs to visit the man, and to decide whether or not he should be taken to the police station. The faithful Giles accompanied me.

The door of the room was unlocked by a sentinel, and swung open. I stepped inside the room. The man was seated on the floor on the farther side of the room. I started to speak. The man looked up, growled and rushed at me.

I had learned, long before, that if mental strength was to govern brute strength, there must be no apparent doubt of its superiority upon the part of the advocate of mentality. So, as the man rushed at me, I kept my hands by my side, and held his eyes with my eyes. In all my experience with these men of the Fifteenth, an experience of almost two years, that was the only occasion upon which violence was ever offered me—by action or even by word. I cannot say whether or not my method of meeting the wild man's attack would have been successful. Something occurred which interfered with the proof.

While I stared at the man, during those seconds in which he arose and rushed across the room, a great hulk of humanity jumped in front of me. Fifteen seconds later, and the man, in a kind of dazed way was picking himself up from the farther corner of the room and, apparently, making ready for another charge.

It was Giles who broke the silence:

"Ef yoo all wants me to t'row yoo over dar agin, yoo all jes cum 'long."

During that long Sunday, I had the pleasure of renewing my acquaintance with the mother of a youngster of my command under circumstances which reminded me of an interesting incident of our tour of duty at Peekskill.

The young man's name was Elmer Partridge. He was one of the best-looking boys in the regiment—fine, clear-cut features, bright, twinkling eyes and a beautiful figure. The boy was a splendid athlete, and very snappy in his bearing. Mentally, the lad was sharp. He had a very fair, common school education, and showed it in his manner of speech. At Peekskill, the 1st Sergeant had brought Partridge to me one afternoon, and reported that the young man had refused to go on guard, although it was his turn, and he had been duly notified that morning to prepare for the guard mounting with the rest of the men of the detail.

I asked Partridge what he had to say. He said the charge was true.

I asked him why he had refused. He said, because he didn't want to go on guard.

I asked him if he was sorry he had acted so, and if he would now obey the 1st Sergeant. He answered that he was not sorry, and that he would not go on guard.

I then gave him a long explanation of the seriousness of a soldier's disobedience of orders. I told him of the disciplinary penalties to the soldier, and I told him of the far-reaching evil results that might accrue to an army, by success coming to the enemy through disobedience of orders upon the part even of one soldier.

I gained nothing by way of expression from the boy of a desire to change his attitude.

Then I gave him five minutes in which to think the matter over, to tell the 1st Sergeant he was sorry for what he had done, and to report with the company's detail for guard.

The young man showed no signs of weakening. At the end of five minutes, I asked him what he had decided. He said he had decided to make no change in what he had already said.

I ordered a corporal and two men under arms to conduct Private Elmer Partridge to the guard house.

As the file approached Partridge broke down, and said he was sorry, and that he would do whatever the 1st Sergeant said. I told him it was too late now to avoid his punishment; but that I was gratified that he had acknowledged his error. I promised to commend him, as a first offender, to the mercy of the court. The next day Partridge was tried before Captain Napoleon Bonaparte Marshall, as a Summary Court.

Captain Marshall was a colored man, a graduate of Harvard, and a lawyer. He held court under conditions of great impressiveness. I have never seen a better Summary Court officer.

There were a number of cases before that of Elmer Partridge was reached. Partridge pleaded guilty. Captain Marshall made a real oration—and fined the boy twenty-five dollars. The sentence was the heaviest of any that had been pronounced. A gasp went up from the group of spectators—witnesses, members of the guard, and other prisoners. Private Elmer Partridge mopped the sweat from a very troubled brow.

The Court proceeded:

"But your captain has asked the Court to exercise clemency upon your behalf, on account of your having made open acknowledgment of your disobedience, and on account of your having said you were sorry, and that you wouldn't disobey again. In the matter of your sentence, therefore, I shall recommend that the execution be suspended until such time as your captain asks that it be put into effect."

Then Captain Marshall made the boy understand that he was free, and would undoubtedly remain free of further punishment for his offense, if he should be a good soldier thereafter.

That evening I was talking to Partridge, and I asked him how he thought his mother would feel about his fine, if it ever had to be collected, and what she would do about it.

"It ain't never goin' to be collected, Sir," he said, " 'cause I ain't never goin' to disobey again. But," and the boy smiled, as if in realization of the fact that he was not answering my question, "but, if my mother should hear about it, and have to lose the money out of my pay, she'd lick me 'till I wouldn't have a piece of skin to my back."

When the mother of Elmer Partridge called to see me at the armory, upon that first day of our service in the army, she told me that Elmer was but sixteen years of age and that she didn't want him to go with us.

I reminded her that she had stated that her son was eighteen at the time of his enlistment; and that when he had tried to hide, the day before we went to Peekskill, so that he wouldn't have to go, she had caught him and brought him to us.

Yes, she remembered that; but there was a reason. He had been so unruly then that she wanted him to go into the army to be disciplined. She had lied about his age then, but she was telling the truth now. Since his return from Peekskill, Elmer had been so changed, so obedient, that she no longer desired to get rid of him.

I told Mrs. Partridge to bring me the birth certificate of her son. Late that afternoon she brought me a letter from the minister of her church saying that, in his opinion, Elmer Partridge was sixteen years of age. But the minister neglected to qualify his opinion as an expert; so I took the lad with me to camp. Subsequently, he went with us to France. When I became adjutant, late in July, I lost personal touch with this soldier; but I have been advised that he did well in France, and returned a noncommissioned officer.

At about eight o'clock in the evening, the 1st Sergeant came to me and asked for a pass for the night.

"No," I said, he should not leave. He was the executive noncommissioned officer of the company; and I must count upon him to keep a tight grip upon the men, and to make sure of the return of the men to whom passes had been given.

Well, he guessed there wasn't much use in being 1st Sergeant anyway. He'd be glad to give up the job for a three hours' leave.

"You are relieved of the 1st Sergeantcy," I said, "and you may have a pass good until midnight."

First Lieutenant Landon was standing by me at the time.

"That was pretty quick!" exclaimed Landon.

"Not so quick as it seemed," I answered. "The man has not

been satisfactory, and for some time I have been merely waiting for an overt act to break him."

Landon, Whittlesey and I then caucused to decide upon a new 1st Sergeant. We all agreed that if Giles could only read and write, and if, in addition, he could learn the necessary commands for forming the company, he would be almost ideal for the job. And we were not trying to be funny in our analysis, either.

Lieut. Whittlesey thought that, with the bright young soldier he was training as company clerk, the business of records would be all right, even if Giles, as 1st Sergeant, couldn't read or write. And I believed that I could teach Giles the necessary commands for his position. So, we sent for Giles.

We explained what had occurred, and what we were contemplating in the matter of a new appointment. Giles listened; but said never a word until I asked him if he would like the job.

"Yassuh," he answered.

"Do you believe you could make good at it?" I inquired.

"Yassuh. Ef de Cap'n kin do jes's he saiz 'bout dat clerk feller, and ef de Cap'n kin tell me dos oders to say, den I kin do et."

"Do you believe that the old 1st Sergeant will try to make any trouble for you?" I asked.

"Nahsuh. Ef de Cap'n kin do all dos t'ings jes's he saiz, nobody cain't make no trouble fo' me, 'cause dere ain't nobody in the cump'ny kin lick me."

So, Giles was appointed acting 1st Sergeant.

# CAMP WHITMAN

*July 16–August 15, 1917*

UPON Monday, the 16th of July, the regiment went to Camp Whitman, N. Y. We started early in the morning and had an uneventful troop movement. The entrainment had not been generally advertised and there were but few people to see us off.

Camp Whitman lay in beautiful Duchess County, about ten miles East of the Hudson River and of Poughkeepsie. We made camp of big pyramidal tents; but we found company streets well marked by permanent mess shacks lined up along "Officers' Row." The Camp was piped for water, and waste-piped to cesspools. Capt. White of the Regular Army and his staff of assistants, who accomplished the mustering into service, were polite, patient and helpful. The custodian of the camp, Lieut.-Col. Lloyd Collis of the N. Y. N. G. Quartermaster Department, (but called into Federal Service as we had been), did everything possible to make us comfortable and happy—and we were comfortable and happy.

Camp at Whitman was made with less confusion than at Peekskill. Company "F" street, which, of course, had my exclusive attention, completed its building before bedtime that first day. By this I mean that, in addition to the erection of all tents and ditching them, we built proper latrines and screened them thickly with evergreen branches. We also set up the field ranges under a big kitchen fly, and built a kitchen incinerator.

Our new 1st Sergeant Giles did splendid work for Company "F" in connection with the making of that first camp. Early in the session he had cut himself a long switch—from a willow tree, I believe. He was all over that street, giving instructions in his own characteristic way.

"Big feller—yoose dat ax! Yas, yoo is de feller Ah mean. Gude! Ah won't talk no mo' ter yoo. Yoo li'l shrimp, git under dat tent an' put de ring on de pole. Yas, da's er way. Co'p'l, yoo all wants ter mak' yoo fellers pull tergedder. Yoo cain't 'xpec' me ter be er-doin' yoo job fo' yoo all er-tahme. Now, w'en Ah cums back, Ah wants ter see dat tent up! Y'understan'? Hey dar! Yoo big feller wid de weel-barrh! Wa's yoo all er-sittin' down fo'? Yoo toddle raht aloang an' git 'nudder lode er stones fer de 'cin'rata. Wa's dat yoo saiz? Yoo's tahed? 'Corse yoo's tahed! Doan let no man 'n Cump'ny 'F' le' me hyar h'm saiz he ain't tahed ter-naht. Dis cumpn'y doan eat, no' sleep ter-naht 'till ev'body in't is jes' all in! Go 'long 'n git dem stones!"

The day after our arrival at Camp Whitman, Col. Hayward discovered a beautiful stream with a rapid current of clear water about a mile from our camp. It could be reached easily by a trail through pasture lands and a small strip of woodland. The Colonel made swimming and bathing a part of our daily schedule of soldier activities. And he made himself the chief of the horde of human beavers who proceeded, by building a dam, to change that perfectly good brook into a fine swimming pool.

The verdure along the banks of the stream was thick with mid-summer luxuriance. One day, Major Dayton, who wore a heavy mustache, almost white, had himself carried across the stream by half a dozen of the bathers. Major Dayton was seated upon an improvised litter of green boughs. He was attired in linen uniform, and broad-brimmed campaign hat. The picture, of which Major Dayton was the central figure, surrounded by several hundred colored men of beautiful physique bathing, required but little imagination to cause a number of us to exclaim —"With Henry M. Stanley, in Darkest Africa!"

One afternoon, orders were received for the companies to march to the swimming hole in Advance Guard formation, with fifteen-minute periods between companies in marching. When "F" Company approached a strip of woods, about half way to the pool, 1st Lieutenant Shaw, a battalion Adjutant, rode up to me from the direction of the pool and engaged me in conversation. I was marching with my Advance Party at the time. When I halted to speak with Shaw the men halted with me. I instructed them to proceed with the march. Half a minute later I looked up and noticed the Point marching gaily down the middle of the road, closely followed by the Advance Party, with flankers closed in. The Point was just entering the zone of the woods. I shouted to them, and warned the sergeant in command, sharply, to put out his flankers and beat up those woods. I was merely going through the motions of a drill, and had no idea of uncovering an enemy ambuscade. Within a few seconds, however, we were startled by the eager shouts of our searchers: "T'row up yoo han's, dare—yoo big feller! T'row 'em quick, befo' Ah knock yoo hayed orf! T'row 'em up quick, yoo li'l feller too. T'row 'em up, all er yoos!"

Looking over into the bushes upon our right, I grinned as I gazed upon our first five prisoners standing waist deep in the underbrush, with arms and hands stretched high above their heads, their faces as sober and chagrined as if the whole thing had been a real skirmish.

Shaw said "Damn it! I thought we were going to gobble you! We've caught every company so far, and you're the sixth."

I was as pleased as a kid; and I shouted my words of praise to the men who had scored a victory for our company.

In the midst of this scene we heard a call from the other side of the road, a few yards farther along:

"Oh suh, Lootenant, Suh! Shall we all cum out now? Ow shall we waiait here fo' de next comp'ny?"

"Hell!" said Shaw. "There goes our last chance." In another minute, our searchers, quickened by the taste of "blood," were parading into the open their second batch of prisoners, with

Colonel Hayward, holding his sides with laughter, the prize prisoner of the squad.

Shaw has always insisted that, if his boob in the bushes had not given the thing away, he could have held me so interested in his crestfallen conversation over the discovery of his first ambuscade that I would have permitted my men to walk into the second trap.

Some of the officers found fault that afternoon and evening on account of ambuscades having been set without warning being given to the companies on the march. Col. Hayward maintained, however, that the order to march in Advance Guard formation carried its own warning. He even went so far, in the aggressiveness of his defense of the afternoon's program, as to suggest that the Germans would not post a sign upon their ambuscades—and that it was training to lick the Germans that was our intensive problem.

The hour devoted each day to Non-Coms' school was, I believe, the hour which accorded me the greatest degree of interest and pleasure in my work. At these meetings I devoted almost no time to drill regulations or matters of military technique. I read to the men from Moss's *Privates' Manual*, and *Non-Commissioned Officers' Manual*, and encouraged a free discussion of the things that we had read. My idea was to try to build, first, a foundation of a sense of great responsibility and dignity upon the part of the non-coms, feeling confident that, later, the precision of drill and command would come all the more easily on account of having a sound basis.

We practiced the forms of speech and the customs of courtesy of the service. The non-coms became very snobbish over the forms of address of "F" Company and claimed superiority over all other companies. Woe to any private who, within hearing of a non-com, ventured to address an officer without permission or in anything but the third personal form!

At our company drills (which were of long hours) I gave the non-coms all sorts of opportunities of command, ranging from independent squad drills to skeletonized parades and guard mountings, with non-coms of all grades taking turns in acting as everything from major in parade and adjutant in guard mounting—down. I even had a skeletonized band with singers for musicians, and with a frequently changing drum-major.

I had the sergeants and four senior corporals serve as an advisory delinquency court and invited advice from them frequently in connection with matters of company discipline. Having thus obtained in advance the sympathetic approval of this important body, there seemed never to be much difficulty in having a sentence of special fatigue duty or deprivation of privileges carried out to the full limit of the sentence as imposed.

It was while we were at Camp Whitman that one of my drill sergeants came to me one day and said: "Sir, Captain, Sir—that new man that you gave me three days ago and told me to train him up in a hurry to catch up with the platoon—well, Sir, Captain, Sir, I can't do nothing with that man—he's so dumb I can't do nothing with him. He's so dumb—why, Sir, Captain, Sir, that man's so dumb that to be any dumber he'd have to be bigger."

Upon one occasion, a non-com who had been very neglectful of duty and who had been reduced to the ranks undertook to gain a disreputable following by making a speech of violence, in which allusions to the captain were in anything but complimentary vein.

This broken non-com of Bolshevic tendencies, I was informed, spoke deprecatingly of my tendency to tyranny, and with disparagement of my pedigree. The speech was shocking to the sense of propriety of the dignified sergeants of the company. That night, the fallen soldier was tried by the non-coms' court, upon its own initiative, and sentenced to be spanked. The sentence was executed in perfect order and in silence, the culprit being held down over a packing case, and the paddling administered by the court—a given number of strokes by each member.

Speaking of company punishment by deprivation of privileges —the Colonel used to tell a story of meeting one of the men

34

walking along the road towards the little village. The Colonel stopped his car and asked the man where he was going. The man answered that he was going to the village to buy some cigarettes. The Colonel asked the man why he didn't get the cigarettes at the regimental *canteen*. And the soldier answered:

"Well-l-l-l—Suh, Kunnel Suh, Ah'll jes tel' yoo de troot' suh. Ah wuz late fo' fo'mation dis mawnin', Suh; and de Cap'n Suh, he dun tak' er-way mah *latrine* privileges."

At both of our early encampments, Peekskill and Whitman, we were compelled by force of circumstances to become experts, to some extent, in the business of inhospitality to lice. It was in those early days of the American's experience in field service, before the little brother and sister of the vermin family became dignified by comic opera lyric and dance under the name of cootie. We had cootie intrusions right from the start. True to the traditions of our conservative families, in those early days, we always discussed the appearance of cooties in undertones. Later, over in France, in the trenches, cooties came to be looked upon as a necessary discomfort, upon a par with mud, and rats, and darkness, and cold, and foul air. After a tour of from one week to twenty days in the trenches, a battalion would be relieved for a period representing half the time of its trench service, and during that period *en repos*, the first couple of days would be devoted to cleaning up. At Peekskill and Whitman we had no sterilizing plants to contribute to the cause of cootie annihilation. We had the choice of burying the clothes, boiling the clothes, or soaking the clothes in gasoline. The first choice was impracticable of adoption because our men had but one suit of clothes apiece. The second choice, also, was impracticable on account of lack of facilities. The gasoline bath, therefore, became the only measure open to us for prompt service.

Every man in the regiment was a self-appointed secret service agent for the detection of lice. The belief of some people that the colored race is unclean in its personal habits was not borne out in fact by my two years of close association with our men of the

Fifteenth. Every few days some man would come and report a suspect. When the inspection would prove the suspicion to be correct, we'd have an orgy of house-cleaning.

Every occupant of the tent in which the man with cooties lived would literally take up his bed and walk. He would also take up with his bed every bit of baggage of every description that he had. The squad, thus dispossessed of a home and loaded with home-making impedimenta, would march to the top of a hill just outside of our camp at Whitman—and strip. There we had a sanitary squad ready to function promptly with a number of wash tubs, some filled with gasoline, and some with gasoline mixed with hot water and soap. The clothing and blankets and web belts were soaked in the gasoline, wrung out, and stretched upon the ground to dry. The men were scrubbed with the mixed solution and sent into a hollow, back of "Cootie Hill" to wait for their clothes to dry. Many an informal game of baseball, and many athletic contests of all kinds, from sparring to just plain tag, with the players in complete nudity, was staged in the natural amphitheatre of that hollow behind the hill.

While the sterilization was being carried on on the hill top, the tent would be swabbed with gasoline along the seams and removed from its ground. Then the ground of that tent position would be burned with oil-soaked straw. Such was the price of freedom from epidemics of lice and the diseases to be bred from such infection. At one time the regimental pet name for lice was "seam-squirrels,"—owing, of course, to the fact that a seam was the favorite place of abode of the unpopular little insect.

Some of our men suffered a great sense of shame when found with lice. Many a pugilistic battle grew out of an incident of a sensitive soldier being spoken of or to as "lousy" by some other soldier of ungenerous spirit.

One afternoon I walked up to the hill to oversee the sterilization of a squad of men in whose tent lice had been discovered, and I was just in time to interfere with what promised to be a bad fighting affair. A young man, not more than eighteen or nine-

36

teen years of age, had drawn his knife and was making ready to annihilate the annihilation squad. The sanitary sergeant in charge of the work had told the youngster to strip and be scrubbed, and in addressing the boy he had told him to be quick, "you lousy kid." The boy wasn't lousy, or so he believed. He had merely been exposed, by being an occupant of a tent in which a man with lice had been found. Words had been passed back and forth and the sergeant had told his men to grab the boy and strip him by force. Then the knife had flashed. I talked to that boy for ten minutes or more. The injustice of the coarse name had ruined him. He didn't care, he wouldn't be washed, those sanitary "fellers" had called him lousy. He was no more lousy than they were. He was a respectable boy. His mother and sisters were respectable. To call him lousy was to insult his mother and sisters. The "Cap'n" could put him in jail for disobedience if he wanted to; but he wouldn't let those "fellers" wash him.

His mother and sisters! There was an idea. I'd try it.

I asked him if he had joined the regiment to fight for his country. Yes, he had.

Had he realized, when he joined, that he might be killed in battle? Yes, he had.

Had his mother and sisters realized that he might be killed in fighting for his country? Yes, they had.

Were they proud of him? He guessed they were.

Were some of his friends waiting to be drafted before they would join? Yes—there were two boys living right in the same house with his family.

Did his mother and sisters boast about him before the mothers and sisters of those other boys? He guessed they did.

And now—did he—who was willing to give his life for his country—propose to upset all that wonderful pride that he had given his mother and sisters a right to feel—just because a man whom he had never seen before had spoken rudely to him? The sergeant was wrong to address him in a shameful way; and he had heard me warn the sergeant not to do it again. But that didn't

37

make it right for him to refuse to obey orders of his captain and his colonel. Couldn't he see that? Was it possible that he was going to let that mother and those sisters hang their heads in shame when the neighbors should ask if it was true that the boy who started out to be a hero had become a jailbird? Was it possible that he, who had been willing to give his life for his country would refuse, now, even to take a bath for his country?

While I had been talking, the boy had brushed away the tears once or twice. Most of these men are very emotional.

As I had finished, however, with my final question, the clouds had blown away. A wonderful, boyish, embarrassed smile came over the lad's face, and for answer he started to unbutton his clothes.

"That's a good boy," I said, "now, you're going to obey, are you?"

"Ah'm er-goin' ter doo jes w'at yoo all wants me ter doo—alwuz—Suh, Cap'n Suh!"

At Camp Whitman Captain MacClinton suffered an accident which came near to scoring a broken arm for him. He was Officer of the Day, and had a guard house prisoner from his own company. The prisoner "escaped" several times, and wandered back to his company street for social purposes. Finally, MacClinton undertook personally to watch for the guard house leak. Presently, the prisoner strolled out and down the street. MacClinton yelled at him and started to run. That startled, also started, the prisoner. In and out of the tent maze they raced—prisoner and Officer of the Day. The race was being won by the colored lad, when—thud—also, kerflop! The Officer of the Day had tripped over a tent guy, and had fallen heavily to the ground. Instantly the laughing fugitive ran to the assistance of his captain. Tenderly, the lad raised his officer and accompanied him to the surgeon. MacClinton's arm, badly wrenched, was treated and hung in a sling. Then he started to talk to his "prisoner."

"What do you mean by running away all the time?"

"Whah Suh, Cap'n Suh, Ah never runned erway. Ah jes' goes over ter see der fellers in der cump'ny."

"Well look here," said the Officer of the Day, "you may not think you're running away; but when you're out of that guard tent without a guard, you are running away. And if the Colonel happens to come along and make an inspection while you're out, I'm in Dutch—because I'm responsible for all the prisoners supposed to be in the guard house—do you get that?"

"Yassuh."

"Well, what are you going to do about it?"

No answer.

"At about five o'clock tonight," continued the captain, "I'll be relieved. There will be a new guard, and a new Officer of the Day. Now, can't you stay in until after that?"

"Whah yassuh, Cap'n Suh," answered the prisoner, "Ah dedn't know et made any difference ter yoo all. Ef yoo wants me ter stay in 'til yoo all's relieved, Ah'll stay in, Suh, Captain Suh."

It was while we were at Camp Whitman that I was appointed Regimental Adjutant.

One evening after supper an army quartermaster blew into camp in a Ford. He asked for the adjutant, introduced himself, and offered me a valise—saying that it contained $42,000 in currency and coin, and that he desired to turn it over to me for the night, for safekeeping. I told him much obliged, but that I didn't care to keep it just for a night; and I offered him a tent and a cot where he could spend the night and take care of the money for himself. The quartermaster insisted, however, that he was serious; and said that it was a regulation or a custom of the army, that if an officer, traveling under orders with public funds, got caught out overnight, he might go to the nearest military post, turn the funds over to the adjutant for safekeeping, and thereby become relieved of responsibility in the event of robbery. It was explained that, at the post, the adjutant has facilities for guarding the funds which facilities are not open to the detached officer.

I took over the money.

I carried the valise into the office and put it against the wall away from a window. Then I had my cot brought over from my tent and placed close up against the valise, so that the valise was, in a sense, locked in. Then I spoke to the three men whom I had sent for to act as guards, told them the situation, mentioned the amount of money in the bag, and asked them if they would volunteer to guard me and the money during the night. I explained that they should stand or sit guard in three reliefs of one hour on and two hours off. They agreed to serve, and seemed to feel honored at being chosen.

I handed my pistol to one, and borrowed other officers' pistols for the other two men—went to bed—and to sleep.

The men I had chosen were all men with records out of the ordinary.

The first man was the giant, Sergeant Giles. He needs no introduction to my friends.

The second man was Sergeant Gaillard who had made a number of trips to Europe during the war upon mule-carrying ships, and who had been on two ships that were caught by the submarines and sunk. Gaillard had spent hours in the water each time, but had been rescued, and as soon as the United States had gotten into the war he had joined the Fifteenth. Gaillard was a giant, as was Giles, and he also had a reputation as a handful in a fight.

The third man was Sergeant Bayard. He was "*sans peur*" but scarcely "*sans reproche*." Bayard was a wonderful soldier and leader of men, very quiet and gentlemanly in manner and speech, and well educated. He is said to have been tried three times for murder—three murders with one trial each. He gained acquittal each time, according to gossip, upon the grounds of self-defense. It is said that the Police of Harlem have a special unit called the Bayard Squad. The duty of this squad is to attend all the colored balls and concerts or other assemblies of fashion, and trail or tail Bayard and his cronies, to the end that any altercations of violence may be nipped in the bud, and Bayard spared the pain of again defending himself at the cost of the life of a fellow-citizen.

These were the men that I chose and armed to guard me and the $42,000. I slept well. I knew my men. These men would sacrifice their lives before they would betray such a trust as I had placed with them.

At *Reveille* I awoke. My three custodians were seated each with his back to one of three walls. Each window was covered by two pairs of eyes, and the door was covered by three. The eyes of the men were bloodshot. I inquired if they had slept in reliefs. They told me that they had not; and, as gently and tactfully as possible, they explained that they thought it would be safer for all to stay awake all of the time; then there wouldn't be any question in the event of anything happening.

"Did anything happen? Did you have any scares, or did any one approach the office during the night?" I inquired, in the hope of getting a good story.

"Nah Suh," answered my own Giles. "Nobody trahed enythin'. We shore ded hav' bad luck!"

# VII

# ON GUARD

*August 15–October 8, 1917*

FOR a couple of days we had had a confidential warning of orders being in preparation for a breaking up of our happy camp at Whitman. Upon the evening of Aug. 7th, while the officers were assembled at their regular school, I was called to the office to take a telephone order from Headquarters, Eastern Department.

A long order, about to be mailed, was read to me over the wire. The occasion for thus beating the delivery of the written order was that one company must be moved the following day. The schedule called for the movement of other units at our convenience, subject to full accomplishment by August 15th.

The Colonel had already determined upon his disposition of troops; but we had not expected the order quite so soon.

The Fifteenth was to be split into many parts, to guard public works and properties.

A battalion was to go to Yaphank, Long Island, where building was to be commenced for the establishment of Camp Upton.

A battalion was to go to Wrightstown, New Jersey, where Camp Dix was to be built.

A company was to go to Ellis Island in the Harbor of New York, to guard interned Germans.

A company was to go to Iona Island, in the Hudson River, a few miles north of Peekskill, to guard naval ammunition stores.

A company was to make headquarters in Albany and establish squad posts along the lines of the Delaware and Hudson R. R.

and the N. Y. C. & H. R. R., covering a radius of about 100 miles from Albany.

A company was to make headquarters in New York and establish squad posts along the line of the N. Y. C. & H. R. R. up to and including Poughkeepsie.

A platoon was to guard the Navy Yard at Erie Basin, Brooklyn.

A detachment was to guard the shoe factories of the Rosenwassers in Long Island City.

A detachment was to guard the clothing factories of the Eisners at Red Bank, N. J.

Two companies were to make headquarters in Newark, N. J., and establish squad posts along the lines of the Penn. R. R., the D. L. & W. R. R., the C. R. R. of N. J., the Lehigh Valley R. R. and the Erie R. R. running out as far as Easton, Pa.

Along railroad lines the particular points to be guarded were bridges and tunnels.

The Supply Company and Headquarters Company were to be stationed in New York. The Band, which was a part of Headquarters Company, was to accompany one of the battalions at Camp Dix or at Camp Upton.

Regimental Headquarters was to be in New York City.

There were between forty and fifty unit posts in all.

As the Colonel read the schedule, he advised the battalion commanders as to the units which he had decided to assign to each headquarters.

A few questions were asked and answered.

Then:

"That is all, gentlemen."

As the Colonel spoke, he added to me the words: "Move your troops."

"Move your troops!"

All the moving I had ever done in all my life up to that time was taking the family to the country and back again to the city, with a variation of a few trips to Europe. And the work and

43

inconvenience of those movements invariably left me all worn out and in need of a few days of recreation! Now I had 2000 troops to move to about fifty stations. I had twelve hours in which to start the movement and seven days in which to complete it.

Cookson was sent to wake up Sergt.-Major Conick. It required several hours of midnight, perspiring effort to get the first order drawn.

After the dictation was completed, Captain Hinton, the Supply Officer, and I worked out the requirements of transportation, of shelter, and of food. The army orders told us where to go and when. It was up to us to work out the how.

We were hampered by lack of facilities with which to work and by lack of professional knowledge and experience. The regiment had no wheel transportation of any kind. Col. Hayward had his own automobile in camp. Capt. White of Company "G" had his car in Camp a part of the time, and 1st Lieutenant Fox of Company "D" had his car in camp most of the time. These officers were generous in supplying the United States Government with transportation facilities. The owners of these cars had to supply even their own gas and oil. I tried to obtain an order to draw supplies for the Colonel's car, which was used 100 per cent in government service; but was refused.

And so commenced the demobilization of the first camp of the 15th N. Y. Infantry N. G., as United States troops. And so, also, commenced our actual war service against the enemy.

Our camp was situated almost two miles from the railroad.

The camp quartermaster, Lieut.-Col. Collis, had a few army trucks. With the surplus time of these trucks, and with some hiring of trucks from the country round-about—we moved out of Whitman. Our impedimenta was by no means light. We moved with full allowances of tentage, ranges, tools and rations. Where movements had to cross New York, we hired trucks to meet our trains.

In connection with a failure of one of our contracting truckmen to meet a troop train on time, an amusing incident occurred.

44

First Lieut. Bates, in command of the M. G. Company *en route* to Ellis Island, telephoned me at about five o'clock in the afternoon, and said that he had been waiting with his company at the Grand Central Depot for over two hours, but that the trucks had not shown up. He said further that he had learned that the boat for Ellis Island would stop running for the night in about two hours and he wanted to know if he had better take the men to a hotel for the night, if the trucks should not come along right away. For many months Bates was teased about his "Biltmore Party."

We all did funny things, and made funny mistakes. *But we never did nothing.*

We asked lots of questions which the regular army officers over us at general headquarters thought were silly; but we found out things. We wanted to get into the war, and we did get into the war. We were told by the Commanding General of our base when we landed in France that we were in the First Hundred Thousand of fighting troops. Many people say that we came out of the war with greater fame than any other single regiment of the American Expeditionary Forces.

What we didn't know of professional technique we made up for by energy, resourcefulness, and indefatigable determination to do the best we could.

All of the small posts were commanded by sergeants or corporals. No officers could have commanded with greater dignity or better discipline than did these colored non-coms. The men made friends with the townspeople wherever they were stationed. In most places the people of the communities, in neighborly spirit, had loaned the soldiers articles of furniture to add to their comfort. Frequent gifts of pies and cakes were received by the men. Many of the posts had talking machines. At these posts the men "fell in" every evening at sunset, and stood at *Present Arms* during the playing of the National Anthem. Where there was no opportunity for music, the squads had their *Retreat* formations just the same, and stood for a moment at salute, in a

45

spirit of patriotic religion, after the manner of Roman Catholic devotees pausing in their activities at the hour of the Angelus.

The official records of the Fifteenth New York on guard show fatal casualties to the extent of about one man per week. Most of the casualties were caused by sentinels being struck by passing trains, although we had drownings, and killings by gunfire and by knife-wounds. One sentinel, apparently, was killed by a Hun workingman at one of the great camps which our men guarded. The soldier's throat was cut as he turned about at one end of his post. Back of a bush close by the turning point were found the marks of the assassin lying in wait for his victim, and a few paces away was found the knife, bound to the end of a long rod.

Upon the other side of the ledger, I believe our men shot and killed one civilian who was upon forbidden ground at night, and who responded to our sentinel's challenge with a revolver shot. Our men also captured a German spy for whom the secret service men had been looking for some time.

But the best part of the Fifteenth's record on guard duty was that no property under our care was destroyed, and that, at the time of our relief, the Assistant Chief of Staff at Headquarters, Eastern Department, in complimenting the Colonel upon a successful tour of service, said that ours was the first organization that had performed this kind of duty against which there had been received no complaint whatsoever of disorder.

During our tour of guard duty, we had the doleful privilege of seeing the 27th Division make its farewell parade down Fifth Avenue before entraining for Spartanburg—to be prepared for war service in France.

We also saw the 69th Regiment march away to become a part of the Rainbow Division—to be trained for war service in France.

Col. Hayward fairly champed at the bit.

He begged to be included in the Rainbow Division—only to be informed that black was not one of the colors of the rainbow.

46

He hinted, I'm not sure but what he begged, for a place in that farewell parade of the New York National Guard. We were not permitted to parade.

Then the big boyish-looking Colonel threw back his head, and laughed, a snarling, cruel, determined laugh. And he said: —"Damn their going-away parade! We'll have a parade of our own when we come home—those of us who do come home—and it will be a parade that will make history!"

And to that pledge and prophecy, all present clasped hands— and said:—"Amen!"

From that time on the Colonel never rested in his efforts to get the regiment started along the route for war training—and France. He attacked the railroads for not guarding their own tunnels and bridges. He ridiculed the Navy for not being able to guard its own munitions at Iona Island, and its own ships at Erie Basin. He agitated a protest against the great National Army Cantonments, Upton and Dix, being filled with newly drafted soldiers under brand new officers of three months' Plattsburg training, depending upon our men for the maintenance of order and safety in their camps while the soldiers of junior service were being pushed ahead of our men in the preparation for coveted service overseas.

And then, one afternoon, out of a clear sky, came to my desk a sheet of flimsy paper carrying a few typewritten lines, ordering the regiment to change of station. The 2nd Battalion at Camp Upton and the 3rd Battalion at Camp Dix, with Headquarters and Supply Companies, were to proceed at once to Spartanburg, there to be attached to the 27th Division, for training. The 1st Battalion and Machine Gun Company were to be relieved from guard duty soon, and to join the regiment at Spartanburg.

Some thrill!

# VIII

# ON TO SPARTANBURG

*October 8–October 10, 1917*

UPON October 8th, 1917, the regiment left its stations in and near New York to journey to Spartanburg, South Carolina. Special trains were arranged for each battalion, and for Headquarters and Supply companies combined.

Col. Hayward, the Regimental Surgeon Major Whittemore, Captain Hinton, Supply Officer, and I traveled by regular express train—making the trip in about twenty-two hours, and arriving at Spartanburg nearly three days ahead of the troop trains.

The sanguinary affair of the 24th Infantry (colored) at Houston, Texas, was still occupying prominent newspaper space. It may be recalled that, stirred to action by a sense of grievance over grave injustices based upon Southern feeling between the white population and the colored people, a serious breach of the peace had occurred during the last week of August, 1917. A considerable body of colored soldiers had violated the discipline of their command by breaking out of camp, invading the city, and, armed with service rifles and ammunition—"shooting up" the town. Seventeen deaths of citizens and more than a score of woundings were reported. An officer (Captain J. W. Mattes) who had attempted by power of command to bring the riotous soldiers to order, had been shot and killed.

During the height of the excitement founded upon the explosion of the mutinous element of the 24th Infantry, the War Department ordered the 15th N. Y. Inf. N. G. (colored) to Camp Wadsworth, at Spartanburg, South Carolina.

Immediately following the publication of the orders, Mr. and Mrs. Worry and Mr. and Mrs. Trouble-Hunter, and all of the relatives and friends of these leading families of Spartanburg, South Carolina, organized to arrange for the reception of our distinguished regiment—which was entirely peaceable in its aims, purposes, and ideals towards all the world—except the Kaiser.

Upon August 31st, the New York *Times* had published the following news item from Spartanburg.

Camp Wadsworth, Spartanburg, S. C., Aug. 30, 1917.
Following the receipt of a report that the Government intended to alter its original plan and include the Fifteenth Infantry, colored, in the troops to be trained at the camp here, the City of Spartanburg officially protested to the War Department against the sending of these troops, on the ground that trouble might result if the Fifteenth refused to accept the limited liberties accorded to the city's colored population. Mayor J. F. Floyd, in his protest, called attention to the recent outbreak of negro troops at Houston, Texas.

That Colonel William B. Hayward's organization, one of the first of the city's regiments to reach its war strength, is unwelcome here is evident from the comments heard in the streets. The whites here are outspoken in their opposition to the plan and predict trouble if the War Department fails to heed the protest.

"I was sorry to learn that the Fifteenth Regiment has been ordered here," said Mayor Floyd to-night, "for, with their northern ideas about race equality, they will probably expect to be treated like white men. I can say right here that they will not be treated as anything except negroes. We shall treat them exactly as we treat our resident negroes. This thing is like waving a red flag in the face of a bull, something that can't be done without trouble. We have asked Congressman Nicholls to request the War Department not to send the soldiers here. You remember the trouble a couple of weeks ago at Houston."

### Chamber of Commerce Objects
While the sentiment against the Fifteenth extended through all classes in the city, the opposition took form through the Chamber of Commerce, which put the matter before the Mayor.

"We asked for the camp for Spartanburg," said an official of the Chamber this afternoon, "but at that time we understood that no colored troops were to be sent down. It is a great mistake to send Northern negroes down here, for they do not understand our attitude. We wouldn't mind it if the Government sent us a regiment of Southern negroes; we understand them and they understand us. But with those Northern fellows it's different.

"I can tell you for certain that if any of those colored soldiers go in any of our soda stores and the like and ask to be served they'll be knocked down. Somebody will throw a bottle. We don't allow negroes to use the same glass that a white man may later have to drink out of. We have our customs down here, and we aren't going to alter them."

It was suggested that the Fifteenth might make an appeal on its own behalf to the military authorities at the camp. The reply was to the effect that it would be futile for the military authorities to attempt to regulate the customs of the country, and that the situation would simply have to be accepted. No attempt, it was said, would be made to alleviate things by the establishment of "Jim Crow" soda stores or restaurants, because there are already a number of such enterprises devoted exclusively to the negroes.

These shops, however, visited by newspaper men, proved to be almost without exception dingy and poorly stocked. It is believed that the soldiers will not be satisfied with these shops and will try to get something better.

In the event that the Fifteenth does come here, it is planned to send a committee of citizens to call upon Major Gen. O'Ryan and ask him to explain to the negro soldiers the difference between South Carolina and New York City. Then, if the Fifteenth is willing to accept the order of things, all will be well; if they chafe under the restriction, "the customs will be observed just the same."

## Plans to Welcome Division

As for the other members of the 27th Division, Spartanburg and the big camp to-night are ready and waiting for them. It is figured here that about thirty hours will be required for the troop trains to reach here. At the camp the regimental camp sites have all been staked out, sanitary arrangements have been completed by a special detail of 107 men from the regular army Medical Service, and it is estimated that it will be possible to put three full brigades under canvas and thoroughly "settle" them within two hours after arrival. At camp headquarters the belief is that a

much larger part of the division will be in camp by Monday night than
was at first planned.

The 30,000 inhabitants of this city have been planning for weeks to
welcome the New Yorkers, and with the report that several of the units
would depart from New York to-night, the folks are having a hard time
restraining themselves from going down to the railroad station and camping there so as to be sure to be on hand when the troop trains get in.

That challenge or threat by Mayor Floyd was discussed
generally and freely throughout our regiment. And the old rule
of trouble hunters usually being successful in their quests was in
a fair way of being justified.

# SPARTANBURG

*October 10–October 24, 1917*

UPON the night of the 10th of October the troop trains commenced to arrive. Before noon on the 11th, all had arrived, and the making of camp was well advanced.

We had a beautiful site for a winter camp—partly on a picked cotton field and partly in a pine grove. A stream ran through the middle of our site, and hills were everywhere. A considerable amount of good drainage had been done by the engineers before our arrival, and some clearing of undergrowth had been done, too. So our men were able to commence at once upon the work of the show features of a camp. Officers and men went about in details to study the landscape gardening effects of the other regimental camps at Wadsworth. Many of the effects were charming. It was a revelation to me to note the handiness of our men with tools. General Orders allowed us two or three days for settling, before entering upon the military training schedule. Our men turned to, like a great pack of beavers, to bring the camp of the 15th Infantry up to the standard of appearance of our neighbors. Picks, shovels, crow-bars, rip-saws, hand-saws, sledge hammers or tack hammers—all hands seemed to be able to use any or all, and to use them well. Teams of horses and of mules were supplied us. Builders' wagons, stone-boats, tackles, grappling irons and dragging chains enabled us to transform a marsh into firm dry ground, bridge a stream with a fine, traffic-bearing structure, gutter and hard-surface a quagmire of a road, and level off inconvenient peaks of hills. At the same time rustic rail fences of artistic design were being erected, and rustic benches built.

Many of the officers purchased lumber, and had the men build them floors and cabin casings for their tents. We found, near a boundary line of our site, the ruins of what must have been a very good stable. A couple of hundred yards away from it was, in state of even greater dilapidation, an old barn. The old barn disappeared from sight; and the material so obtained, in the skilful handling of our men, repaired the stable and gave us fine, dry and clean shelter for twenty horses.

And all the time these men worked—these colored men, rated and insulted by Floyd, Mayor of Spartanburg, as disorderly, almost obscene, wholly undesirable,—all the time they worked to make their home as attractive and healthy as were the homes of their neighbors (white soldiers)—they sang.

My old friend Giles had not been satisfactory, as a sergeant, to the new Captain of Company "F," and he had been returned to the ranks. Giles obtained permission "ter speak ter de Adjutan'," and begged me to take him into Headquarters Company. I was delighted to have Giles for one of the horse orderlies. He understood the care of horses, and, for me, he was a model of fidelity. While we were settling our camp I handed Giles a little sketch of a wash-stand and towel rack that I desired built for my own tent, and asked him if he could make it for me.

"Yassuh," answered the giant optimist.

"Do you think you can find the necessary tools?" I went on to inquire.

"Yassuh," once more came the answer. "Ah kin find 'um, Ah'm sure. Ah's got er hammuh a'reddy. An et's mah own. Ah knows et's mah own, 'cuz Ah stole et."

A few days after our arrival at Camp Wadsworth, Spartanburg came within a very few minutes of qualifying for the front pages of all the national daily newspapers—with headings in two inch Gothic type.

Mayor Floyd had started something. If it hadn't been for an element of great luck, combined with hair-trigger promptness of plucky action upon the part of Colonel Hayward—the Devil would have been in at the finish.

The day after the regiment arrived at Camp Wadsworth, Colonel Hayward had assembled the full strength of officers and men in an open field, and had them crowd up in mass in front of a bath house. Then the Colonel had climbed up onto the roof of the bath house, and asked if there was any man in that crowd who could not hear him when he spoke. After some testing, it was well established that every man could hear the speaker. Then Colonel Hayward made a speech.

He referred to the disorder of the Twenty-fourth Infantry at Houston, Texas, and to the statement given to the press by the Mayor of Spartanburg. He did what he could to offer excuse for the unfriendly attitude of the people of Spartanburg, basing the excuse upon the grounds of ignorance and misunderstanding. He explained that the Southern people did not appreciate the fact that the colored man of New York was a different man than the colored man of the South—different in education, different in social, business, and community status, different in his bearing of a sense of responsibility and obligation to civilization.

He pointed out to the men their opportunity to compel the South to recognize the differences which the people of the North already appreciated, simply by accepting the Spartanburg situation as an opening for the educated colored man to prove his moral worth as a citizen, by refusing to meet the white citizens of Spartanburg upon the undignified plane of prejudice and brutality which had been so unfortunately advertised, by Mayor Floyd, as the standard of the community.

The Colonel pointed to the situation confronting the regiment as a great opportunity to win from the whole world respect for the colored race, with an advance in the elimination of existing prejudices to follow.

The Colonel appealed to the men upon the grounds of self-respect and urged them not to try or to want to go to places where their presence was not desired.

He warned the men that, in spite of all their forbearance, it was by no means unlikely that physical abuse might be offered them. He urged them to stand such abuse with fortitude, and without retaliation; and to come and tell him, with full particulars, of any incident of outrage that might occur. He illustrated the extent to which he urged forbearance upon the part of the men, by asking them to refrain from striking back even if the local people should strike them. "See to it," plead the Colonel, "that if violence occurs, if blows are struck, that all of the violence and all of the blows are on one side, and that that side is not our side. If wrong by disorder is to occur, make sure and doubly sure, that none of the wrong is on our side."

Colonel Hayward concluded his oration by asking every man to promise, by the raising of his right hand, to refrain from violence of any kind under every condition. A sea of hands shot up over that sea of heads—and the meeting was dismissed.

The men kept their word to the Colonel. No soldiers were ever better behaved than our men when they went to town on pass. The Band played an important part in the effort to establish good will in that community of unfriendliness. Open air concerts, by the regimental bands of the Division, were given two evenings a week from a band stand erected near the principal hotel of the town, and upon a great public square. Our Band (Jim Europe's) was conceded to be the best at Spartanburg, as it was later to be hailed as the best of the American Expeditionary Forces; and General Phillips had the schedule rewritten, so that the Band of the 15th New York Infantry should play the concert of the first Saturday evening after our arrival.

The program was carefully chosen. Drum-Major Noble Sissle, a true artist and our barytone soloist, sang delightfully. The Colonel and about a dozen of his most reliable officers attended that concert. We didn't occupy seats, and we didn't pay very close attention to the music. With overcoat collars hooked close at the neck, so as to hide the numerals on the crossed rifles of our blouse collar-ornaments, we scattered through the audi-

55

ence. If disorder had been started in that assemblage every colored soldier present would have been able to find at least one officer's face that he knew. And our men, with their own trusted officers leading them, would never (and never did) go wrong.

The talk which some of us overheard through that crowd, during the early stages of the concert, was by no means reassuring. At first it seemed, almost, as if an error of judgment had been made in forcing the colored regiment into prominence at so early an hour after our arrival. But there must be something in the time-honored line about music and its charms; for, gradually, the crowd grew larger, but the noises of the crowd grew less and less, until finally, in that great public square of converging city streets, silence reigned. Lieutenant Europe conducted, as was his custom, with but a few seconds between numbers, and the program appeared to be short. When the final piece had been played and the forty or fifty bandsmen had filed out of the stand in perfect order with the "Hep—Hep—Hep—" of the sergeants as the only sound from their ranks, the flower of Spartanburg's citizenry looked at each other foolishly, and one could be heard to say:—"Is that all?" while another would say:—"When do they play again?"

That evening, a committee of business men found Colonel Hayward, before he got started back to camp, and invited him to have a little chat in a private room of the hotel. I attended the meeting with the Colonel. According to my recollection, Major Morris and Captain Hinton were also present. The sense of the informal meeting was that the interview of Mayor Floyd as expressed in the daily newspapers did not represent the true spirit of the conservative or responsible citizenship of Spartanburg. The gentlemen present at that meeting appeared to deplore the expressions of the Mayor. They were quite frank in criticizing the War Department for forcing such a delicate situation as had developed by ordering a colored regiment to a Southern state; but they offered us full cooperation in striving to prevent the delicate situation from becoming an indelicate one. They agreed that we had made a good start. They invited all of the officers of the regiment to consider themselves honorary members of the Country Club. They requested the Colonel to let the Band play for dancing at the club dance the following week, for which services they desired to make up a purse.

They invited the Colonel to be guest of honor at a Rotary Club luncheon the following week, and to make a speech.

We were getting along too well.

Efforts were made to re-create ill feeling. A colored officer, Captain Napoleon Bonaparte Marshall, was insulted, on a trolley car upon which he was riding, and upon which he had paid his fare. He was ordered off the car. Captain Marshall, in civil life, is a lawyer. He knew his rights. He was by no means lacking in appreciation of the wrongs of his race. But Captain Marshall had volunteered to help lick Germany, not to force a social or racial American revolution.

So—Captain Marshall accepted the indignity, and got off the car.

Upon the outskirts of the camp were a number of little shops where soft drinks, tobacco, and candies were sold to soldiers. The proprietors of some of these shops talked too much. Some soldiers of the Seventy-First and Twelfth Regiments (white men, of course) visited a number of these shops and asked if "any of those colored soldiers were going to be served here?"

"No!" usually came the answer, with plenty of abusive side trimmings.

"Then," said the white soldiers, "you might as well put up your shutters. These colored soldiers are all right. They're fighting with us for our country. They're our buddies. And we won't buy from the men who treat them unfairly."

One evening, in Spartanburg, a colored soldier was thrown off the sidewalk of the main street and into the gutter. He was attacked by two men. There had been no words or altercation of any kind. The colored soldier's sole offense was in being on the sidewalk. The boy picked himself up. Then he picked up his hat. By that time a crowd had gathered to see the fight.

"Ah dun promise mah Kunnul dat Ah woo'den' stra'k back ef yoo all er-goes ter licken me."

The boy—who, a few months later, was to prove against German raiding patrols that he was not afraid to fight—shuffled off.

"Well, I didn't promise my Colonel to keep my hands off you bullies!" It was a clean cut youngster, in Seventh Regiment uniform, who spoke.

"Nor did I!" shouted his companion. And before anybody had time to interfere, these young gentlemen soldiers (of the regiment that furnished to the Army in the World War half as many officers as West Point furnished) jumped in and knocked the town toughs into the gutter from which their victim had just arisen.

All this time the officers of the Fifteenth were working, I believe, as no officer had ever worked before. We had taken up the regular schedule of training of the 27th Division. We were from three weeks to six weeks late in commencing. In addition we had formal Guard Mounting every day, and Evening Parade two or three times a week. These ceremonies served well in promoting the popularity of the regiment with visitors at the Camp and with the men of other regiments who would gather as spectators. Ceremonies, also, always seemed to us to be good for the regiment in the up-keep of morale. With the strains of martial music ringing in their ears, the men were always snappy. And snappy soldiers are almost always good soldiers.

In addition to these open duties the officers stood frequent reliefs as policemen in order to nip in the bud any possible trouble. A number of officers, by arrangement, walked the streets of Spartanburg every evening, until all soldiers had returned to camp.

Despite our vigilance, one morning, at the beginning of our second week at Camp Wadsworth, the trouble promoters almost scored. Affairs had been going along so smoothly that, it is possible, an unconscious relaxation of watchfulness may have taken place. At all events, a couple of young officers failed to recognize a danger sign in a coincidence of two reports that did not fail to take violent hold upon the imagination of a group of enlisted men.

A truck driver from town (a local white man) told some of our men, gathered along the roadside, that two colored soldiers had gotten into a fight with a policeman in town, the night before; and that the soldiers had been hanged in the yard of Police Headquarters.

Then came the report that two men (mentioned by name) had been absent from *Reveille* Roll Call—these two men having had passes for town the night before.

It took but a few minutes for the circumstantial story to be whispered through the ranks that Privates Blank and So-and-So had been lynched by the police of Spartanburg. It was agreed by many of the men that the promise to the Colonel must be declared off. But, of course, the Colonel was not advised.

At about ten o'clock in the morning, I was out in a field, about two hundred yards from the road running through our camp, overseeing some drainage work. The Colonel was bossing the building of a foot bridge near the road. We had been talking back and forth, more or less constantly. Suddenly, a Sergeant, Harry Leonard, from Headquarters Company ran in from the road towards the Colonel, and saluted to speak. The Colonel cocked his head over to listen; and then, without a word, ran as fast as he could up to the road. The Colonel's car was waiting, with engine running, at the top of a little hill beyond the bridge. Up the hill the Colonel hobbled, hampered by his lame heel, scrambled into the car, pulled the sergeant in after him, and gave the signal to be off!

I smiled—put the scene down to some long distance telephone call—speculated as to the Colonel's eagerness—reached a conclusion—smiled some more—and proceeded with my work. An

59

hour and a half later, I was seated in my office. An orderly reported.

"Suh, Adjutan' Suh, de Kunnul dun send hes comp'ments, an' would de Adjutan' please cum ter der mess shack ob Cump-'ny 'X'."

When I reported, a few minutes later, I found the mess shack filled with soldiers, and a number of company officers listing the soldiers' names. Upon the mess table running the length of the room were from forty to fifty service rifles and a quantity of ammunition.

The Colonel looked up as I entered, and said that he wanted arrangements made to keep all these men under guard. When a note had been sent to the Officer of the Day, the Colonel motioned for me to sit down on the bench beside him, and there, in an undertone, he told me the following story:

"Did you see me run out of that field, where we were working this morning? Of course you didn't know what it was all about. I couldn't take the time to call to you, to tell you, or to take you with me. God! I knew it was seconds or ruin—with the chances all in favor of ruin, anyway! You saw Sergeant Leonard come and speak to me? He told me that a half company of men had started, more than an hour before, for Spartanburg. That they had rifles and ammunition, and that they were going to shoot up the town. I didn't wait for any more. We raced to the car.

"I told Reese to drive as he had never driven before.

"That old car, I guess, made the record this morning, between camp and town. The M. P.'s all along the route tried to stop us. I yelled for Reese to go faster—and yelled to the M. P.'s to clear the road. I'm not very religious, as you know! but, between curses at Reese to go faster, and at the M. P.'s to get out of the way—I prayed to God! I prayed to get us there in time to save our regiment from disgrace—to save the population of that town from destruction! Seventy-five men with service rifles—seventy-five men whom we had taught with such pride how to shoot—seventy-five men with belts full of ammunition—these seventy-

60

five men, with pent up grievance and wrongs (some real, some fancied) bursting their hearts—marching upon that town—to kill!

"I thought that car would never get to town.

"We ran into the main street from the middle of the town, down by the railroad station. All was quiet. The town, in contrast to my expectations and fears, seemed to be asleep. We ran quickly up main street to the end of the town where most of the traffic comes in. And there, sure enough, was our company. Only it wasn't a company. It wasn't even a half company. I believe there were forty-three or forty-four all told. They were standing at ease in column of squads. As I approached, they were brought to attention, and the leader saluted me in perfect order.

"I demanded an explanation. The leader explained that they had heard that Privates Blank and So-and-so had been lynched by the police, and that, if it were so, they had come prepared to shoot the police—all of them, if they could find them, and any other people of the town who might interfere or try to assist the police.

"The leader said that he had sent a detail of two men to the police station to make inquiries, and that he expected them back shortly. Then he threw back his head with pride, and said the men had been handled under perfect discipline, that not a man had spoken except to give orders as acting officers, and that marching salutes had been given on the road to a number of officers in automobiles whom they had passed.

"I placed Sergeant Leonard in command, with instructions to stand fast until I returned. Then I had Reese run me, in the car, down to Police Headquarters.

"At the desk two of our men, with belts on and rifles at the order, were standing at attention, making inquiries in regard to our missing men. The police officers undoubtedly took them to be provost guards. When the men saw me, they saluted, and permitted me to do the talking.

"I questioned the police people closely. They reported that

61

they knew nothing of our absentees. None of our men had gotten into trouble of any kind. They examined their blotter and offered me the blotter to read. With the permission of the police our two men and I inspected the jail. None of our people were there.

"I drove back to the head of the street, taking the two provost guards with me. The detachment was standing in perfect order. Quite a little crowd of civilians had gathered. I got out of the car, told the two men with me to fall in, called the detachment to attention, gave the orders to put them into march and in the direction of camp—and home we came.

"Those men never drilled better in their lives. As they swung off, and snapped their pieces up to right shoulder, that crowd of civilians applauded!

"Can you beat it, Little? Just to think! That town was, for a half hour or more, just balancing between tragedy and normality, and they didn't know it. They don't know it yet; and they mustn't know it until the war is over and the regiment is mustered out. My, it was a narrow squeak! And the police showed those men through the jail, never realizing that they had been facing death at their hands a moment before, and until answers to questions had been made satisfactorily!

"Little, you should have heard that street crowd applaud the men when they stepped off. Knowing what I knew, but what, of course, the crowd didn't know—it was the most incongruous demonstration I've ever seen.

"As I drove slowly home behind the men, I almost had hysterics."

As the Colonel finished his story, the 1st Sergeant of Company "X" entered the building, and reported to his captain:

"Suh, Cap'n Suh, Privates Blank and So-and-so, A. W. O. L. at *Reveille* Roll Call, has jest reported. Day saiz as how dey turned ter der left instaid of ter der rahght, w'en dey waz er-comin' home las' nahght, and dey gits loast, and goes ter sleep in der fiel's, and dey's jest now cum in, Suh, Cap'n, Suh."

The conservative element of Spartanburg, the element represented by the peace-promoting group of business men, to whom reference has been made, worked constructively for the betterment of conditions. While they tried to make things pleasant for our officers, at their clubs, they arranged entertainments for the men as well. These entertainments, for the most part, took the form of dances, to which the best class of the civilian colored population was invited. The well-to-do colored citizens also made a point of inviting our men to join their family parties at church, on Sundays, and to enjoy with them afterwards, Sunday dinners of home cooking. The business men's self-appointed committee encouraged and helped to steer these developments, and went to a lot of trouble to arrange for smooth-running transportation facilities. In all of these affairs full consideration was given to the Southern tradition. The conservative and constructive elements of both sides were striving to make the best of a difficult situation.

A social atmosphere of great promise was developing at Spartanburg. We feared that our regiment would be forced to spend the winter at Camp Wadsworth, and we prepared to make the best of it. Already, the families of a number of officers of other organizations were settled in town; and both officers and men of our regiment spent much of such spare time as they had, in house hunting.

Every afternoon at *Retreat*, our Band would play a short concert in front of Regimental Headquarters, immediately following the playing of the National Anthem. Many of the ladies, and officers of other organizations, whom we had met at Division Headquarters, would drop in to hear Europe's Band. General and Mrs. Phillips honored us several times upon such occasions.

Our orderlies usually managed to rustle up some hot biscuits, or cake, or pie, and, of course, tea or coffee. Our visitors bid fair to become as deeply interested and attracted to our men as we ourselves had become. And the men always appeared to enjoy these little parties of the officers, as much as any one. Each orderly's pride in his particular officer, and his fidelity to him, were

63

things that made it easy to understand how a successful officer of colored troops usually will be found to express a preference for service with colored troops to any other class.

First Class Private Orderly Cookson was one of the features of these twilight hour informal parties. Cookson was hospitality and politeness personified. He would pass everything to everybody, and then post himself to watch for opportunities to offer second helpings. Usually, some lady would ask for a glass of water.

"W-h-y c-e-r-t-a-i-n-l-y!" Cookson would just make that lady glad that she had expressed a wish for water. He *could* roll out those two words! There was one lady who enjoyed so much hearing that "Why certainly!" that she would always decline everything when first passed, in order to admit of an opportunity to claim a change of mind, and ask Cookson to pass the dish again.

And Cookson never failed. "W-h-y c-e-r-t-a-i-n-l-y!" went with every cup of tea, and with every biscuit.

Of course Col. Hayward had reported to Gen. Phillips the incident of the detachment of outlaw soldiers, which incident had come so near to developing into real trouble. And the General kept himself well informed, as to the extraordinary efforts of the officers of our regiment to prevent a recurrence of such an outbreak. The affair had been kept secret. Only two or three of the newspaper-men covering Spartanburg and Camp Wadsworth had gotten on to the thing, and they had been so high minded as to agree to the policy of secrecy when its necessity was explained to them.

In spite of the surface appearance of smooth running, Col. Hayward and his headquarters officers and enlisted personnel knew that the trouble hunting element of the town was still bent on trouble making. General Phillips knew it, too.

One morning the General dropped in at Col. Hayward's quarters, informally, apparently for a social call. There was a real reason for his call—something more than for the making of a social appointment.

"Colonel Hayward," said the General, "I have been watching your regiment here, very closely. I have been deeply impressed with the conscientious manner in which you and your officers have accepted your responsibilities in these matters of race feeling, and with the manner in which your men, as a whole, have responded to your leadership. So far, you have been wholly successful in avoiding trouble. In a number of incidents, your success has, to my mind, taken the proportion of miracles. But we can't count upon miracles; and if we could count upon miracles, it would not be fair to ask you and your regiment to continue working, indefinitely, under the strain which you have been compelled to accept since you came to Spartanburg. Moreover, it would not be of any profit to the military service. Our first task in this camp should be to prepare our troops for combat with the German army. Of course, that has not been your first task, here —it could not be, and cannot be your first task. Your first task has been, is, and must continue to be, to guard against a clash with the townspeople, upon the grounds of racial prejudice. I've thought a great deal about this situation, and I've decided that your regiment should be moved out of here, and sent to a place where no prejudice against men of the colored race exists. But you've done well. It would not be fair to have your regiment moved under circumstances which would admit of the violent element of this town claiming a moral victory. The only first class answer possible, to such a public expression as that given by Mayor Floyd to the newspapers, is the answer which you and your regiment have given.

"For that answer, and for that record, your regiment should be rewarded, even while it is being placed in a position so that all further danger of the kind which has confronted you may be eliminated. To my mind, your regiment has established its right to be classed as 'Disciplined.' Having attained discipline, your regiment is fit to represent our country in foreign lands. In

France, there is no color line. In France, your regiment can complete its training for modern warfare. To France, every fighting regiment of our army must go, sooner or later. Colonel Hayward, I have made up my mind to take the initiative and recommend to the War Department that the 15th N. Y. Infantry, N. G. be sent at once to France."

Then the General explained that he expected to be called to Washington on official business, within a few days; and he suggested that it might be a fine thing for Colonel Hayward to be with him when he made his report and recommendation about sending the regiment away. The General doubted the propriety, however, in the circumstances, of ordering the Colonel to travel at public expense—and he wondered if the Colonel thought he could afford to take a trip to Washington, at his own expense.

The Colonel thought he could.

As he related this portion of the conversation to me, the Colonel executed something very much like a wink. And I understood the look. From my own knowledge of the Colonel's affairs, as bearing upon his ability to afford a trip to Washington at that time, and at his own expense, I too—thought he could.

The next day, General Phillips advised Colonel Hayward that the matter, which he had expected would call him to Washington, had been settled by mail. So, it was arranged that Col. Hayward should go alone to see the Chief of Staff, and, with the permission of the Chief of Staff—the Secretary of War. General Phillips provided Col. Hayward with a very strong letter of introduction and recommendation.

For obvious reasons, the greatest secrecy in regard to the cause of the Colonel's absence was maintained.

The Colonel and I agreed upon a simple code to use in telegraphing to each other, night and morning, as to developments at either end. Over and over again, with that earnestness with which a mother impresses underclothing advice upon a boy taking

66

his first departure for boarding school, the Colonel begged us, and warned us, and begged us again—to "Ride herd."

Then he boarded the train for Washington.

The evening of the second day Major Morris and I, according to our promise to the Colonel, spent in town. We established a communication center at Police Headquarters, and kept the telephone operator there informed, constantly, as to our whereabouts.

At about half past eight o'clock we were notified that there was a riot in progress at one of the hotels on a side street. We were no more than two or three blocks away, and we reached the scene of the excitement very quickly.

The report had been exaggerated. There was, and there had been, no riot. The street was crowded with men and women of both races, civilians and soldiers; and there was a considerable degree of suppressed excitement. But there was no disorder and a number of men of our own provost guard were quietly but insistently making the crowd move away from the hotel.

The full guard was immediately assembled, and under the direction of the officers in charge, all of our men on pass were rounded up and held at Police Headquarters. We had a system of making all men on pass register, when they arrived in town; so, in course of time, we were able to determine when all of our men were present at our round-up. Then they were marched back to camp. Passes for that night were cancelled.

While we waited to check up on the clearing of the town, Major Morris and I examined witnesses, and found out about what had taken place.

Lieutenant Europe and Drum-Major Sissle (colored men, but artists of genius and of high musical education, and gentlemen, by instinct and by bearing) were walking past the hotel. A white man (apparently a head waiter) stood in front of the hotel door. Mr. Europe inquired of this man as to where he could purchase a New York paper. The man directed him to the newsstand in the lobby of the hotel. Mr. Europe asked if it would be all

67

right for a colored man to go in there. The man assured him that that would be all right. Sergeant Sissle then offered to go in and buy the paper for Lieutenant Europe.

He went in, bought the paper and paid for it, and was half way across the lobby on the way out of the hotel, when a man (said to be the proprietor of the hotel) rushed at Sissle, struck him in the head, and knocked his hat off. The man followed his blow with loud and abusive language.

Sissle is about as peaceful appearing a man as can be found. Also he was wearing glasses. He made no attempt at defense or counter attack; but stooped to recover his hat, preparatory to getting away.

While Sissle was bending over, and reaching for his hat, his assailant kicked him, knocking him over. Then, as Sissle scrambled towards the door, the assailant followed him, kicking and striking and cursing, until the unfortunate Drum-Major landed in a heap upon the side-walk.

The action was over, of course, in shorter time than that in which it can be described. Within a few seconds, however, the lobby of that hotel was in an uproar. Forty or fifty white soldiers, lounging there, had witnessed the outrage. Somebody yelled:—"Let's kill the so and so, and pull his dirty old hotel down about his ears!" A rush was started, and Sergeant Sissle's assailant was in a fair way to find himself in more trouble than most men ever live through; when suddenly, a voice of command was heard above all other voices.

"ATTEN . . . TION!"

It was an officer who spoke; and those men, of subconscious spirit of obedience, stood fast.

"Get your hats and coats and leave this place, quietly, and walk out, separately or in twos, to Main Street," the officer continued.

And again the men obeyed.

As the last of these white soldiers stepped out into the street, the man who had assaulted Sissle, raised his voice once more—

this time bellowing at the officer whose brave action had probably saved his property and his life:—"Get out of this hotel—you blank blank blankity blank, how dare you step in here after I've just kicked your blank blank blankity of a blank side partner into the street!"

The officer who had quelled that riot by the power and majestry of command was a black man, a full blooded negro, 1st Lieutenant James Reese Europe.

He hade no response.

For a moment Jim Europe's eye held that of the man who was insulting him. There was no sign of fear in the glance of the negro.

Then, with quiet dignity, he turned his back, and walked into the street.

Most of the officers of the regiment wanted to rush Sissle's assailant into arrest by civil authorities, and seek satisfaction by criminal prosecution. Major Morris refused to permit such action. His course was most unpopular, with officers and men. His impulse was for red-blooded action by legal prosecution of a quality which would have been wholly satisfactory to the most ardent of talkers.

After winning Major Morris over to the policy of waiting for the Colonel, the best part of the night had to be spent in securing the fruits of the victory—silence. Every newspaper representative in town had to be found (some of them waked up) and begged not to report the story of the Sissle and Europe affair. One by one they promised to hold off if all held off. Then, after the last promise was secured, the whole field had to be covered again, to confirm and verify the unanimous agreement, in order that no evil might come from misunderstanding.

Finally, a full report of the facts of the case were telegraphed to Col. Hayward.

The following morning Major Morris and I called upon General Phillips and reported in full upon the affair of the preceding night. The General told Major Morris that he had done well.

That afternoon I received a telegram from Col. Hayward, which gave me to understand that he had succeeded in his mission; and that he would be with us upon the evening of the second day following the mix-up.

Upon the second morning following the affair, we received formal orders through the Chief of Staff of the 27th Division, to prepare to move the regiment upon Oct. 24th. We had about two days to clear up our paper work and pack up.

# GOODBYE TO SPARTANBURG

*October 24, 1917*

EARLY upon the morning of October 24, 1917, the regiment broke camp, marched to a great parade plain, and was there formally reviewed by General Phillips.

The breaking of camp was, compared to other experiences of regimental movement, a simple matter. Tentage was left erected, and turned over to the Division Quartermaster, all ready for use by some new command. In the land to which we were bound tents would not be useful as shelter for troops; and ocean-going freight space was too precious to warrant the transportation of anything but necessities.

After marching in review, we hiked to the railroad siding, a couple of miles or more from camp.

Our movement was secret, and our destination unknown; but as we swung along through the camps of the Twelfth, Seventy-first and Seventh Regiments, in the course of our hike, thousands of brave New York lads of the 27th Division lined the sides of the road-way, and sang us through, to the tune of *Over There*. At the railroad siding most of the Division Staff were present to wish us Godspeed. Gen. and Mrs. Phillips remained until our train pulled out.

We moved in three train sections—one train to each of the 2nd and 3rd Battalions, and one to the so-called "4th Battalion" of special units, under my command "in addition to his (my) other duties." It should be borne in mind that the 1st Battalion had not gone to Spartanburg. It had continued its duty of guarding railroad bridges and tunnels until about the time of the issuance of our overseas orders.

Colonel Hayward, accompanied by two or three staff officers, journeyed North by regular passenger train, to report to the Commanding General, Port of Embarkation, Hoboken.

About this time, our regimental sobriquet, "The Saluting Fifteenth," underwent a change. For a number of months, we were to be spoken of by many officers upon general staff duty with whom we came in contact both in the United States and in France as—"The Travelling Fifteenth."

As we waved good-bye to our friends at Spartanburg, as the train pulled out, upon the beautiful sunny morning of October 24th, 1917, we did not know exactly where we were going.

We did know, however, and in the knowledge we felt thrilled with a number of emotions, of which by no means the least pronounced was—elation, we did know that—we were on the way.

# THE PORT OF EMBARKATION

*October 26–November 11, 1917*

OUR trains to the North made fast time. My section (the first) accomplished the run in about forty-two hours—which meant a cut of nearly thirty-five percent in the schedule of the troop trains which had taken the regiment South about two weeks before.

At about eight o'clock upon the morning of October 25th, our train ran into a railroad center with siding facilities of considerable proportions. There I arranged with the railroad officials for a stop of an hour and a half. The men, with the band playing at the head of the column, were paraded for a snappy march of a couple of miles, into the country and back again.

A baggage car had been converted into a kitchen car, and there, upon our field ranges, set up and imbedded in clay-filled packing cases, our "chef-cooks," formerly of the Pullman Dining Car Service, prepared for the officers and men of the Travelling Fifteenth—three hot meals a day.

Our next stop was Washington. We rolled into the great train-shed at about midnight. For something less than an hour we were held here. During that time a Red Cross Canteen unit served us with hot coffee, sandwiches, and cakes. The workers of that unit were ladies of the highest social and official standing of Washington. The fame of individual officers, at that time, developed Ham Fish as an easy leader, and Jim Europe as a creditable second. But, while these ladies were charming in their graceful interest, and wholly delightful in that wonderful and indescribable comradeship which the war service bred between men

73

and women of normally formal relationship, still, they never relaxed from their intensive duty of serving the midnight lunch. While our train waited, the other two sections came in. And while we all waited, Southbound troop trains arrived.

Several thousand soldier boys crowded the station and clamored for refreshments.

And as these noble women cooked, and served, and washed pots, and scrubbed tables and floors, they recognized no color line.

We had finished breakfast upon the morning of the 26th (our sailing day) when, glancing out of the car windows, we recognized the fact that we were crossing the Jersey Meadows.

Orders were sent through the cars to prepare for detraining. A few minutes later we found ourselves in the tube, under the Hudson River. Then, out into the open of the Pennsylvania yards we glided; and, a few seconds later, once more we were in darkness in more tubes.

What did it mean? Long Island, of course. But why?

Presently, our train found its way into daylight and open country, and sped along. Embarkation from Montauk Point, from about that time, had come to be the favorite guess of the rumor mill.

At about nine o'clock the train stopped. Sentries took post at the base of the steps of their respective cars. I descended from my car, to have a look about.

A civilian stepped up to me and inquired if I was Captain Little.

I admitted that much.

"Well, sir, this is where you detrain," said the civilian.

"May I know who you are, and where this is?" I inquired.

"Certainly," smiled the civilian. "I am the Assistant Superintendent of the Long Island Railroad, Mr. Blank, and this is a siding for troop movements for Camp Mills, near Garden City."

"Have you some military orders for me, sir?" I inquired.

"Why, no," said Mr. Blank, "but if you think you should

74

have orders before acting with me, my motor car is at your disposal, and Camp Headquarters is within a couple of minutes run."

At Camp Headquarters, I learned that something had gone wrong with the ship upon which our sailing had been planned, and that the regiment was to go into camp, and wait for the make-up of another convoy.

We were two nights at Camp Mills and then moved over to New York, with the several units quartered in four of the city's armories.

For two weeks we worked under high pressure, first locating and then drawing complete equipment for overseas service. Our original equipment had been shipped with the convoy of October 26, and there was no probability of our ever finding that in France.

We had to administer several kinds of inoculations to every man and officer in the regiment.

We had a staggering amount of paper work to accomplish, covering every field of recording known to the service.

At last—on the afternoon of November 8th, the regiment paraded in Central Park, for review before General Hoyle, Commanding General, Eastern Department.

The exercises were staged upon the Sheep Meadow opposite the Mall.

In addition to the formal Review, the ceremony of Regimental Parade was performed; and after the parade, the Band gave an open air concert.

We were not permitted to talk about going overseas; but everybody knew we were going. Dramatically and sentimentally the spectacle was a notable success.

During the Standing Review, while General Hoyle was driven in motor car around the troops, the Band played *Auld Lang Syne*. For sound off, while the Band trooped down the front of the regiment and back again to its place in line, Europe played *Religioso March*—a kind of half syncopated arrangement of *Onward Christian Soldiers* and *Come Ye Disconsolate*. For the march in review, the music was *Over There*.

Upon the morning of November 11, 1917, the regiment marched by separate battalions to a pier at 96th Street and the East River. The excursion steamer *Grand Republic* was waiting for us. The freight and baggage of the regiment had been loaded upon our transport in Hoboken, during the several preceding days.

Our embarkation upon the *Grand Republic* was accomplished almost completely without the attracting of public notice. Police lines at the street end of the pier kept all civilians away.

The *Grand Republic* steamed quietly down the river, around The Battery, and up the Hudson to Hoboken, and the Hamburg-American piers. There the 15th N. Y. Infantry transferred from the river steamer to the ocean transport, *Pocahontas*.

That evening, when darkness had descended, the *Pocahontas*, with all lights extinguished, pulled out into the stream, sailed quietly down the bay, and poked her nose out past Sandy Hook to carry New York's regiment of colored volunteers to great adventures.

# WRECKED

*November 11–November 13, 1917*

EARLY upon the morning of November 12, 1917, I awoke and dressed.

After breakfasting, I went on deck for a bit of exercise.

The day at sea was fine.

We had passed out of the harbor shortly after midnight, and we were out of sight of land. All about us, however, were other ships. There were a number of transports and three or four of the speedy destroyers of our navy.

The sea was calm. Good health and high spirits prevailed.

The night before, as we had slipped down the bay, in stealthiness and darkness, we had all indulged, more or less, in red-blooded sentiments of boyishness.

I remember, well, how Colonel Hayward slapped me upon the shoulder, as I stepped out on deck to take my farewell look at the shore lights, and exclaimed, "Well, you old pirate and buccaneer—we're on the way! Isn't it wonderful?"

It did seem to us to be wonderful. We had come pretty near to beating them all.

In April, the regiment was an organization on paper—and not so very much of that. In August, when New York's Division was organized, General O'Ryan had been either unwilling or unable to find a place for us with his gallant 27th. And certainly, no officer of the 15th N. Y. Infantry had felt like expressing anything more than disappointment over the situation.

But we were human; and that night, as we sailed for the battle fields of France, and realized that the 27th Division was

77

in winter quarters at Spartanburg—we chuckled, and I must confess that, in a good-natured, friendly spirit, we even gloated a little.

There was much administrative work to do. With Sergeant-Majors Conick, Cheesman and Hooper I retired to my cabin-office to do it. I stopped only for a hasty luncheon and then back and hard at it.

Early in the afternoon Capt. Hinton stopped for a moment at my door.

"Well, we've turned about, and we're going back to New York," said Hinton.

"Yes," I grunted, "too bad, isn't it?"

I couldn't afford the time to stop work. I sensed a practical joke, and was determined that no one should get a rise out of me.

At dinner, everybody seemed low in spirits. I paid no attention. I had work to do. Too bad these youngsters all get so grouchy when they're idle, I meditated. Then I thought of the orders almost ready to issue; and I reasoned, grimly, that if idleness was to be blamed for the depressed spirits, the next day should find a ship's company of positive hilarity.

At dusk, I went on deck to walk. Hinton and MacClinton joined me.

"It is remarkable," I said, "that in this half light, we can see nothing at all of the other ships."

"But," Hinton responded, "the others must be, by now, two hundred miles away. We've been running in opposite directions for six or seven hours. I'm expecting, very soon, now, to see the Sandy Hook lights."

"What are you talking about?"

"Why, I told you, shortly after noon, that we had turned back, and you answered as if you knew all about it," said Hinton.

And then, I learned all about it.

We were a hundred and fifty miles, or so, out, when one of our engine's piston rods went out of commission. That had meant that the *Pocahontas* would not be able to keep up with the convoy; so we had turned about, to limp home again on one screw.

At about midnight we swung into our old berth at the Hamburg-American pier, and Colonel Hayward went ashore, to report to General Shanks.

MacClinton told me, afterwards, that he had never before seen Col. Hayward exhibit sorrowful emotion; but that, as our ship had turned about that morning, and headed away from the other ships of our expeditionary convoy, to carry us back to New York, the Colonel had stood upon the Captain's bridge, crying, like a great big handsome college boy, with the hopes of a long season's training smashed—by some other man's fumbling of the ball.

Our wireless had prepared a reception for us. We were to disembark in the morning, and go by train to Camp Merritt, near Tenafly and Englewood, N. J.

# A DREADFUL THREE WEEKS

*November 14–December 2, 1917*

CAMP MERRITT was a great cantonment—under construction. We experienced very cold weather during the entire period of our stay there of almost three weeks; and we suffered many of the inconveniences of pioneering.

A few days after we had settled at Camp Merritt, the consolidated morning report showed about 850 men, A. W. O. L. The families of most of the other 1152 men were in camp, visiting their hero sons, husbands, and brothers.

We expected and hoped for sailing orders every day. Under such expectations, we tried to get along without unpacking—much. The result was discomfort, and the poorest mess arrangements that we had at any time during the history of the regiment, except during actual fighting.

We had provost guards out all the time, and in every direction. The police of New York, Brooklyn, Jersey City, Newark, Hoboken, and twenty smaller cities and towns were in constant touch with us, reporting the apprehension of our men, absent without leave. The men, for the most part, had no intention of deserting. They just wanted to see their families.

Our problem was to get those 2,002 men and 50 officers into camp, and to hold them there, to be ready to re-embark when our orders should come.

Life, for the officers, was scarcely worth living.

When we received word of our men from the police, we had to send after them promptly. We could not afford to depend upon the ordinary practices of the Army Regulations for getting our men back into control. All large groups of men (either as provost guards or as prisoners) had to be commanded by officers. The mere money cost, to the officers, in getting our men back, amounted to more than three thousand dollars. But we had to have the men. If we didn't have them, our sailing orders would be cancelled, and all our ambitions and hopes sacrificed.

There were many amusing incidents in connection with our runaways; but we didn't laugh much in those days. We were too sore in our minds and too tired in our bodies.

We had one rather remarkable case of railroad fare-beating by a colored soldier. A private was homesick to see his mother. The mother lived a few miles west of Pittsburgh. The private had no money; but he determined to see his mother. He saw her. He made the railroad trip by boarding local passenger trains all along the line and riding upon each train until put off. He was never put off between stations. The stopping and starting of a train is too expensive. So, by patronizing every train upon the time table, this soldier got home.

To bring him back to the regiment we had to send Sergeant Lee of the Supply Company all the way to Pittsburgh, at private expense, to make the arrest.

Another interesting incident lay in the jail delivery of a dozen or more of our A. W. O. L. men from the police headquarters of a nearby city.

A telegram had come from the chief of police to Regimental Headquarters. Word was wired back that a guard was on the way to take the prisoners from the police.

A corporal, whose buddy was A. W. O. L., and who sensed, from learning the destination of the provost guard that was being organized, that his buddy was locked up and in trouble, put on his belt and bayonet, and jumped an army truck—out of camp.

A couple of hours later he walked up to the officer at the desk of police headquarters of a city of the State of New Jersey and reported that he was Corporal So-and-So (assumed name), of the 15th N. Y. Infantry, and that he had been sent to take the prisoners back to Camp Merritt. The prisoners were turned over to the bogus provost guard; and with every appearance of discipline the squad marched away. A half hour later the real provost guard, under an officer, reached the station house, and the ruse was discovered. The prisoners, with their friend the corporal, all got back to camp without being caught.

During the latter days of our sojourn at Camp Merritt, our Guard House consisted of two large two-story barracks. And the Guard House was filled, all the time.

Every officer and man of the regiment was nervous and irritable to an advanced stage. There was no available space in the camp for drill. All the companies could do for exercise, to take the place of drill, was to march in column of squads along the roads, and to execute the manual of arms, on the march.

And to add to the mental distress of the period, every officer and man of the command, every day, and sometimes and in some cases several times a day, had to say to some person or persons with claim to his affection—"Good-bye."

At Camp Merritt we had to make up new Embarkation Lists, to take care of the changes in enrollment that occurred between November 11th and December 2nd.

We had hundreds of Summary Court trials to conduct, to dispose of our runaways.

We had forty or fifty Special Court trials.

We had a murder case—the most cold blooded murder in all the history of the regiment. And homicides in our regiment were not particularly sensational on account of infrequency of occurrence.

Two men had been in a gambling game. One had left the game owing the other two dollars. The creditor was confined to quarters with some ailment which had almost paralyzed his legs. This man was a full blooded Zulu by birth; and he had served in the British army during the Boer War. He was seated upon his cot, upon the afternoon of our last Sunday in America, when the man who owed him two dollars entered the barrack room.

The Zulu called to the man, and demanded information as to when he was to receive the money due.

The debtor gave an evasive answer.

The Zulu (who was a sergeant) picked up his service rifle, loaded it, took deliberate aim at his victim (not more than fifty feet away) and fired.

The man who owed the two dollars never had to pay. He rolled over on his cot—dead.

The other men in that part of the room, dived out of windows.

At last, after three weeks that seemed like three months, we received word that the *Pocahontas* was once more ready for us.

Early upon the morning of December 2nd, 1917, we marched out of Camp Merritt and proceeded to Hoboken, where, for the second time, we embarked for France.

XIV

# FIRE

*December 2–December 12, 1917*

THE two days of our first voyage on the *Pocahontas* made us feel like seasoned transport travellers, when we stepped aboard for the second time.

The ship was crowded. All of the junior officers, and some of the captains, had to be crowded in, three or four in a cabin.

There were forty casual officers aboard, and three hundred and thirty-seven so-called casual enlisted men, although of this number there was a company of automobile assembling men, all experienced mechanics. These men had with them a full machine-shop equipment; which fact was destined to be proved, some ten days later, of great value to us.

Col. Hayward was in command of all troops on board.

During the day of December 2nd, we watched our neighboring transports being loaded. We expected to pull out when darkness should fall. During the evening, we learned that some of the other ships of the convoy were not quite ready; so we settled down in patience, for another day of waiting.

During the afternoon of December 3rd, a rumor found its way about, that the ship was on fire. At first the rumor was laughed at; but, just before evening, it was confirmed.

The coal at the bottom of the port bunkers was burning, apparently from spontaneous combustion. It would be necessary for the bunkers to be emptied, cooled, and painted. Then fresh coal would have to be taken aboard. A week would probably be needed for the *Pocahontas*, once more, to be made ready for sea.

That evening, we gathered upon the after deck, and watched

84

the shadowy forms of the other ships of our convoy back out into the stream, and disappear, down the river towards the bay.

Our convoy of October 26th, we never even joined at the starting point.

Our convoy of November 11th signalled us "good-bye" a hundred and fifty miles out at sea.

Our convoy of December 3rd, left us with nothing but a stubborn hope—at Hoboken.

During the recoaling of the ship, the regiment and the casual soldiers were kept on board.

We were held aboard ship at Hoboken for eleven days. During all that time no communication with the outside world was permitted.

We were all concerned in regard to the anxiety which would soon commence to be suffered by our families when they failed to hear of our safe arrival on the other side.

Officially, there appeared to be nothing that could be done. Everything in regard to our regiment must be kept in strict secrecy. Our families must not be permitted to suspect that we were still in Hoboken. Only the Germans, through their spies, must know that. The *Pocahontas* was moored next to the Lackawanna Ferry; and every twenty minutes, during each of those eleven days, the passengers upon the upper decks of the ferry boats could, if they so desired, learn that the colored soldiers were still aboard; and that the *Pocahontas* was still in port. And German spies could travel back and forth upon those ferry boats, as often as they pleased, at three cents a trip.

There was a very efficient Red Cross woman, Mrs. Amy G. Olney, who visited our ship several times while we were waiting. Through Mrs. Olney the men were fitted up with sweaters, and knitted helmets, and woolen gloves.

She knew that we were worrying about the worries of the people at home. So, when she left us for the last time, she took a list with her of the names and addresses of the families of the officers, and of the relief association for the men's families, and

85

telephoned them that we were all safe. Mrs. Olney was very careful and conscientious in regard to the necessity of maintaining secrecy as to our whereabouts. She gave a very brief message, saying that she wanted to report, based upon official knowledge, that everybody in the 15th N. Y. Infantry was well and safe, that the mail would be delayed, and that that was her reason for telephoning.

Upon the afternoon of December 12th, 1917, at about 3:15, we left our pier and dropped down the bay, and anchored a few miles inside of Sandy Hook, to wait for the other steamers of our convoy.

We waited all night, and all the next day.

All day long upon December 13th, a storm threatened. The weather was very cold. As darkness came, the storm broke—a blizzard of snow. No lights were permitted on board ship. In sheep-skin coats, with collars turned up, and with knitted helmets under our campaign hats, we huddled on deck in darkness, and in the storm—waiting, and wondering, as to our next move.

## XV

## COLLISION

*The Night of December 13, 1917*

AT 8:45 P. M. a despatch board ranged alongside of our anchorage; and a megaphoned voice came out of the darkness:—"On board the *Pocahontas!* Get under weigh and carry out your orders!"

A few minutes, and the anchor chains creaked. Then came the throb and vibration of the engines.

The night was such a one as a writer of fantastic sea tales would describe in choosing an appropriate setting for the running of a blockade. Pitch dark, and snowing, with a gale of wind, and very cold.

All the officers and most of the men were on deck to see the last of the country to which they were offering their lives. Over our heavy storm coats we wore the life preservers which regulations required to be worn constantly.

The *Pocahontas* moved forward slowly, fairly creeping—as if groping for its course. Other vessels were all about us. Several times we came so close to other ships that a baseball could have been tossed aboard, from one to another. Twice we stopped and backed, to avoid a catastrophe.

About the upper deck were little knots of men formed in circle groups—singing—close harmony in school, love and longing in theme.

I found myself up forward in the center of the promenade deck, looking directly out over the bow.

Down roared a voice from above me:—

"On the main deck forward—take the soundings!"

87

"Aye-aye, Sir," came the answer.

Two minutes passed:—"By the lead—thirteen fathoms!"

An officer beside me muttered:—"That settles it. Thirteen fathoms, on the thirteenth of the month, and we've already had two mishaps for this regiment and this ship in combination. What a dirty night! It's tempting Providence to try to make it out tonight."

"Nine fathoms!" came from the deck below.

A ship loomed up over the port bow. Not a light to be seen— just a great dark mountain standing out as an inky spot on a gray black screen. We stopped, and reversed engines.

"Eight fathoms!" came the report of the man with the lead.

"That was close enough," spoke the superstitious man on my left.

"Six fathoms!"

"Let go the port anchor!" The voice of command came through the darkness from the bridge over my head. Two seconds, and the engine's bells to stop were drowned in the rattle of a great chain, paying out.

Everybody went indoors to stamp their feet warm, and to rumor as to whether we would stop for the night or attempt to go on.

"Attempt to go on!" exclaimed our pessimist, who believed in ill omens. "Attempt to go on! Do you think they're crazy? We've got to get our third mishap. I hope they stay right where we are and get it inside here where we've got a chance. *We're* anchored; but everybody else in the world isn't; and if we don't get rammed tonight, it'll be because we're doomed to be torpedoed, later in the week."

It was ten o'clock. I went to bed.

I awoke with a start. Someone was shaking my shoulder.

My night orderly was speaking:—"Suh, Cap'n suh, der uff'cer of der Day saiz ter let der Adj-den' know der ship 'as been struck bah anudder ship. Dar's a big hole fo'ard, an' he t'inks der Adj'den' 'ad bettur git up!"

"Has the Colonel been called?"

"Yassuh."

"Very well. Have the Lieutenant Colonel's orderly help you, and call every officer at once and quietly. You go down this side of the ship, and have the other orderly go down the other side. Tell the officers that the Commanding Officer directs that they dress, with side arms, and go to their company quarters. The men are not to be awakened, or permitted to get up."

"Yassuh. I und'stn' Suh."

I turned on my blue light. My watch gave the hour 2:45 A. M.

On deck, a half dozen men were stirring. With the Colonel, we went forward, to check up damage and estimate needed action.

Beside us lay an oil tanker (British). It had dragged anchor and drifted into us. Its bow had torn three or four plates away from our starboard side, on the main deck—well above the water line, and no great danger was apparent. But the night had brought on an increased volume of storm. The decks were crusted with ice on top of snow, the wind was blowing terrifically, and the oiler was hugging up close—making us quiver every time a sea would drive her up against us. Her anchor chain was afoul of ours; and we were tied together.

The officers kept their vigil until broad daylight at 7 o'clock. Then the chains were freed, the oiler slipped away, and inspection by daylight and repairs commenced.

It is a curious thing, the way little incidents, during periods of stress and importance, will stand out in one's memory.

At about five o'clock that morning Ham Fish appeared in the little lounge, up near the Colonel's room, with an enormous loaf of freshly baked bread, hot from the oven. Captain Fish had made a raid upon the baking galley; and then protected himself from the consequences of his iniquity by dividing his spoils. That bread tasted fine. Nine and a half months later, the name of Captain Fish was to become once more associated in my mind with very welcome bread. Upon the latter occasion there was something more involved than the mere daredeviltry of robbing a bake-shop.

There was a command of two battalions of our regiment (or what was left of them) in a very uncomfortable position, as a result of a battle, and the descent of darkness. Food was required for the men of that command. And Captain Fish who was at Regimental Headquarters in the rear, as an observer and visitor, and in no sense serving in an official capacity, joined a little volunteer squad, organized by Sergeant Major Marshall, and brought forward to us, through the darkness of three or four kilometers, about eighty round loaves of bread. But I am running ahead of my story. The story of the bread relief will be a part of the story of Sechault.

When a daylight inspection had developed the fact that the damage to the *Pocahontas* was confined to the superstructure and the smashing of a couple of life boats, we became keen to go ahead under temporary repairs.

At first, Commander Helwig of the Navy and Lieutenant Commander Green, the Executive Officer, felt that they must put back again and lay up for repairs. Colonel Hayward, however, did some of his best talking; and backed his talking with very practical offers of assistance in the repair line.

We had in our regiment about every kind of laborer, skilled and unskilled, known to building, mechanical, and engineering industries. The automobile assembling company, to which I have already referred, had a lot of clever and keen young men, skilled as steel workers. This company was commanded by a very energetic young lieutenant named J. B. Streit. The unit was a volunteer organization, gotten together and equipped by efforts based upon a determination to succeed somewhat similar to that demonstrated by Colonel Hayward in forcing his colored regiment to a position where it had to be recognized.

Lieutenant Streit had brought aboard a complete and absolutely up-to-date machine shop equipment, including drills which could make holes in the great steel plates of the ship structure, as prettily as a dairyman can cut through a hard form of butter.

Point by point Col. Hayward demolished the objections of the Navy men, and showed them how to overcome obstacles. The last point was that there were no steel drills about the ship, and that the kind of repairs needed couldn't be made without them. The Colonel met that point with a grin. He had had quite a row with young Streit over those steel drills, while the *Pocahontas* was laid up at the Hoboken pier. The drills had not been delivered with the rest of Streit's stuff, and the young man had just made the Colonel's life miserable, until he got permission to go to General Shanks for authority to go over to New York to secure the things. As the Naval Officers talked, all that stubborn persistency of the young automobile officer came back to Colonel Hayward. Only this time it didn't annoy him. He sent for Streit.

Streit reported, wondering what he had done this time to get on "the old man's" nerves, and almost collapsed, upon finding himself patted on the shoulder by the big Colonel, who had been so cross with him a few days before, and welcomed as "Streit, my boy."

Well, when the decision was made to go to work and repair ship, it was a beautiful picture of industrial cooperation, to see the way everybody on that job tried to do his bit.

The ship's carpenter knew his business, and he planned the work. The sailor men, the automobile mechanics, and the colored doughboys were all partners in following those plans. There was no lost motion, and no slowing down of effort. A number of reliefs were formed. The weather was severe, and it is impossible to work with bare hands, in the open air with a ten degree thermometer registration, for very long periods, without becoming numb—and slow. Then too, during most of the day, four or five men at a time were working from slings, hanging over the side of the ship.

So, the reliefs worked for short periods and hard; and then went inside to warm up, to be ready for their next turn.

The Flag-Officer of our convoy had sent word to our captain that he couldn't wait for us beyond the scheduled hour for sailing; and that we shouldn't accompany the convoy unless our damages were soundly repaired, and our freeboard painted.

That meant that we must be ready to sail at dusk. And I believe that no less than ninety per cent of the soldier men on that ship would have burst into tears, if we had failed for the fourth time to accompany the convoy to which we had been assigned.

But we didn't fail. At 6:20 P. M. our last painter was dragged up over the side, his hands so cold that he dropped his brush; but the cheer of his comrades must have warmed the lad's heart.

Our third mishap had been met and conquered.

Our superstitious man was beaming. His pessimism of the night before had given place to jubilant optimism. We were now to proceed in safety upon our mission.

Already reports and orders had been exchanged with the Flag ship.

At 6:25 upon the evening of December 14, 1917, once more we felt that vibration of the shaft. The engine had started.

# THE VOYAGE

*December 14–December 27, 1917*

THE voyage of the *Pocahontas*, the troopship of the 15th Heavy Foot, was, I imagine, very much like most of the voyages of most of the troopships which carried American soldiers to France.

We had no disasters. We had few scares. We had many rumors of danger. And, probably, we were, a number of times, in greatest danger when we didn't know.

That voyage cured me of any desires which I may ever have sensed, of visiting any land of continuous darkness for a given season. For almost a full two weeks, we existed, during the shortest days of the year, without the convenience of artificial light during the hours of darkness.

In addition to being in darkness we had submarine drills after we entered the zone where those boats were known to operate.

Now there is something about the activity of a hostile submarine, with your ship as a possible victim, that is food for thoughtful consideration. When the call comes, "stand by to abandon ship," in the middle of the night that consideration is intensified.

On one of those occasions we were all standing at our assigned positions. Life boats had been cleared. Every nerve was tense. We were waiting for that torpedo to strike—keenly aware that the blackness below was the cold, wet Atlantic. Nerves can stand about so much without relief. This time relief came in the typical 15th New York way. Out of that tense silence rose a soft voice:—"Is there any man in Company C who'd like to buy a brand new wrist watch—cheap?"

During the evening of December 20th we had a scare.

I was sitting with the Colonel and two others in his room, about eleven o'clock (in the dark, of course), when an orderly came to the door and said: "Suh, dar's er raid laght jes' erhaid 'vus, an' ter der raght!"

We all rushed out to the forward deck.

The night was clear and mild—moonlit. The heavens full of stars. A night at sea for lovers! But such nights were not welcome with us. They favor, too much, the designs of the submarines.

The red light was just where the orderly had said—and it was moving slowly across our bow. We had slowed down to a speed of not more than three or four miles an hour. Two or three minutes, and we were abreast of the strange craft.

It was a small schooner (or appeared to be), apparently a fishing boat. But the "subs" had, according to reports, been rigging up that way, so as to get the steamers up close to them; and we all waited for the torpedo.

The schooner had crossed our bow, and was passed on our port side, not more than a hundred feet away. She couldn't have missed us with a shot. Our guns were trained, and if any sign had come of hostile action upon the part of the stranger, she would have been sunk with us, if not before us.

We all held our breath. We passed the schooner. She seemed to be almost hove-to, riding out a heavy swell for the night.

After the schooner, at a distance of about a hundred and fifty yards, floated a number of planks. They looked like wreckage. We feared it might be the structure for a floating mine. That was said to be one way they had of working a mine—dragging it after an innocent looking boat, and trying to get the ship to cross, between the boat and the planks, so as to strike the rope, and draw the mine up against the far side of the ship, where it is exploded.

We steered clear of the wreckage. We never knew whether

KITCHEN AND DINING QUARTERS IN TRENCHES, MAY 4, 1918, BOIS D'HAUZY

CHAPEL IN SECTOR HELD BY REGIMENT, MAY 4, 1918, BOIS D' HAUZY

we were near to death, or not. The ship's captain was inclined to the opinion that we were.

One day we slowed down, for target practice. Jim Europe, who had lots of pluck, but who joked all the time about being scared, was in bed and sea-sick. When the first big gun boomed, Jim made a jump, and was on deck almost in time to see the shell splash the water near the target. Later, he was laughing at himself, and telling the Colonel how he felt sure we were in a battle, and probably sinking.

The Colonel said: "Jim, did you stop to put on your life preserver?"

"No Siree!" answered Europe. "I didn't do no stopping. But, when I calmed down, I found I had my life preserver on— and Cheeseman's too."

Jim used to promise somebody, every day, that, if ever he should reach the country of his name, he would stay there.

Sunday, December 23rd, was like a beautiful Spring day, at sea.

We had religious services on deck. There was no chaplain on board, so the Colonel conducted the service. He did it well, too. The Band played *Onward Christian Soldiers, Nearer My God To Thee, Rock of Ages, Holy, Holy, Holy*, and *Come Ye Disconsolate*. The men all sang—officers, too.

Everybody was very serious. We were in the so-called "danger zone"; and the church service seemed to emphasize the gravity of our mission.

At about nine o'clock in the evening of December 24th, I was in my cabin, and lying down. That was all there was to going to bed; because, in the danger zone, we were under orders not to undress. Everybody had been blue all day. Scarcely anybody had spoken, except on duty.

A pounding on my door interrupted my musings. MacClinton shouted to me to come on deck, quickly, to see what was coming to us as a Christmas present.

On deck, all was excitement and enthusiasm. Our augmented

convoy, for which we had been looking and hoping for two days, had found us. From all directions, signal lights, from way down low, near the water, were flashing.

We turned in again, an hour later, quite happy.

In the morning, we counted seven of the wonderful little destroyers, darting about, hither and yon, searching the seas, after the manner in which bird dogs search the fields. And we felt that our goal was in sight.

Upon December 26th we ran into heavy seas, and strong winds. Everybody was so accustomed to the ship that the motion caused practically no inconvenience to anybody.

The wireless brought news to us of six submarines operating in our part of the world.

During the afternoon, our convoy was divided into halves. One half turned east, to make port at St. Nazaire. We kept on north-east, for Brest.

A few hours after leaving us, the half of our convoy making for St. Nazaire was attacked by submarines. The Germans were beaten off.

At midnight of December 26th-27th, the wireless advised us of the sinking of a big ship, near us. It was a Pacific Mail steamer; and sailing in the opposite direction to us. And we escaped!

The superstitious man of the night of December 13th was right.

We sighted land at daybreak, December 27th.

And upon that morning, once more our convoy was augmented—this time by seaplanes, flying very high above our ships, and serving as sentinels for our safety.

At about eleven o'clock in the morning, we sailed into a beautiful harbor.

France was decked in Spring-like sunlight. Chateaux and well appointed country places—even lawns (apparently, from the distance from which we made our survey) were passed by, in inspiriting panorama. The sea, or bay, was as calm as the proverbial mill pond.

We dropped anchor close in under the sea walls of Brest, amid the usual scenes for such occasions. Bumboats surrounded our ship. Soon, an official boat came off from shore. An aide of the commanding officer of the port came aboard, called upon the Colonel, was turned over to me, and, all the afternoon, I had to read orders signed, "By Command of General Pershing."

But everybody was happy, because, at last, the 15th N. Y. Infantry was in France, and actually a part of the American Expeditionary Forces. We were ready to look up to John J. Pershing—almost as a god.

# XVII

## ST. NAZAIRE

*January 1–February 12, 1918*

O N New Year's Day, we landed in Brest; and, within a half
hour, we entrained for St. Nazaire.

As our tender pulled away from the ship which had been
our home for a month, the Band played *Auld Lang Syne*, and
the ship's company saluted us. The Captain, and the Executive
Officer of the ship said we had kept and left the cleanest ship
they had ever known. They seemed sorry to part with us.

Our trip by rail was extremely interesting. It lasted from
10:30 A.M. January 1st to 3:30 A.M. January 2nd. Everybody
was cold, all the time, and thoroughly uncomfortable; but we
were all so engaged with the novel sights presented to us throughout that day that everyone was cheerful.

Our men, of course, saw something comic at every turn. When
they first crowded into the little freight cars marked *"Chevaux
8, Hommes 40,"* the cars which in France served as passenger
coaches for soldiers, they giggled, as they unslung packs and tried
to find spaces in which to stretch out, exclaiming in their almost
inimitable language:—"Well, it's all right about the 40 men. It's
going to be crowded; but that will help us to keep warm. But,
after we all get in, where in hell are they going to put 8 horses?"

At about 3:30 in the morning, upon January 2nd, our trains
rolled into St. Nazaire. We detrained at once and departed upon
our hike to the camp, about two miles out from the city.

St. Nazaire is a picturesque city, and, as we marched through
the silent and dimly lighted streets, during the still cold of that
night, we looked it over with keen interest. We had seen nothing

of Brest. Our trains had been made up down by the water front. The small towns through which we had passed by railroad were mere villages. So, St. Nazaire was, to about ninety-nine percent of the members of our regiment, the first French city, or foreign city of any nation, which they had ever seen.

We stumped into the great camp, to which we had been directed, at about 4:30 in the morning, 51 officers and 1949 men strong, upon 4000 frozen feet.

A labor battalion, the name of which I regret I cannot recall, which had been in camp some time, through its cooks and kitchen police, greeted the men cordially with an invitation to hold out their cups. Into those cups they poured steaming coffee, and thus cheered, the men stumbled into the Fabyan barracks assigned to them, wrapped themselves in their blankets, and lay down upon the frozen ground to sleep.

The General commanding had the regiment temporarily assigned as laborers to the engineers. There was important work to be done. At Montois (six kilometers from St. Nazaire) a vast swamp was being reclaimed, several miles of store-houses were being built, and railroad tracks laid to serve each street and every store-house. It was planned to provide a six months' supply of all material for an American army of five million men. In addition the engineers were modernizing the docks to do away with lighterage, and they were also building a dam for a great reservoir.

This pick and shovel work was most destructive of the morale of men who had enlisted to fight. We put up with it, and the incidental indignities, for a long time, however, but the condition was not one to be endured indefinitely.

About the first of February, Sergeant-Major Conick came into the office and reported—"The Colonel's compliments, Sir, and would the Adjutant please step over to the Colonel's room to confer?"

When I reported to Colonel Hayward, he told me he had made up his mind it was time for us to try to do something towards extricating ourselves from the dirty mess of pick-swinging and wheel barrow trundling that we were in. We had come to France as combat troops, and, apparently, we were in danger of becoming labor troops.

Col. Hayward had written a letter to General Pershing, or the Chief of Staff, American E. F., asking for front line work, and it was in order to have me read that letter and criticize it, that he had sent for me.

The letter was a corker—very interesting, giving in summary form the complete history of the regiment, step by step, from conception in New York, through prevention of race rioting in Spartanburg, to dam building in St. Nazaire. And all through was the plea for service as a fighting regiment of doughboys.

"What do you think of it?" the Colonel asked, after I had finished reading.

"It's great!"

"It's too long," said the Colonel, "would you shorten it?"

"I should make it longer," I said.

"Why?"

"Because," I answered, "this letter is likely to come before the eyes of General Pershing himself, and, if that should come to pass, there is one thing that we have the right to say which you have not said, that will probably impress General Pershing more deeply than all of the other things combined."

"What is that?" Col. Hayward inquired.

"What one thing is the most talked of thing in all the literature issued from Army Headquarters over here? What one subject appears to take the space of about sixty per cent of all orders and circulars from G. H. Q.?"

"Prophylactic against venereal disease," answered the Colonel, without hesitation. "But why?"

"Because," I answered, "this regiment has not had a new case of venereal sickness develop for almost three months."

As a magazine publisher, I had been one of the pioneers of the country in promoting public opinion along the lines of sex hygiene and the prevention of spread of disease by methods which have now become general by law and by practice.

With Colonel Hayward's backing, I had issued orders as far back as August 20th, 1917, for the enforcement of prophylactic treatment. And I had followed up those orders for enforcement —to my own great unpopularity amongst the officers of the regiment, who, at first, had taken no interest in the matter.

The Fifteenth, therefore, had been learning of the advantages of this important feature of the care of soldiers, for more than a third of a year before we landed in France. I had paid the penalty of being a pioneer and a crank, and I was proud of the record which had grown out of my unpopularity.

After Colonel Hayward had sent for the Surgeon's records and verified my statement, he wrote an additional paragraph, as suggested. Then he looked up—"Anything more?" he asked.

"Yes, sir, one thing more," I answered. "I think you should ask permission to report in person at General Headquarters. You are without a doubt, the best fixer in the world; and if you can get to General Pershing, face to face, we'll get into the trenches within a week."

So, that feature was added, and the letter forwarded.

When the time came for General Walsh, Commanding General, Base No. 1, to endorse the letter for forwarding, he sent for Colonel Hayward, and checked up on that venereal record. Then he forwarded the letter, with requests approved, and told Colonel Hayward that he believed that record of ours was the most remarkable record ever established in the United States Army.

General Walsh was a good friend to our regiment, and a delightful officer to serve under. He had commanded colored troops in the Regular Army for twenty years or more; he understood them and he loved them, and he gave us good advice in our problems with them.

One evening, while dining with us, General Walsh expressed a desire to meet the 1st Sergeants of the regiment. He made them a little speech, and then shook hands with each Sergeant as I pronounced the name in introduction.

When it came the turn of 1st Sergeant Gillard Thompson of Headquarters Company, General Walsh flashed a look of recognition. "Thompson!" he exclaimed, "I know you. You were in Troop B of the old 9th Cavalry when I commanded Troop C, and we used to have drill contests, weren't you?"

1st Sergeant Thompson almost burst with pride.

One of the duties of officers which afforded some entertainment at first, but which soon became a dreadful hardship, was the censoring of mail. Each company had from 150 to 250 men. Each company was supposed to have six officers. During the entire period of our service we averaged about two officers to the company, for duty.

Our men were sentimental and affectionate. They wanted to write letters home, frequently, and it was right that they should. If we estimate that an average of 200 men per company wrote two letters each per week, and that each letter was of four pages in length, we find that, with an average of two officers to the company, each officer would have had to read and censor 115 pages per day. That is by no means an extravagant estimate of what our officers had to do in the censoring line. And most of the letters were written with lead pencil.

Before censoring got to be a sore subject, the officers used to joke with each other over some of the funny things they read.

Many of the letters indulged in extravagance of imagination. While we were at St. Nazaire, two hundred miles or more from the front lines, numerous accounts of actions of great dramatic quality went back to the girls our men had left behind them in Harlem and in Brooklyn. Two months or more before our men ever heard the shriek of hostile shell or the whistle of a bullet, some of them wrote descriptions of our bloody and desperate work, with touching pen pictures of the groans of the wounded and the heroism of the dying.

One of the men of Headquarters Company made a practice

of telling his wife three times a week that he was "failing dear, failing rapidly." One day after the receipt of mail from home, I noticed that this man seemed depressed. I inquired if he had had bad news. He answered: "Nahsuh, no bad noos 't *is* noos; but mah warf dun seems ter be so wurr'ed an' skeert 'bout me all de tahm."

One day, Captain Hinton read in a letter which he was censoring that a man of his company had sold his service shirt for fifteen francs. Hinton ordered inspection, and, upon finding the shirt missing led the man, by clever questioning based upon inside information, into a great state of alarm. The man promised to produce the shirt at a later hour; and he kept his promise. The next evening, Captain Hinton read in this man's letter home, that—"my captain sure has a touch of a he witch in him. After I sold my shirt the other day for fifteen francs, the captain found out all about it. He knew how much I got for it, and he knew that I sold it to one of those drafted stevedore fellows. It just made me feel kind of queer like as if I was haunted. But I went right off and got the shirt back, I was that scared! The bad part of the thing was that that drafted stevedore fellow held out for a profit, and I had to pay him twenty francs for the shirt."

The system of mail censorship served some purpose, for the U. S. Army, beyond that of preventing the enemy from getting news of our movements.

During the latter part of January we received orders to select a couple of personal orderlies for Gen. Pershing. It was a matter of pride for us to know that the men sent in pursuance to that order were kept by the General all through the war. They were assigned to duty on his private railroad car.

With the regiment's long hours of daily work in the mud— on the dam, and in the swamp, we suffered constant nightmare that our men would forget their habits of snappiness and of neatness, and fail when the test by inspection should come, to decide as to our fitness to serve as fighting soldiers.

Regimental Parades and Formal Guard Mountings were put

on whenever work and weather permitted, to help defeat the danger of slouchiness; and to inspire neatness of appearance. Col. Hayward inaugurated a series of inspection contests for prizes.

There was a prize for the best turned out man in each of the sixteen companies. There was a contest for such a prize every Sunday morning. And the prize was a silver identification tag and chain marked with the successful soldier's name and organization.

The Colonel paid for the first set of prizes, and we older officers each in turn paid for a set.

The results were superlatively successful. The method of procedure was by elimination. Each man showing any blemish, was told to drop out. After the first contest, the men prepared for these inspections with such energy and skill that there would always be a few men left in each company, after the great majority had been thrown out, who were practically perfect. To reach a decision from such a picked group it would occasionally be necessary to have the men undress, piece by piece. In some cases the decision was made upon the basis of the state of the soldier's undershirt.

The American Expeditionary Forces had the American law-making habit to an exaggerated degree. Orders were ground out more rapidly than they could possibly be read and digested by anyone who had anything else to do. And as for remembering them—such a thing was just out of the question. But they were there, in black and white, and they stood as law, to serve the powers that be in almost any situation of punishment or of buck passing that might become desirable or necessary.

Some of these law-making orders were comical. There was one that was presented to us just before going ashore at Brest that always impressed me as being a perfect example of the product of a small man in a big place. And I don't know who wrote the order, either. In effect this is what it said:

Officers are not permitted to be seen in public with women of bad reputation; and a woman of bad reputation, for the purposes of this order, will be considered to be, any woman who may be seen in public with an officer.

In our camp at St. Nazaire it was forbidden to permit any woman to put foot inside of a barrack. This rule was enforced to such an extreme that the French laundresses were compelled to stand out in wind and rain and mud to deliver to us our freshly washed and ironed clothing.

A number of times, distinguished ladies visited us. They had to be received out on the wind-swept plain. The only place in which they could find shelter was in the Y. M. C. A. hut, at least a quarter of a mile away from our area.

In such a miserable way were we compelled to show our eager hospitality to the ladies who came on Saturday and Sunday afternoons to see Regimental Parade.

Mrs. Winthrop Ames came with her husband, and with Mr. Edward H. Sothern. They too occupied chairs in the mud. Mrs. Walter Kernan, representing the Director of the Knights of Columbus paid us a call. She never saw the inside of our barracks. The splendid young women of the Y. M. C. A. canteen and welfare workers, who associated in the healthiest kind of spirit all day long in the Y huts with soldier men, had to abide by the fixed rule. There were no exceptions. In St. Nazaire there dwelt a number of ladies of the Navy—wives of Officers. There dwelt also several French families of high social station—families of title, of the old nobility. They all visited us; but they had the sky for a roof.

Mrs. J. Borden Harriman blew in one afternoon. I happened to be entering the barrack building which served as both sleeping quarters and office for Capt. Fox, the Supply Officer, and myself.

Mrs. Harriman had called to see Ham Fish, Whitney Kernochan, and Jim Europe; and she asked me to send for them. I told her that they would be in from their work details within an hour. She suggested that she would like to wait in my room.

105

I told her that I would like to have her, but that it was *defendu*. Then she flashed a kind of roving commission (signed by very high authority) and thought it would be all right to sit inside, as an inspector; and I thought so too. So far as I know, Mrs. Harriman is the only woman who ever set foot inside of that sacred chamber.

In closing my reminiscences of life with the 15th Heavy Foot at St. Nazaire, I will tell a serio-comic story of Kid Cotton, the prize-fighter, and his tender hearted philosophy of observation.

Kid Cotton stood six feet six inches in his stocking feet, and weighed, in ring side form, some two hundred and sixty pounds. His colossal size added a whimsical effect to the words which I am about to quote. He was attached, as a member of the regimental police squad, to Headquarters Company. He was frequently stationed at the Adjutant's Office. I became well acquainted with him, and enjoyed many a conversation in which the heavyweight professional exhibited greater evidences of mental nimbleness than we are accustomed to look for in men who make their living by fast foot work and hard punching.

One evening, Cotton said to me, in language showing almost none of the broad pronunciation peculiar to his race:

"Sir Adjutant, Sir, did you ever stop to think about our blessings over here, in the midst of all the poverty which the French people are suffering?

"I saw a sight this afternoon which made me think about it, a lot.

"You know I was on duty down at the dumping grounds, where the army trucks throw out the waste from the camps up here. There were hundreds of old men and women and children swarming over those fields, to pick food and fuel from our refuse. Just think of it, Sir Adjutant, Sir, the stuff we throw away as waste, supplies all the food and heat that those poor people have, to keep them from starvation and cold!

"And some of our fellows kick! It makes me think.

106

"It was awful cold and windy down there today; and there seemed to be a larger and hungrier crowd than usual. I noticed one young girl who kind of got on my nerves.

"She was pretty, and oh so thin! I guess she was about seventeen. That girl didn't have nothing on, in all that cold wind, but a little calico slip of a dress. She was so eager to get something good to take home, that she tried to beat the crowd, by running out and climbing up on top of one of the big truck loads, to pick over the stuff before it was dumped out on the fields. And that's how I found out that she was so thinly dressed—that she didn't having nothing on under that calico slip.

"When she got up on top of the truck, the wind caught hold of that thin dress, and just blew it up, right over her head!"

"What did the poor girl do, Cotton?" I asked.

"Oh, Sir, Adjutant, Sir, the girl didn't do nothing. She just kept looking for food and wood. Except that she straightened up for a minute, to make a grab for her skirt, and said, in a funny little shrill voice:—'Oo-o-la-la!'"

# XVIII

# THE COLONEL'S STORY

SOME little time after our arrival in France, Colonel Hayward received word, to the effect that request had been made and favorably received to and by General Pershing, to have the band of the 15th New York Infantry ordered detached, for the entertainment of the first United States soldiers on leave, due to arrive on Washington's Birthday, at Aix les Bains, which had been named as one of the principal leave area centers. That information, of course, started lots of rumors, but it also presented a number of problems.

The band had been built, almost instrument by instrument, and note by note, by First-Lieutenant James Reese Europe, known to the world of entertainment throughout the United States, as Jim Europe. But Lieut. Europe was a line officer, and his work with the band was officially "in addition to his other duties." United States bands, at that time under the tables of organization, were not commanded by band leaders of commissioned officer rank. Our band was officially under the command of Band Sergeant Eugene F. Mikell, a splendid man, a highly educated musician, and a cornet player of great ability; but as compared with Jim Europe as a leader of men, or as a band leader, he wasn't in the same class. As a matter of fact, nobody was in the same class with Jim Europe, who was a most extraordinary man without qualification of limitation as to race, color, or any other element.

The rumor came down from Chaumont that a white officer would have to go in command of the expedition, and that Lieut. Europe would not be permitted to go at all, as he was not officially connected with the band, and could not qualify as a white officer merely as a military commander.

Colonel Hayward started one of his fixing campaigns, so as to provide that Lieut. Europe could go in addition to Band Sergeant Mikell, and that he should go as a specially designated band leader, so that the expedition could have the benefit of his genius in direct leadership over the musicians.

While the fixing program was being pushed, however, Colonel Hayward strung a second string to his bow, by arranging for a special series of evening concerts and afternoon concerts in the town of St. Nazaire, under the leadership of Bandmaster Mikell, with Lieut. Europe as critic and instructor— not of the band, but of the Bandmaster. The difference in the quality of the music played under the preparation and leadership of Mikell and that of Europe was quite pronounced, although our band, even under Mikell, compared favorably with the best of the rest of the army bands, and would have rated way ahead of the average.

One evening, during the latter part of the first week in February, Colonel Hayward was giving a dinner party to General Walsh and the officers of his staff. A few hours before the time for the dinner, he walked into the Adjutant's office with one of those boyish grins on his face that I had learned to read as an indication of an accomplishment in the field of putting one over, and he said: "Little, I want you to have Jim arrange to lead the band at the dinner concert. General Walsh was up here a few nights ago and we gave him a good time, but if we can get Jim inspired tonight, we can stand that Headquarters crowd on their heads, and I think we'll have won our point about having Lieut. Europe tour France with the band, and in command of it."

That plan was carried out. Nobody in printed or written words can describe the effect upon the audience's emotions when Jim Europe led that band, but something happened to General Walsh and his staff. When General Walsh rose to say good-night, he said to Colonel Hayward: "Something must have happened to your bandsmen tonight, Colonel, I have never heard them play so before, in fact, I have never heard such music from a military band in all my life. You must have been putting them through some wonderful practice since you got the preparing orders about that trip to Aix. I have listened to every concert down in the Park, and of course, I have dined with you a number of times and heard them, and I have even sneaked in on the outskirts of the crowd and listened to your general afternoon concerts here, but nothing ever happened such as happened tonight. I'm all stirred up."

And then Colonel Hayward was able to go back at General Walsh and explain to him that he'd had Lieut. Europe, who built the band and who had arranged most of the music for the band, lead tonight in honor of the last concert to be given to General Walsh, and that he felt just as unhappy over the prospect of having to have that band travel under the assistant leader, Mikell, without the benefit of Europe's presence, as General Walsh had expressed himself confident of the great hit that the band was to make during its tour—only the two sets of feelings were at opposite ends of the poles.

Well, the thing worked. Before General Walsh left he had promised to make a personal plea for a revision of the program of command, and ask to have the orders from S. O. S. when published, provide for Lieut. Europe to accompany the expedition.

After General Walsh left, the band played one or two more pieces for the regimental officers, and the company broke up. Most of the officers drifted off to their quarters.

The Colonel's mood seemed to change. During the evening, while he was operating on General Walsh, he had been brilliant, aggressive, good-natured, cynical, humorous, winning and forceful in every way for which he was famous; but, as the band and the officers departed, and there remained only a few of his more intimate friends who had been seated at his table during

DRILL AT VIENNE LA VILLE, COL. HAYWARD SENDS A MESSAGE BY CARRIER
PIGEON

11914

DRILL IN THE TRENCHES, MAY 4, 1918, LIEUT. WALTER R. LOCKHART IN
COMMAND

the evening's entertainment, his manner seemed to take on a wistfulness, and presently he looked up and said to the three or four of us who remained: "You fellows aren't in a hurry, are you? Let's have a little talk."

We made ourselves comfortable around the old-fashioned heating stove that we had had set up in the mess barracks. Then the Colonel talked.

He talked for several hours, sometimes repeating, occasionally correcting, but he talked as if in a kind of a dream at times, and his talk was filled with sentiment. He unfolded one of the most wonderful stories of accomplishment I have ever heard.

The Colonel commenced by telling the four or five of us present that he looked upon us as his old reliables, and that he wanted us to know, no matter how impatient he might be with us sometimes, that he believed in his heart that he never could have built and led our regiment to the point that it had gotten to, with the assistance of even one of us left out of the picture. And after that preamble, he just drifted along with his story without interruption:

"We have all heard the sneers directed at us, characterizing the 15th N. Y. infantry as a smart piece of political development. We have heard people say that it was conceived in politics, born in ridicule, and reared in opposition. Well, the rearing and the borning characterization may be all right, but they're all wrong about the spirit of the conception. Governor Whitman and I up in Albany found the record of the law sponsored by Governor Sulzer, authorizing the building of an infantry regiment of colored soldiers. The making of that law predated Governor Whitman's first term by a number of years. It is not for us to say whether that was conceived in politics or not, but if it was, it was damn poor politics, because after the law was put on the statute books, nothing was done about it.

"The Governor and I started to talk about it, and we agreed that either that regiment ought to be built and given a fair chance of proving itself, or the law ought to be repealed. Gradually the details of the program for the building of the regiment were worked out. Governor Whitman was perfectly sincere in his feeling that the great colored population of New York ought to be given an opportunity to shine in the National Guard field without prejudice; and as you men know, I felt very deeply on the subject of the negro problem, and the unfairness with which it was being met. When the Governor invited me to accept the designation as Commanding Officer of a regiment that did not exist, under a detail to active service from the supernumerary list of Colonels in which my name had been placed by a transfer from the supernumerary list of the National Guard of Nebraska, I accepted the opportunity in all seriousness, and in full appreciation of the probable difficulties which lay before me. The absurdity of being Colonel of a regiment of which the Colonel was the only member struck me as a necessary absurdity to accept. Enlistments and equipments and training cannot be accomplished without authoritative leadership, and a Colonel is the proper authoritative leader for a regiment.

"I never batted an eye when I called upon John Purroy Mitchel, then Mayor of New York, and told him that I wanted an appropriation for quarters to serve as an armory for my regiment; and I was grateful when Mayor Mitchel sent me to Lawrence V. Meehan (Larry Meehan now, to us) who was the superintendent of the Armory Board, for expert assistance as to the ways and means of getting what we were after. We got a lease on that little dance hall on the second story of the building at 132nd Street and 7th Avenue, and we got a lease on the corner store that had been a cigar store on the corner of the same building at 131st Street and 7th Avenue. We called the larger room on the second floor the "armory" and with that went the cellar, which we decided to use for uniform storage, rifle and ammunition storage, etc. Of course, we didn't have any uniforms or rifles or ammunition, but that's another story. Also, how we got them is another story.

"Larry Meehan in some way found for us a little bit of office furniture, and he stuck it in the cigar store at 131st Street and 7th Avenue, and we put a sign up in the window advising the public that the recruiting of the 15th New York Infantry, colored regiment of the National Guard, was under way.

"I spent a part of every day there; old George Hinton over there spent the other part of every day there; Boley Lee—Dr. George Bolling Lee, my personal friend and physician and one of the great surgeons of New York, as you know, and the grandson of General Robert E. Lee, he spent a part of every day with me. Business was kind of slow in starting, and then one day a big, strapping young fellow named Bunting came in and allowed as how he'd like to be a soldier. Well, Boley Lee submitted him to all the indignities that a soldier has to submit to in a physical examination, and passed him as sound. I told him to put up his hand and I administered the oath of allegiance. George Hinton stood at attention and cried while I was administering that first oath of enlistment, and then I shook hands with Private Bunting of the 15th New York Infantry, and allowed as how there were now two of us!

"That evening the Colonel of the 15th New York Infantry, and Private Bunting sat down and had a long conference as to the future of our regiment, and we agreed not only that we were going a long ways, but that we were going to the top. I offered Private Bunting the job of First Sergeant of Company A, but he declined it. He said he didn't want to be anything but a private, that that would be glory enough for him.

"Well, we kept on working, enlisting and building, and followed the rule that we figured ought to appeal to human nature: The first twelve men enlisted were made First Sergeants of the 12 rifle companies, and the next twelve men were made Supply Sergeants of the 12 rifle companies, and the next 12 men were made Mess Sergeants, and the next group were assigned as Duty Sergeants—one company at a time. And so the regiment in the early stages was built from the top down, instead of from the bottom up.

"I had a terrible time securing the services of officers of experience. And finally, as you know, we had to start in with officers of little or no experience.

"When the National Guard was mobilized for guard duty on the border between Mexico and the United States, we got a bit of a boom; and when the National Guard came home from border duty, we got a further bit of a boom. A lot of fine young fellows from the 7th Regiment and the Squadron had learned that they'd just as soon be officers if they had to go out again, and so they gave up their jobs as non-commissioned officers with the old established organizations, and threw their lot in with me. George Hinton got a transfer from the National Guard supernumerary list of some Western state, just as I had, and Monson Morris got himself picked up from the supernumerary list of New York State National Guard in which he had formerly been a Major of the 12th Regiment. Gradually we commenced to function, even though rather lamely, along the lines of organization.

"One afternoon a nice looking middle aged man came into our headquarters offices in Harlem, and applied for enlistment. He explained that he was professionally a bugler, and that he was employed by the Right Rev. Bishop David H. Greer for duty in connection with the Episcopal Cathedral up on Morningside Heights. After he had passed his physical examination and been sworn in, I invited him to take charge of the office for a couple of hours if he had time, stating that I had to go downtown for a luncheon appointment, and promising him that when I returned I would look up in the regimental roster to see what non-commissioned office might be open to him, and we would assign him to such an office. When I returned several hours later, I found on my desk a neatly written report of everybody who had called either in person or by telephone, together with the messages left, and then glancing down at the bottom of his report, I found that it would be unnecessary for me to assign this recruit to office, because he had found his niche, appointed himself to that office, and was filling it perfectly. At the bottom of the sheet of this very comprehensive report appeared the words:

'Respectfully submitted,
David P. Wendell
Receiver of Messages'

"The recruiting of a regiment is to a considerable degree a question of showmanship. We figured that the best way to get recruits was to have parades, but figured that a necessary part of a real parade was uniforms and a band. From the semi-professional National Guard Quartermaster's Department, where I had to go to apply for uniforms, we received no assistance.

"If it had not been for the determination of Governor Whitman and of his Adjutant General, Louis Stotesbury, who helped me go through with the enterprise, I doubt if we could have ever even gotten a start. Whenever I got up against a blank wall with the Quartermaster's Department and their prejudices against us, I would have to go either to Stotesbury or to Gov. Whitman himself, and get such stuff as I could get in the way of supplies, by specific orders, and even in these specific orders at times the Governor found such opposition and obstacles in his path that he had to indulge in some pretty rough alternatives. I never did find out what the prejudice was all about, but I never had any doubt that it was there. I cannot be cruel enough to figure that it could have been racial prejudice, and so I have kind of accepted the weight of the prejudice as applying to me personally, and I guess that is where it belonged, because I was able to take care of myself, as events subsequently proved.

"We paraded around with broom sticks and what-nots for so long that the people of Harlem commenced to believe that the whole thing was a fake, and that we were not going to be soldiers at all. I figured that if we could get some rifles that that would be of great help to us, so I went over to the State Quartermaster, took my hat in my hand, and asked for rifles. Of course I didn't get any. But I didn't get right out, either, and some of the laborers over there at the Arsenal commenced to develop human instincts, and commenced to whisper to me a little bit about where I could find things that I needed, if I only knew how to look for them. I found that there were between 500 and 1,000 rifles available—all nice new ones too—which had been earmarked to be reserved for civilian shooting clubs. This civilian shooting club idea, I believe, was an off-shoot of some of General Leonard Wood's military preparedness program. He couldn't get any action from the government in the line of military preparedness, but he applied his resourcefulness to seeing what he could do about getting preparedness under a camouflage. So he got either a law or a regulation put on the books, encouraging the formation of civilian shooting clubs, or rifle clubs, with the right to draw rifles from the Ordnance Department of the United States Army.

"Well, I started the darndest set of rifle or civilian shooting clubs that you ever heard of. There was a regular boom. Practically everybody in the regiment in the early days became the president or the secretary of a civilian shooting club, and we put in our requisitions and got the rifles delivered to us. I suppose if an ordinary business concern had been handing out those rifles, some smart Aleck might have discovered that the presidents and secretaries of all these different shooting clubs all lived in the same place, namely, the office of the Public Service Commission in the Municipal Building in New York; but bureaucrats of the army do not look far beyond what they find printed in a book, and so nobody did discover it until we had all the rifles that were available for shooting clubs.

"Then dear old Jim Europe joined the regiment, and when I discovered who he was, I asked him to build a band. In the beginning the band was pretty bad, but it made a noise, and at the time we had 28 bandsmen it made 28 noises all at the same time, mostly not in tune or in rhythm, but the band, such as it was, plus the uniforms, such as they were, plus the rifles, without bayonets, of course, because civilian shooting clubs had no use

116

for bayonets, all contributed to our parades through Harlem, and the parades all contributed to recruitment.

"Finally the day came when the Governor agreed that it was time that we had a stand of colors.

"My spirit of showmanship then was called upon, and it was decided that the colors should be presented to the regiment on Fifth Avenue, in front of the Union League Club, and presented by no less a dignitary than Governor Charles S. Whitman.

"A very impressive parade was arranged for the receiving of the colors. I borrowed a lot of officers—one of the officers I borrowed was Bert Williams, who had had a commission once in a National Guard outfit of a Western state. I invited him to ride on my staff.

"Well, everything went along pretty well until the band struck up. I had had the bad judgment of arranging to have the staff ride. I suppose it was to some extent a matter of personal vanity, because I figured that I looked just lovely on a military charger, and I couldn't see myself riding out ahead of a regiment with my staff walking. Be that as it may, when the band burst forth, the staff burst right out and rode off in all directions! Bert Williams pulled a John Gilpin for several blocks and might have been going yet if his horse hadn't spied an open doorway in an apartment house. The horse entered the apartment house without knocking, clattered right down to the end of the corridor, and halted in front of the bank of elevators. Bert Williams looked helplessly around him, and seeing a nice red plush sofa within reaching distance of one of his feet, dismounted by way of the sofa and reached the ground in safety. At this point, the apartment hallman rushed up to him with a great deal of indignation and said: "Now, you just take that horse right out of here!" And Williams in his blandest tone, which we were accustomed to pay $8.00 a seat to hear at the Ziegfeld Follies, said: "Mah friend, if you wants to take that horse out of here, you jes' take him out yo'self. I'm sure you must know more about that horse than I do." Capt. Bert Williams thereupon walked with great dignity out to the street, got into his automobile which had been following him all the way, and reported that he would continue as a staff officer in the rear of the regiment, by automobile.

"Our men didn't have carfare sometimes to respond to an order for assembly. Many times they didn't have money to buy their meals. While our officers were teaching right hand salute with their voices, they were exercising right hands in the change pocket for themselves, almost as frequently with their own gesture as with the teaching of the military gesture.

"A lot of our men had no place to live, and we gave them cots and blankets and permitted them to live in the so-called Armory Headquarters.

"We established the second battalion, with headquarters in Brooklyn, at 191 Harrison Avenue, and put Major Monson Morris in command.

"When the mustering-in nights occurred for federalization as National Guard units, we kept the telephones hot. Fortunately, we were mustered in by companies, and I'd hate to have to take disciplinary punishment for all the duplications that I strongly suspect were worked by company commanders in getting the necessary "Here!" answers to roll calls, to comply with the minimum number per company necessary for the establishment of a unit.

"Our roll calls were accomplished by companies largely because we didn't have room to do it in any other way on the floors of our so-called armories. I have heard rumors that some of the Captains, in order to make it not too difficult for the mustering officers under General Bridgman to fail to recognize repeaters in the several companies, clubbed together and hired a couple of busses to bring men over from Brooklyn, armed to answer the roll call in the Harlem companies, and then a couple of nights later, reversed the operation. There is also a story to the effect that one night they had to have just one more man, and they went out on the street and shanghaied a man with a wooden leg and draped it up in uniform trousers and had him stand in the rear ranks and answer "Here!"

"Of course, I as the Colonel of the regiment wouldn't have countenanced any of these things if I had known about them, and naturally I didn't know about them.

"But all these things that I am telling you men tonight (and I strongly suspect that you already know about them) I am merely repeating as hearsay.

"I wonder how many of you fellows know how we came to get the money with which to build our band? I am going to tell you because it leaves a kind of nice taste in my mouth, as the story has a direct bearing upon the public-spiritedness of one of the kind of men that the demagogues of politics and press and pulpit who seek to build class prejudices in America, like to refer to as the "criminal rich" or even "malefactors of great wealth" if they want to go back to the days when Theodore Roosevelt was President.

"Jim Europe came to me one day and persuaded me that the army band of 28 pieces which was all that a band needed according to the tables of organization, was an entirely impracticable combination of instruments to play well-balanced music. He had it all worked out and he figured that 44 was the minimum number that a regimental band should have, and that 60-odd would be better. Well, of course, we couldn't get instruments for 44 men when the tables of organization only allowed for 28 men, and we couldn't get music scores, and we couldn't enlist bandsmen. We figured out that the latter difficulty could be met by having soldiers detailed for special duty with the band and excused from their regular infantry company duties, while performing this special duty.

"But the need of money presented quite a problem. Europe convinced me also that we ought to have a few key men for each of the important instrumental sections of the band, just as we had squad leaders and platoon leaders in line companies. And he knew where he could get such men, but they couldn't afford to serve for the regular army pay, unless we were able to pay them premiums out of our own pockets. Well, I touched the officers as far as it was safe to touch and then I found I was still short thousands of dollars on a reasonably set up budget.

"In a spirit almost of despair, I called upon Mr. Daniel C. Reid, sometimes described as 'The Tin Plate King,' or 'American Can King.'

"I told my story to Dan Reid, and he was very nice, gave me all the time I wanted, and said: 'What do you want me to do?' I said, 'I'd like to have you give me letters of introduction to 30 or 40 of your rich friends, and ask them to let me talk to them, and then if they will let me talk to them, I am going to try to touch them for $500 a piece.'

"Dan Reid said to me: 'How many of the 30 or 40 victims do you expect to land for $500 a piece?' And I said I hoped to land at least 20 of them. Mr. Reid reached into a drawer of his desk, took out his check book, and wrote me a check for $10,000 and said: 'That's a damn sight easier than writing you 40 letters of introduction, and it will save you a lot of time too. Here are your 20 victims at $500 each.'

"Then we were heeled with money for the band.

"Jim Europe one day explained to me that the reed instruments, that is, clarinets, flutes, saxophones, and one or two other instruments, served the same purpose in a military band that string instruments serve in a symphony orchestra, and he said there was a great scarcity of reed instrument players in the United States among the colored people. He explained that the difficulty had something to do with the lips of the colored man— I don't know whether it was thick lips or thin lips—but Jim Europe knew, and I asked him what the answer was. He said the answer was Porto Rico. When I got over my astonishment over that answer, he explained to me that there were a lot of really good reed instrument musicians in Porto Rico, that their lips were all right, and that they were all well educated; that he had corresponded and found out about it, and then he un-folded a most amazingly ambitious plan.

"Europe suggested that if we could give him proper orders to go to Porto Rico and enlist musicians for his band, that he could get the pick of the crop and build the best band in the army, if I would permit him to pay some bonuses where needed for the key men for each set of instruments.

"Well, we fixed Jim up not only with military orders, but with money orders, and within less than three weeks we had 18 of the best reed instrument players in the world, as full-fledged members of the 15th New York Infantry.

"Jim also went to Chicago and got one of the greatest cornet players in the world, Frank de Broit. As you know, de Broit is right next to Eugene Mikell in rank and authority in the assistant leadership of the band. As you don't know, I am slip-ping him $100 a month personally, out of that $10,000 fund, which in addition to his highest grade pay that an enlisted man can get as one of these super staff sergeants, plus his overseas percentage, gives him quite a moderate income when you consider that he also has his clothes and board and lodging paid for in addition.

"Little, here, has had quite a lot of perplexity over de Broit. Of course, de Broit is a prima donna, and that moustache that he wears in itself marks him as a bit eccentric. I overheard Little protesting with Europe one day about the way de Broit sits with his cornet on his knee, and doesn't play it at concerts; but Europe climbed right into de Broit's corner and said he didn't have to play at concerts, that the mere fact that he was there ready to start every new theme for him, made the difference between the successful rendering of a piece and an unsuccessful one. He said very frankly that de Broit likes to look around the audience and see the girls admiring that moustache, and that very likely he *does* think of himself as a counterpart of the Kaiser in appearance, but that his job is really that of what a pace-maker would be to a laboring organization, and that he's invaluable. So then Little changed his opinion, and started to treat de Broit like the genius that he is, and he even went so far one day as to arrange for de Broit to give a musical lecture to the members of the band and he invited me to listen and it was really tremendously interesting. De Broit explained the meaning of every instrument, and what it came from, from the earliest days of barbaric music.

"There was another pretty nice incident of courtesy and generosity along the same lines as that of the donation of Mr. Daniel C. Reid. Our regiment, of course, as a brand-new regiment, was at a disadvantage in comparison with the old established National Guard regiments, on account of having no company funds with which to buy luxuries, such as phonographs, phonograph records, books and magazines, for the recreation and entertainment of the company members. Eventually we were sure to be able to remedy that handicap on account of our savings from mess funds, but in the early days our poverty presented something of a problem, not only in administration costs, but in the fields indicated.

"During the month of August, Little here had a talk one day with a man who was a close friend and even an associate in a sense, with Mr. John D. Rockefeller, Jr. I'm pretty sure Little didn't ask for anything, but I'm also pretty sure that he hinted pretty hard. As a result of that talk, Little received a check from Mr. Rockefeller a few days later for $500, with the request that no advertisement of the donation be indulged in, but with best wishes for a cure of some of the difficulties which had been experienced.

"A couple of weeks later, having made a report as to the uses that were going to be made of that money, or which had in part been made of it, Mr. Rockefeller sent another check for $500, still with the same request that no advertisement be made.

"Well, Little kept his promise, and I obeyed the spirit of his promise. No advertisement of that gift has been made before tonight, but I feel that I ought to make you fellows all acquainted with these important incidents of the regiment. It is almost a certainty that we won't all go home, and when we get home, it is a complete uncertainty as to what the future is going to hold either for our regiment or for our country. We are almost sure to go through economic and social revolutions. If the tide should ever turn so that the Daniel Reids and the John D. Rockefellers should need the friendship of our crowd, that day should not find any of my intimates unprepared as to being able to appraise our obligations.

"Somewhere in one of my trunks, I have a photograph of one of our early recruiting parades in Harlem. In a way it's a pitiful thing, but when I look at this magnificent regiment today, and then when I look at what we all hope this regiment is going to be after the war when we return in triumph to our own country, that miserable little parade of unorganized and ununiformed straggling individuals, takes importance in my mind, ranking in a sense as the Plymouth Rock must rank to some of these Mayflower descendants' associations.

"We fellows around this table have gone through an awful lot. I have been reminiscing with you tonight, and I can tell from your faces that almost everything that I have been talking about, one or more of you know as well as I know. Still, there is a kind of a spell upon me tonight, because I have a feeling that within a few days we are going to receive orders from A. E. F. Head-quarters ordering that blessed band of ours down to Aix les Bains, and it seems to me that may mark the beginning of a long list of casualties, as it might be called, which this regiment from that day on may never cease to experience. I have a hunch that while that band is away, we may receive our orders to go up to the front line zone. And I have a hunch that by the time that band rejoins us some of us may have made the supreme sacrifice, in their country's service.

"And so I am sitting here with you old stand-bys tonight, just reviewing some of the high spots of the hell that we have gone through, and gloating in anticipation of some of the triumphs that we may register.

"Way back last August, when the 27th Division had its farewell parade in New York, upon the eve of leaving their home stations for Spartanburg (we were of course detached from the 27th Division at that time, and we were doing special duty in guard service covering railroads, bridges and water works and the big cantonments at Wrightstown, New Jersey and Yaphank, Long Island), I applied for permission for our regiment to make that farewell parade to Little Old New York with the 27th Division, and my application was denied. I felt wounded and I felt bitter. I went back to headquarters, and I sat down by Little's desk in the Adjutant's office, and I don't remember whether I actually cried or not, but I know that I wanted to cry. And I told Little what had occurred.

"I put up my right hand, as if I were taking an oath, and said: 'I swear to you that even if they won't let us parade with them in going away, that we will have a parade when we come home that will be the greatest parade, in one sense, that New York will ever have seen, and I swear to you that we won't let any division have us attached to them for that parade.' And then I asked Little to stand up and swear to me that if he survived and I didn't that he would carry out that same pledge. And now, my friends, you are the stand-bys of the building of this regiment. We are upon the eve of a great mile-stone in the history of this regiment, and I want you all to stand with me and take that oath together—that whichever of us may be in survival as commanding officer of this regiment when we get back to New York, that we see to it that the glory and honor of the Negro race of America may be served by having our welcome home parade celebrated all alone—in the same manner in which we have been born and trained and shipped to France and received in France."

The Colonel's vision that night was in a sense prophetic. Within a few days the band did start on its tour of France as an independent unit. Within three weeks the regiment did journey to the danger zone.

And with the exception of four or five days during the latter part of August, when all the units of the regiment were united in a training camp in the central part of France, we never again were all in the same post until we assembled at Le Mons to be refitted preparatory to our embarkation back to America after the war was over.

# THE BAND TOURS FRANCE

*February 12–March 20, 1918*

UPON February 10, 1918, the special order quoted below was received at our camp:

LINE OF COMMUNICATIONS

BASE COMMANDER, BASE SECTION NO. I

FRANCE

Special Orders⎱                              February 10, 1918.
  No. 41      ⎰            EXTRACT

* * * * * * * *

3. Pursuant to telegraphic instructions, Headquarters, L. of C., dated February 1-4-26, 1918, the Band, 15th N. Y. Infantry, and detachment Hqrs. Co., that organization, consisting of two officers and fifty-six men, with necessary cooking utensils and eighteen days rations, (under command of Captain A. W. Little, Adjutant, 15th N. Y. Inf.), will proceed from this Base to Aix-les-Bains, so as to arrive at that station not later than February 15, 1918, reporting upon arrival thereat to the Provost Marshal for duty in connection with the opening of the Rest Station at that point. This detachment will remain at the above mentioned station until March 2, 1918, on which date it will return to its proper station, at these Headquarters.

The Quartermaster Corps will furnish the necessary transportation and travel rations and coffee money for eight days for the journey to and return from Aix-les-Bains.

The travel directed is necessary in the military service.

By command of Brigadier General Walsh.

ORRIN H. WOLFE
Adjutant General.

Copies to:
C. O. L. of C.
DQM (3)
FIN (2)
RTO
C. O. 15th N. Y. Inf.
Capt. Little.

Line of Communications (L. of C) was, at that time, the name of the department of the service subsequently known as Service of Supply (S. O. S.).

I was provided with two 3rd class coaches for the men, one car for freight and baggage, and 1st class reservations for Lieutenant Europe and myself. We took with us about eight tons of rations.

At about 1 o'clock in the afternoon of February 12th, 1918 (Lincoln's Birthday, and exactly one year before the return of our regiment in triumph to New York), Lieutenant Sattler reported to me that my cars were completely packed and ready to be moved, that two trucks were waiting for the men outside of the company quarters, and that we should entrain at 3:45 P. M.

Our first stopping point was Nantes. The run was but a short one—about an hour and a half.

At Nantes, our cars were detached from the train and held in the station, over night. The men detrained, and marched to some French barracks, where they were quartered and messed as guests of the U. S. Military Police detachment of Nantes. The officers and men of this command were most cordial in their hospitality.

The Band was scheduled for a concert at the Opera House, at nine o'clock in the evening. The concert was in honor of Lincoln's Birthday, but for the benefit (financially) of a French charitable institution.

The Opera House faced a plaza of about two hundred yards square, bounded by handsome buildings. This entire plaza was crowded with an audience which maintained silence during the playing of a number—and then made up for lost time, by wild applause. With the French, a shrill whistle, or "cat call," is the supreme effort of applause. The thoughtful French manager had explained this to our men. He had been informed, so he said, that in America such sounds are indulged in to denote disapproval; and he desired no incident to mar "the happiness of the evening of this beautiful day."

127

I elbowed my way through the crowd, and reached the Opera House in time to hear a couple of pieces. Then, the band went inside, to the back stage, to prepare for the formal appearance; and the doors were opened to the public for general admission. Subscribers for boxes and orchestra seats had been admitted by side doors during the playing of the advance concert. Most of the audience seated in these reserved sections were in evening dress. The galleries were crowded, and all standing room was occupied. I doubt if any first night or special performance at the Metropolitan Opera House in New York ever had, relatively, a more brilliant audience.

The French people knew no color line. All they seemed to want to know, that night, was that a great national holiday of their ally was being celebrated—and that made the celebration one of their own. The spirit of emotional enthusiasm had got into the blood of our men; and they played as I had never heard them play before.

Upon the morning of February 13th, 1918, our detachment resumed its journey, leaving Nantes at 9:27 A. M. with our cars attached to a regular train, with destination—Tours.

At about half past twelve our train stopped at Angers. There we had lunch. The Band played in a public square, near the station, for a quarter of an hour. At about two o'clock we resumed our journey.

Tours was reached at about six o'clock in the evening.

No advance agent had arranged for us in Tours. After some delay, orders were given to attach our cars to the south bound express, leaving Tours at 3:18 A. M. In the meantime, I had been fortunate enough to find at the station another hospitable military police officer; and the men, under command of Lieut. Europe, had been piled into trucks, and carried off to barracks, for a hot supper.

The railroad business attended to, I strolled off to find the office of the Provost Marshal. As I presented my orders, to be stamped, the A. P. M. (I can't recall his name; but I believe he was Lieutenant Colonel) looked up and smiled. "So you've got a band with you! Can they play?"

"They can, sir. Also, they would like to—if you can arrange a couple of concerts for us," I answered.

"Fine! Any suggestions as to where or when?"

"Yes, sir. I should like to go out to the Commanding General's place and give him a surprise serenade, if you know some staff officer out there with nerve enough to help me stage it. After that, I'd like to play a formal indoor concert, in the biggest theatre you can get for us at this late hour."

"All right, I believe I can fix you up both ways," said the Assistant Provost Marshal. He was a regular fellow—that A. P. M.!

He started a clerk telephoning a series of calls, while we waited, and our conversation was resumed.

"Have you got a good band?"

"Pretty good," I said. "It's the only one I've heard over here; but I believe it's the best in the army."

"Well, I dunno," the colonel came back, "I dunno about that. Some of our young officers here came back from St. Nazaire a couple of weeks ago, and they've been talking ever since about some colored band they heard down there. They say that's the real thing in bands—about double the size of the regulation article, and wonderful to listen to. The leader, I believe, is a chap by name of Europe—Jim Europe, who used to play dance music in New York for Mr. and Mrs. Vernon Castle, when they were all the rage. Ever hear that band?"

"That's the band I've got out at your barracks, right now," I answered.

"Well, I'll be damned!"

Presently, Mr. Europe came in to tell me that the men were waiting outside, in trucks, ready to go to the house of the Commanding General.

We found Major General Kernan quartered in a beautiful little chateau on top of a steep hill upon the outskirts of the city.

The serenade was a surprise and a success. After a number of pieces had been played, the General requested some of his favorite Southern melodies; and then, he said he would like to make a little talk to the men.

General Kernan complimented the men of the Band upon their music, and he thanked them for the pleasure they had given him. He prophesied that the tour would be a great success from the viewpoint of the entertainment to be given to American soldiers on leave. But he appealed to the men to remember that their duty throughout the tour was not merely to consist of playing music for the entertainment of the crowd. He explained that where we were going, no American soldiers had as yet been; that, according to the impression left by us upon the minds of the French population of the great territory through which we were to pass, so would rest the reputation of American soldiers in general. He told the men that France recognized no color line. He begged the men not to be the cause of the establishment, in the minds of French people, of a color line. He told the men that they were upon a mission of great importance; that they were not merely musicians and soldiers of the American Army but that they were representatives of the American nation. The eyes of France would be upon them; and through the eyes of France, the eyes of the world.

Major General Kernan, in his manner of appeal to our men, proved himself a master student of human nature. The men of our regiment, when appealed to in that way, never failed to respond in satisfactory manner.

The men of the Band and Headquarters detachment made a splendid record all through their tour. They left behind them enviable reputations—everywhere.

The cause of the colored race suffered in no particular on account of their representation through the peaceful territory of France by the men of the 15th Heavy Foot.

The American Army in general had no cause for complaint in its representation by the men of my command.

After playing for Major General Kernan, at Tours, that night of the thirteenth of February, the Band returned to the city, and played before a large and appreciative audience in the rooms of the Red Cross Club.

After the concert, the men were taken to barracks for a few hours' sleep.

Shortly before half-past three upon the morning of the fourteenth of February, our train left Tours.

From Tours we visited Saincaize, Moulins, Bessay, La Ferte, Varennes and Créchy. Our tour also included St. Etienne, Lyon, Culoz and St. Germain des Fossés. We arrived at Aix-les-Bains on Feb. 15, 1918.

Our first official duty at Aix-les-Bains consisted of participation in a parade, as a part of the formal ceremonies in the opening of the Leave Area.

The first troop train, filled with American soldiers booked for seven days of rest and recreation, arrived at about noon. The city was *en fête*. The Mayor made a speech of welcome, in French. The Chairman of the Citizens Committee seconded the motion, in English. The Assistant Provost Marshal declaimed a few well chosen threats. Mr. Franklin S. Edmonds, the head of the Y. M. C. A. for that area, told the boys that he and his assistants loved them. A French band of school boys played the Star Spangled Banner (at least their leader told us that that was what it was). Our band responded with the Marseillaise. Then, the head of the committee waved his hand and the parade started.

I have never been able to figure out exactly why I happened to be picked upon to lead that parade, when there were so many persons present of such superior eminence. But, as Tennyson told us, a soldier's lot is not to reason why. I had my orders. I led the parade. A couple of French detectives served as guides. Their conception of duty seemed to be to march as close to me as possible; and, I regret to report that, upon a number of occasions— owing to the fact that our Regulations provide that a soldier's eyes shall be "straight to the front,"—I stepped on the guides. Outside of that, everything went all right.

The Band played splendidly and without ceasing, the citizens cheered, the officials rode with dignity in their carriages, and bowed with graciousness. The Sun shone. The three thousand soldier boys (*permissionaires*) marched with the snap of Americans—and wondered when that "rest and recreation" was to begin.

Our original orders for Aix were for two weeks. Upon February 26th, telegraphic orders from the Commanding General, S.O.S., were received providing for an extension of our service in the Leave Area for an additional fortnight.

So, the Band had a full month at Aix-les-Bains, and a total of about nine days on the road.

While at Aix, the Band rehearsed every morning in the Casino theatre. Every afternoon, it played a concert—Tuesdays and Fridays in the Park, and upon the other days in the general assembly hall of the Casino. Every evening it played a big concert in the Casino Theatre as a part of the professional vaudeville show, put on under the direction of Mr. Winthrop Ames, and including among its personnel Mr. E. H. Sothern.

Not long after this there was a considerable discussion running in the newspapers at home having to do with an accusation against the American command of unfair treatment of negro troops. The following clipping came to us. It was written as a contribution to the discussion mentioned. It is a matter of no small satisfaction to be able to present it here.

*N. Y. Herald, Monday, April 17, 1918*

To the Editor of the Herald:

It is good to see the Herald and the Telegram declaring that sinister statements that our colored troops are abused by their officers are false. Of course they are vilely false.

I had the pleasure in company with Mr. and Mrs. Winthrop Ames, about six weeks ago, of being the guest of the Colonel and officers of the Old Fifteenth New York Infantry in France. Our mission, concerning the entertainment of the American troops, led us to the post of this regiment. We passed half a day there and were entertained by the remarkable band of the regiment, conducted by the celebrated Mr. Europe. Colonel Hayward talked with great enthusiasm of his men and of certain prizes he had established for cleanliness and for perfection in equipment and behavior. He especially was proud of his regiment's record for health and gave his soldiers great credit for their discipline. His officers stood by and echoed his enthusiasm. We talked with the men, who were equally proud of their colonel and his aids. There was no question of the genuine affection and regard these colored soldiers had for their officers. Later the quite remarkable band of this regiment was permitted to take part in the opening ceremonies of the rest camp at Aix-les-Bains. Here Captain Arthur Little, who was in charge of the fifty musicians, and the men themselves were quartered in our hotel. We saw them constantly, and it was easy to observe Capt. Little's pride in his band and their affection for him.

Colonel Hayward raised among his own friends $10,000 to provide instruments for his regimental band. It was the bright particular success of the opening at the Aix-les-Bains season. I am sure that no one would resent the reports of ill treatment more vehemently than the colored soldiers who serve proudly under Colonel Hayward.

E. H. SOTHERN.

New York City, April 13, 1917.

Upon a number of occasions, during intermissions at the park concerts, civilians would hand Mr. Europe a sheet of music, and request that the Band play the piece at the next concert. Such requests were invariably accompanied by a glimpse into a family's heart yearning. It might be a song written by a daughter who had died. It might be a valse composed by the firstborn son of the family now serving at the front. Europe's sympathy and courtesy went out to all alike. No such request was ever refused. One morning, I noticed that Mr. Europe's eyes had the appearance of great fatigue. I inquired if he was unwell. He said that he was quite well, but that he had been up most of the night, arranging the orchestration for one of those amateur musical compositions. As Europe expressed it, he had written three million notes, representing over twenty different instrumental scores. Of course the three million estimate was an exaggeration; but in Europe's Band no more than two men ever played the same score. His arrangements were always marvels of effective harmony. No one instrument was ever offensively distinguishable.

The Band played several formal and several other informal concerts at Chambéry, the fascinating old cathedral city a few kilometers from Aix.

I once figured up roughly that my black babies and I travelled, during that tour, almost 2000 miles in France; and the Band furnished music in more than twenty-five cities or towns.

Upon the morning of March 11, 1918, I was horrified to read in *Le Progres*, of Lyon, in a column devoted especially to affairs of Aix-les-Bains, a squib, which I publish in the original French as well as in translated form:

133

Extrait du journal le Progress
du LYON lundi 11/Mar/1918

Aix-les-Bains—Le negre et la Corsetiere
Un brillant musicien pour obtenir les faveurs d'une jeune corsetiere lui offrit 1000 francs, celle ci accepta de grand coeur les 1000 francs et le negre mais le lendemain lorsqu'elle voulut changer le billet de mille francs, la banque ou elle se presenta lui fit remarquer que son billet etait un billet de la sainte-farce et n'avait aucune valeur.

La corsetiere le coeur bien gros compta sa mesaventure au commissaire de police qui eut le sourire. Quand au negre avec un rire caracteristique il declara "Moi promis billet mille francs donne bille mille francs, moi pas promis billet bon." La corsetiere n'en revient pas.

Extract of the French newspaper
"Le Progress" of Lyon
Monday 11th March 1918.

Aix-les-Bains.
The Negro and the Corset Dealer—A brilliant Musician in order to gain the good will of a young Corset maker offered her 1000 francs. The latter accepted gladly the 1000 francs and the Negro, but on the next day when she wanted to change the note the bank where she entered called her attention to the fact that her note was one payable to Holy-Farce and had no value.

The Corset maker with a very heavy heart, related her adventure to the police commissioner, who did nothing but smile. As for the Negro with a characteristic smile he declared: "I promised her a 1000 franc note, she was given a 1000 franc note, I did not promise her a note that was good." The Corset maker has not yet recovered her equanimity.

A thorough investigation convinced me that the item had no foundation in truth, and that it constituted a libel upon my command in general. The police commissioner assured me that he had received no such complaint, and had had no such interview as described in the newspaper publication.

I made formal complaint against the author; and the following afternoon, the journalist was brought by subpoena from Lyon.

After a brief examination in the office of the Mayor, the journalist admitted that the item was one of invention and not of news. He agreed to publish a retraction; and I was considerably relieved in my mind two days later to read his confession and apology:

Extrait du journal le Progress<br>du LYON lundi 11/Mar/1918

Aix-les-Bains—Le negre et la Corsetiere.
Nous avons publie sous cette rubrique dans notre numero du 11 Mars dernier une information humoristique inexacte en fait. Nous regrettons l'incident qui s'est produit et assurons les autorites Americaines presentes a Aix-les-Bains de notre vive sympathie.

Extract of the French newspaper<br>"Le Progress"<br>Thursday 14th, March 1918.

Aix-les-Bains.

The Negro and the Corset Dealer:
We have published under this title in our paper of the 11th of March last a humoristic information not true in fact. We regret the incident which happened and assure the American authorities now at Aix-les-Bains of our best sympathy.

Not only did our men follow the example of the woman in the nursery book, who has rings on her fingers and bells on her toes, who, as it may be remembered, is represented as making music wherever she goes; but, in addition to that, the men of the Band of 15th N. Y. Infantry, made friends wherever they went.

During the entire thirty-seven days of our absence from the regiment, not even one complaint was made by civil authority or by military authority outside of our own command, in connection with the deportment of our men.

The city of Aix-les-Bains, represented formally by the Mayor, presented our band with a splendid silver vase.

The City of Chambéry, in equally formal presentation, gave a gilt laurel sheaf with long streamers of the colors of France, with gilt lettered inscription.

We also received many bouquets of flowers, and many verbal bouquets, some oral and some printed.

The official resolutions of the Y.M.C.A., issued in the form of a printed card for mailing, I quote as follows:—

Y. M. C. A.—A. E. F.
SAVOIE LEAVE AREA
MARCH, 17, 1918

*An Expression of Appreciation*

The Secretary and Workers of the Y.M.C.A. in the Savoie Leave Area wish to express to Capt. Little, Lieut. Europe and the Members of the 15th New York Infantry Band, their heartfelt appreciation of the service rendered by them to the American Soldiers on leave at Aix-les-Bains and Chambéry during the past month.

The music of the Band has been easily the most important single element in the programme provided for the amusement and refreshment of the men sent here from the camps and trenches.

The Band has responded in the most cordial manner to every request. In the evenings their music and minstrel show have added greatly to the vaudeville, and their special programmes have been enthusiastically received. In the afternoons their concerts in the Casino or in the Park have given great pleasure, not only to our own boys but also to the citizens of Aix, and this has aided greatly in cementing the friendly relations between the two nationalities.

The willing co-operation and courtesy of all the individual Members of the Band have endeared them to the staff, and their stay here will always be remembered by us with the keenest pleasure.

FRANKLIN S. EDMONDS
Secretary.

Far too many interesting, inspiring and sentimental incidents occurred during our tour to permit mentioning many. But some cannot be neglected.

At Chambéry, for example, the band gave a concert at the Orphan Asylum.

How those children did enjoy the music!

136

One little fat faced kiddie made me homesick. He was fascinated by the gestures of Lieutenant Europe, in conducting; and, standing behind Jim, he followed every movement in imitation. The crowd laughed, and Europe turned to catch the little fellow in the act.

And then followed one of those delightful incidents of inspiration by a big hearted man.

With a crash of brass wind and cymbals, Jim brought to a close the piece which he was playing. Then he walked over to the little fellow, placed the baton in his hand, led him out in front of the band, gave instructions to his men for the playing of a piece of simple time, walked over to the side lines to stand beside me—and the little French orphan led the Band.

That crowd just went crazy!

I couldn't help thinking of the words of Major General Kernan, as he started our men upon their mission—that they were representatives of the American nation—that the eyes of France would be upon them; and through the eyes of France, the eyes of the world.

As I watched the faces of the crowd, while that little French boy led the *orchestre militaire Américaine*, I knew that in so far as the eyes of France might be centered upon the spirit of America, through the representation of Jim Europe and his colored band, that the *entente cordiale* between our two countries was safe.

Upon March 14th telegraphic orders were received for us to proceed upon completion of our tour of duty at Aix to Connantre, Department of the Marne, to rejoin our regiment.

Upon the evening of March 16th, 1918, at the conclusion of the usual vaudeville entertainment in the Casino Theatre, Gerry Reynolds, the Y man in charge of entertainment features, a man of remarkable personality, and an indefatigable worker, stepped out on the stage to make a speech—to bid good bye to the Band, and to thank them for their services.

Mr. Reynolds said:—

137

"Ladies and gentlemen of Aix-les-Bains—men of the Army: It is my sad duty to announce that we have listened to our last concert by the Band of the 15th New York Infantry. Orders have been received for them to rejoin their regiment. Tomorrow, these men, who for a month have given us so much pleasure, proceed to the front lines, to serve in the trenches against——"

Cheers interrupted the speaker. The audience of that theatre rose *en masse*. Men and boys yelled and whistled. Women cried. The civilian orchestra played; but no sound of music could be heard. Flags, hanging from the balcony, as decorations, were torn loose and waved.

Gerry Reynolds never finished that speech.

On the stage, the colored soldiers who had been spat upon in Spartanburg, rose and bowed—and grinned.

When I returned home, after the war, I found that, in some circles, it had become fashionable to abuse the Y. M. C. A. and to belittle its war service. It is neither my purpose nor my privilege to offer testimony in defense of the acts of misfeasance or malfeasance with which, I am told, officers of the Y. M. C. A. have been charged. I know nothing about the matters against which criticisms have been directed.

I do know something, however, about the work of the Y. M. C. A. for the American soldier in the establishment and maintenance of a home for soldiers on leave, of which each man was supposed to get seven days, exclusive of travel, every four months. I know a lot about that. In fact, I believe there are very few officers who know any more, or as much.

For more than a month, I watched the Y. M. C. A. men and women work for the health and morale of the men of our army; and I can offer specific testimony towards a conclusion that Mr. Edmonds and his staff worked with a patriotic and humanitarian fervor almost fanatical. And the fanaticism was operated along lines of constructive and practical efficiency.

March 17th was a busy day for us. We were scheduled to leave at 7:58 in the evening; but our cars were spotted for us during the forenoon; and Supply Sergeant Holliday and Mess Sergeant Granville Malichi and their details had their hands full in packing and trucking and loading.

Our meals, during the trip South, had been too irregular for comfort; so, for the return trip, we decided to rig up a kitchen in one end of our baggage car. Our rations were fairly well used up, so we had plenty of room. We set up a field range in a clay-filled packing case, as we had learned to do in America. I had bought the cooks and kitchen police men white jackets, aprons, and caps, such as are worn by chefs; and when the people of Aix crowded in under the station shed to see us off at train time they saw the cheery sight of a cooking supper about ready to be served—a neat kitchen on wheels—and four immaculately dressed "chef cooks," who would have been a credit to the Pullmans.

It was Park concert day; and the Band played during the afternoon. I had calls to make, and callers to receive, and packing to superintend. The hours slipped away.

At six o'clock I went to my room to harness up in marching order. M. Leder, proprietor of the de l'Europe, met me as I entered the hotel. He begged that I join him in a bottle of champagne.

M. Leder had been a delightful and generous host. His son was a Blue Devil, and a prisoner of war in Germany. My son had driven ambulances for the Blue Devils. There was a little bond between us. Frequently, we had dined together. We were friends.

The champagne was delicious. M. Leder's cordiality was inspiriting. I tore myself away, to hurry to the hoted where the men were quartered.

The streets were already crowded with civilians, waiting to see us march by. I had about a third of a mile to walk, from my hotel to that of the men. Scores of demonstrative French civilians rushed out and delayed me—to shake hands with the men and women, to kiss the cheeks of the babies held up to me.

I reached the Hotel Exertier, to find the band assembled and waiting, with hundreds of men, women, and children crowded about them. Mr. Europe was in front, beside 1st Sergeant Thompson, the Drum-Major. As I approached, they both saluted, as though to report formation.

"Are you all ready?" I shouted to make myself heard above the din.

"Yes, Sir."

"Then we'll start right along," I said. And I moved out to take my post.

"My God, Captain," Europe protested. "You'll break that landlady's heart if you do. She's been waiting for you the last hour, with a bottle of champagne."

"Jim, it can't be done. I've just finished one with Leder, and the afternoon was a busy one before that."

But the landlady and her sister cut short the argument by rushing out and drawing my arms through theirs. Mr. Europe followed, and the bottle was divided between four—for which I was truly thankful.

Some more babies were kissed; and the parade to the station started.

The Chief of Police had reported, and placed himself and a squad of men at our service to clear the way. The school cadet corps band had been reported by the dignified old master at their head—as an escort of honor.

Three times we were stopped in our march to listen to speeches; and twice I had to respond. The third speech was made by the Assistant Provost Marshal, in front of his headquarters.

He praised the men generously for good behavior and splendid service, which was a source of delight to me, as he had been none too friendly in his manner towards us at the time of our arrival, a month before.

I thanked Major Alcorn.

He asked me if there was anything he could do for us.

I asked him to speak of us in his official report, as he had just spoken to us in his farewell.

He promised to do so, and later mailed me a copy of his report, which I am proud to publish:

HEADQUARTERS ASSISTANT PROVOST MARSHAL
AIX-LES-BAINS

Mar. 17, 1918.

From: William F. Alcorn, Major 102nd Inf. A.P.M.
To: Colonel E. D. Isbell, P. M. Tours.
Subject: Report.

1. Pursuant to telegraphic instructions I have ordered the Band and Headquarters detachment 15th New York Regiment under the Command of Captain A. W. Little and 1st Lieutenant James R. Europe as Officers to proceed to Connantre Department of Marne, and they are leaving to-day March 17th at 9:56.

2. The Band has been in this leave area since Feby. 16th and while here have provided a great deal of amusement to the men on leave and have assisted greatly in making their vacation a pleasant one, the conduct of the men of the Band has been of the very highest order and their work deserves high commendations.

3. Would request that a Band be kept here at all times.

WILLIAM F. ALCORN
Major 102nd Inf. A.P.M.

Throughout the line of march to the station, the police failed utterly to keep the street clear. I marched, of course alone, at the head of my command; but I was so closely surrounded by civilians that the greatest care had to be exercised to avoid stepping upon them. Between me and my orderlies, five paces to the rear, marched a solid phalanx of civilians from curb to curb; and the distance between the orderlies and the Band, fifteen paces, furnished marching space for no less than from four hundred to five hundred old men, women, and children. Of young men, there were none in France outside of the army.

When we arrived at the railroad station, a lane had to be forced, to admit of our getting through to where the trains were to be boarded. And when the train rolled (or rather crept) in, a guard of police and railroad attendants had to precede it, to clear the tracks to avoid wholesale carnage. During the delay attendant upon attaching our cars to the train, the Band played its farewell; the crowd cheered without ceasing; women and children wept. When, at last, the call *"En voiture"* passed down the line, the cheeks of the few remaining unkissed babies of that town were presented to me for attention; and, joy and glory be; as the train commenced to move, two ladies of high caste dressed in mourning black, stepped upon the running board of the car as I leaned out of my window—and made my farewell complete.

# GIVEN A NEW NAME

OUR journey to the North was uneventful until the time of our arrival at Connantre—as we supposed, our destination. We stopped successively at Lyon, Dijon, Langres, Chaumont, Romilly, and at many less important towns.

During the daylight hours of our last morning before arriving at Connantre, we ran through the country of the great battles of the Marne. For the first time, we saw a country devastated by modern warfare—wrecks of buildings, miles upon miles of meadow land torn and horribly disfigured by shell burst or by pick and shovel, the sole crop awaiting harvest, barbed wire entanglements.

We saw, also, little wooden crosses, marking the graves of patriots of the supreme sacrifice—thousands and tens of thousands—some carrying a wreath of the tricolor of France, some bearing marks identifying the dead of Germany; but all respected by the wonderful French, with their ideals of sentiment.

At about 10 o'clock upon the morning of March 20th, our train stopped at Connantre.

When we had received orders at Aix to proceed to Connantre, I had tried, by discreet questioning, to find out what kind of a place it was. An American major of artillery just down from the front had told me that Connantre was a wilderness, also a railroad junction, serving as a forwarding point for troops going into the front lines. By sending troops freely from all parts of France to Connantre, and routing them from that point by secret, oral orders, information as to the disposition of troops was kept from the spies of the enemy, as well as could be.

1903

RECREATION, MAFFRECOURT, MAY 5, 1918

1901

NO-MAN'S LAND
FORMERLY THE RAILROAD EXPRESS LINE——PARIS TO BERLIN

We found that that artillery major was right, or nearly so. Connantre, if not a wilderness, ought to be.

But, as we approached Connantre, we had no idea of any such state of affairs. We believed we were going to find our regiment in camp, waiting for us to complete its happiness with the wonderful music of which it had been deprived for more than five weeks.

The train stopped, and the band assembled, as planned. Four red-brassarded orderlies took their position in front, each man bearing a trophy or gift, after the manner of the Greeks of ancient days. The commanding officer of the detachment, with an air of nonchalance which he did not feel, stepped to the front to do his part, looked about, and found nothing there but— France.

Several hundred yards away there were a few barracks that looked like buildings which the illustrated papers show in connections with western mining camps. To those buildings I set off, alone, in search of information.

When I got there, I found a number of French officers, extremely polite, but extremely French.

The 15th Foot was unknown, unexpected, unheard of, undesired, unheralded and unsung; and, if we had been cavalry, no doubt we should have been unhorsed.

Bearing in mind our having come from a farewell of that never-to-be forgotten scene at the station at Aix it may, perhaps, be possible to imagine our feeling of deflation as we stood there in the bitterness of our awakening on the threshold of the wilderness.

After about an hour and a half of effort with the French language, I found out who, what and where we were.

The 15th N. Y. Infantry had died a peaceful death in General Orders; but like the Phoenix of mythology it had risen again in greater glory from the ashes of its pyre, to be known as the *Trois Cent Soixante Neuvième R. I. U. S.* This *369 ème Régiment d'Infanterie U. S.* had been temporarily detached from

143

the United States Army and assigned to the 16th Division of the French Army.

Shortly after our arrival at Connantre rain commenced to fall, and continued for a full 24 hours.

We left Connantre by railroad train at about two o'clock in the morning.

We were in the advanced zone, air raids were common, and lights were forbidden. The night was one of pitch darkness. Our special cars had been taken from us at Connantre. We piled into the train which stopped for us, with no sense to serve us in finding places but that of touch. The train was already crowded with French casual soldiers returning from *permission*.

At 11 o'clock, March 21, we reached the end of our railroad journey, Givry-en-Argonne.

As we detrained, we recognized some of the men of the regimental supply company at work transferring baggage and freight from railroad freight cars upon a siding into two-wheeled French Army carts.

Upon the edge of a woods a hundred yards away, were two or three army tents, and from a fly at the end of the row curled smoke from the fire of a field range.

The cook of that supply company detachment looked to our men like an angel without wings; and flap-jacks and coffee was the menu.

We hiked from Givry-en-Argonne to Noirlieu, a distance of no more than nine or ten kilometers. At Noirlieu, the 1st Battalion was billeted; and there, also, was Regimental headquarters and the home of the Band.

The 2nd Battalion was billeted three kilometers to the South at St. Mard-sur-le-Mont.

The 3rd Battalion was billeted at Remicourt, about a kilometer to the West of Givry, and on the road to Noirlieu.

We found the regiment in the highest of spirits, and filled with ambition and determination to accept worthily its opportunity to win a real place in history, as the first, and possibly, the only American regiment to take its place in the firing line of the Army of France.

Officers and men were swanking in French helmets and gas masks, and chattering in the most atrocious and wholly ununderstandable French.

The French General who had welcomed the Colonel had, I believe, given out the flattering statement that our regiment had carried the Stars and Stripes to the point farthest north in France that they had ever been carried by a military organization.

That funny little organization of Harlem, which had been called by the scoffers and cynics "a glorified Mulligan Guards," was getting on.

As I am confining myself only to things that I know, I think it will help my readers to catch up with the progress of the regiment, during my absence with the band, to insert here the text of a letter written by Col. Hayward.

France, March 18th, 1918.

Colonel Reginald L. Foster,
52nd Pioneer Infantry,
Camp Wadsworth, Spartanburg, S. C.
My dear Colonel:

Your interesting letter of February 6th has just reached me. I am glad that you have a command again and think the results you had with the 12th indicate great success and efficiency for the new 52nd. There is so much to write you, and the censorship is real and strict. I have carefully read the American Censorship Order and feel that what I am about to tell you violates neither the letter nor the spirit of same. If it does, I hope that any censor who reads this will send it back to me. In addition to this, I have asked our Division Chief of Staff (French) and he has told me that what I wanted to write you and others, is quite all right. So here goes.

The most wonderful thing in the world has happened to this regiment. A fairy tale has materialized and a beautiful dream has come true. We are now a combat unit—one of the regiments of a French Division in the French Army, assigned to a sector of trenches and it is now a question of days when we will be holding it, the same as each of the other regiments of our wonderful division is holding its sector. We have with us about fifty French instructors, giving us our finishing touches and specialistic training.

It is all so wonderful, especially following the monotonous tour of duty during our first two months in France, I hardly know how to write about it. The last few days of December, we landed at a port in France and were taken sixteen hours by rail to a great base where for two months we did everything under the sun—engineering, provost, patrolling, guard duty, labor, horse and motor transportation, working on the line of communication. I realize what a wise selection I made in my officers and what a competent list I had—especially when they began to take them away from me. We furnished the entire personnel for one General Court, which sat for weeks; the entire personnel, except three, of another General Court; two Special Courts; and an efficiency board for officers of other organizations. I furnished Aids for Generals, Assistant Chiefs of Staff for headquarters, an Inspector General, Intelligence Officer (Secret Service), Acting Quartermasters, Lecturers, for teaching the French the American Insignia and Army organization. We made wonderful maps of the whole country for headquarters, incidentally discovering a wonderful new range finder, which Colonel Pickering has dubbed "Pris-mil ranging." We furnished orderlies and strikers for the American Headquarters from top to bottom; made range cards and position sketches; and when we marched away from that base, it was with the commendation of the base and camp commanders we had served under, and I believe to the sincere regret of every officer and man we had come in contact with.

Then came the message from the A.E.F. Heaven.

145

# FROM HARLEM TO THE RHINE

I loaded the wandering, saluting, laughing 15th N. Y., the only unit ever in France with a state name, on about a million of these little French cars, still carrying our State colors, and under sealed orders for the second half of the journey, puffed away into the night on a strange mission—the most wonderful adventure which ever befell a regiment in our army or any other army since the war began.

The French army moved us and we were well taken care of. They evidently believe in the comfort of their colonels for I had the bridal suite on a sort of private car and everything that went with it, except the bride.

We went on and on for two days; passed the phoney destination which had been announced as our destination, through great supply depots; passed acres and acres of piled up munitions; passed wonderfully camouflaged armored trains of big guns—the "long Toms" pointing up into the air; passed aviation centres where the aeroplanes looked like great flocks of birds; through miles of barbed wire entanglements; and finally stopped at a place I had never heard of before, and when I stepped off the train, the first thing I heard was the "boom-boom" of the big guns a few miles away. A French Staff Officer came up and asked me if I was the *"Trois cent soixante neuvieme Régiment d'Infanterie, Americain";* and I allowed I was.

We had heard unofficially of our change to the new number, but this was the nature of the passing of the old 15th New York. So you see, we carried the name and the colors through seven states, across the Atlantic, through the submarine zone, in two great bases in France and clear to the firing line. Of course, the French know only the new name and in our division we are the 369th R. I. U. S. It's a good thing we are not artillery, for I would hate to substitute an "A" for the "I" in this designation.

The regiment is billeted in a group of three villages a few kilometers apart—one battalion in each. I would not be allowed to tell their names, but nobody ever head of them anyhow.

It is all very interesting being lulled to sleep every night by the distant boom of the guns; and at night it looks like some one was continuously taking flash light pictures. One morning since we have been here, we saw a peach of an air fight—or shall I say a bird of an air fight, in which large forces were engaged, and in which our crowd had none the worse of it.

There are no American troops anywhere near us, that I can find out, and we are *"les enfants perdu,"* and glad of it. Our great American general simply put the black orphan in a basket, set it on the doorstep of the French, pulled the bell, and went away. I said this to a French colonel with an "English spoken here" sign on him, and he said "Weelcome leetle black babbie."

I think my official interpreter, detailed to me from the French Army, expressed the sentiment of the whole outfit when we discovered where we were going when he said "God gracious—we go to the front lines."

The French are wonderful—wonderful—wonderful. I have never been more profoundly impressed with a feeling of certainty and security, and efficient direction, supply and management, than here. Incredible as it may seem, there is no red tape here. You should see and talk with our division general. What a man—what a soldier he is! And when he sayed *"Attendez, mon Colonel!"* you should see me click my spurs together and "attende" in my best pidgin French.

I thought I raised, organized, trained and brought this regiment here, but I now believe that All Mighty God had more to do with it than I did. To be sure, I and most of the other officers have worked twenty-five hours a day, and we have struck for the best and highest each time, but it is clear that anyone who would have prophesied what has actually come to pass would have been locked in a mad-house. You know, I shall never get over my disappointment and chagrin, even if I live through this party, at being left out of the wonderful 27th Division, which I even yet say is the finest body of troops I have ever seen together. However, a quotation from Holy Writ keeps bobbing into my head away up here. I don't know what book it is in and haven't time to look it up, but it goes something like this—"And the stone which was rejected by the builder has become the corner stone of the temple."

I didn't mean to write so much, but I started and couldn't stop. All of your friends among my officers send to you their greetings and congratulations on your new command, and none more than I. Will you also be good enough to remember me to General O'Ryan and our friends down here.

Our address is the same—c/o A.E.F. via New York, and our mail will be sent from A.E.F. to the French and passed along to us. You may rest assured the latter know where we are, if no one else does.

Yours very truly,

WM. HAYWARD,
Colonel.

P. S. I had planned to write our friend Wainwright and tell him of our great good luck but I'm so busy, guess I'll send him and one or two others a carbon of this letter to you. I'm busy counting and playing with *fusils, mitrailleuses, fusil-mitrailleuses, grenades, grenade V. B.'s, 37 m/ms, gaz masques,* steel casques and other homicidal paraphernalia. I'm like a rich kid, Christmas morning, don't know which toy to start on half the time. And a funny thing is happening psychologically to me. I, who always hated and loathed even the Spanish War, the military business with its rank and precedence and arbitrary or accidental authority conferred on men of small calibre, who in civil life couldn't stand a squad, and its uniforms, pomp and display and lockjaw, am beginning to like it. Probably it was the peace time tin soldier end of it I despised, but now it is a regular he-man job. As I have progressed in my temporary and

146

emergency profession, I have felt less and less like a camouflaged civilian, and now feel quite a soldier. I suppose when it's over and I go back to trying law suits, if I go back, in whole or in part, I'll feel like a camouflaged soldier trying to be a lawyer. But just now that "going back" stuff seems very remote and hazy and I guess we'll be soldier men a long, long time. Anyhow, we're pretty fit and, I believe, unafraid from colonel to cooks.

The boys keep looking at the big flashes in the north, and saying "God damn, le's go" and we've formally adopted "Le's go" as the motto of this brunette fighting outfit.

I may have a scalp or two to send the next time I write, because before this reaches you, we'll be in it up to our ears. On the other hand, there may not be any next time and some Bosche "oberdt" may be sending my fair hair across the Rhine, but he'll know he's been in a dog fight, Foster, if he does, 'cause I'm a "two gun" man now.

W. H.

# EARLY DAYS WITH THE FRENCH
*March 21–April 13, 1918*

WE had to turn in our American ordnance. We had to draw French ordnance complete. When we got through with that transfer, our men wore and carried nothing American but their clothes. Our trusty Springfield rifles, with heavy knife bayonet, were exchanged for Labelle rifles with long rapier-like bayonet. We felt that a poor exchange had been made; but, undoubtedly, a necessary one. Rifles without ammunition are but little better than clubs; and, as a unit of a French division we had, of course, to look for ammunition to the French bases of supplies.

Four days after my return to the regiment we received orders to move forward—not to the front lines, but nearer. The move was but a short one, averaging, for the several battalions from their respective stations, approximately ten to twelve kilometers. Regimental Headquarters, and eighty percent of the regiment were stationed at Herpont; the balance at Herpine, a smaller town three kilometers to the East.

Our regiment had to be entirely reorganized to conform to the French Tables of Organization.

During our first fortnight with the French there came to us five French officers to be attached to our regimental and battalion staffs. We were also given French sergeants or corporals as drill instructors, in the proportion of about one to each platoon or, at most, five to a company. We also had interpreters assigned to our staffs.

And so, by the means which I have briefly mentioned, our

regiment was given its intensive training of preparation to take its place in the fighting lines of the Allies.

To these officers and non-commissioned officers the 369th Regiment owes much.

In connection with this subject, I must tell one of the favorite jokes of our command.

Upon the day of our arrival in the Advanced Zone, General Le Gallais of the 16th Division of France, of which we had become a part, explained to Colonel Hayward all about the training in store for us. At the conclusion of his instructions, the General suddenly altered his manner and said to the Colonel:— "And now, my dear Colonel, I have to ask you a serious question. You have undoubtedly heard of the new drive which the Germans are starting. It is to our West. We are hopeful that the enemy may be stopped before they gain any important success. It is doubtful, at any rate, if they spread over as far East as our sectors. But, we must be prepared for all things. We must guard against surprise. If they should come through here, we must have our defences ready. Now, Colonel, what I want to ask you is as to just what we may look to you for, even before you complete your training under our instruction. Your training will take some weeks; but the enemy may not wait so long. What could we count upon your regiment doing right away, in the event of the Germans piling through here? What could we count upon the 369th doing in—say—four or five days?"

Colonel Hayward gave the only answer that he could give. He knew that we didn't know much of the science of warfare. So, he said that we could be counted upon to do the best we could —and that, of course, no men could do more. And the Colonel smiled his smile of winning confidence.

The General Le Gallais said:—"*Bon!*" and he took his departure.

As the Colonel walked away with the General, to see him to his car, the group of officers remaining exchanged glances of significance. And from the rear of this group came the voice of

Dr. John Bradner, a modest officer, up to that time unsuspected of humor, saying:—

"What could we do if the Germans should attack here at once? What could the 369th be counted upon to do in four or five days, if the enemy should come piling through here? What could we do? Why if the Germans should come piling through here this very night, in four or five days, the 369th could be counted upon to spread the news—all—through—France!"

And in the laugh that followed, every man in that group had a mental picture of little groups of colored men from Harlem, wearing the uniform of the United States, and French equipment, rushing through France—2000 self-constituted Paul Reveres, spreading the intelligence all over the towns and cities, from Verdun to Marseilles.

We developed a terrific *Esprit de Corps,* and went about our work with heads up and chests out, assuring each other that our regiment was undoubtedly the most talked of regiment of the American Army, the natural successor, in the World War, to the picturesqueness, in the Spanish War, of The Rough Riders.

And then, one day during the first week in April, along came a perfectly delightful man of the world, with every reason to know what he was talking about—to tell us that it was all true; that we were, so to speak, in Paris, in Chaumont, in France, actually the talk of the town.

This man of the world was, by force of circumstances and for the period of the war, a soldier, a liaison officer attached to the personal staff of General Pershing. But by profession and by birth, he was a banker and an aristocrat. His name—Herman Harjes, the American Banker of Paris, of the great firm Morgan, Harjes and Co., and one of the founders of the famous volunteer war ambulance corps: The Norton, Harjes Unit—Major Harjes of the U. S. Army.

Harjes blew in at Herpont upon the morning of April 5th. Col. Hayward had General Le Gallais on his hands; and it fell to my pleasant lot to take care of Major Harjes.

150

We walked about during the morning, to see the troops at work; and Harjes discovered a number of his friends of New York—men of the Racquet Club, the Knickerbocker and the Union. At lunch he found more of his friends.

After lunch, the Band gave one of its inimitable concerts, the quartette surpassing itself in quaint harmony and grotesque dancing.

Then we walked over to my office, to relax a bit. Harjes laughed, a long, true laugh.

He said:—"I'm laughing at having discovered the mysterious Three Hundred and Sixty Ninth Colored Infantry.

"All over Paris and at Chaumont people are talking about you; but everybody has some different idea about you. They don't know where you are or what you're doing. And there are all sorts of conceptions about *who* you are or, perhaps I should say *what* you are, as to personnel. There's a general idea that you are getting along all right because we never get any complaints from you or about you; and then, some people have had an idea that you are all (including the Colonel) colored men, and that that accounts for your not kicking at the things you have to put up with.

"Latterly, some of our people have come back from visiting you and carried very complimentary reports to Headquarters, and gradually the mystery is beginning to blow away. And now, today, I drop in here and find myself, not in the wilderness of France, as the surrounding country would suggest, but in New York—in a joint meeting of half a dozen interesting clubs.

"One of our officers recently said that Colonel Hayward was, in his opinion, one of the men who would go far in this war, if the war lasted; and I believe that the report was a just one, and that the Colonel won't have to go far—alone.

"I'm going to bring General Pershing up to see you. You are the most refreshing things I've seen in the American Army."

Of course we all liked Harjes. Most people approve of men who, with apparent sincerity, speak well of them. But Major

Harjes never made good on that promise to bring General Pershing to visit us. A short time after Harjes spent the day with us at Herpont he became a victim in a serious automobile accident; and for weeks he was reported as lying in a hospital at death's door. I understand that the Major did, after a long time, recover from his injuries. He had our well wishes.

There was a comical incident in connection with the departure of Major Harjes from our Headquarters at Herpont. His handsome limousine car drew up in front of Colonel Hayward's house, the driver, a Frenchman, with cap pulled well down on the head and held there by chin-strap. It had been explained that fast time must be made as the Major had an important official dinner engagement in Paris that evening.

Harjes opened the door of his car, and packed away some documents and an overcoat. Then he stepped back (leaving the door open) to shake hands with the Colonel and me, in farewell.

The car moved slowly away. Nobody gave a thought to the movement—another car was approaching, and it was necessary to make a bit of room. As the car moved along, one of our boys (to save the door from being damaged) slammed it shut—the driver opened his throttle, and the car sped away.

Major Harjes was still standing with the Colonel and the Adjutant of the 369th Infantry—all three open-mouthed with astonishment.

A rush was made for telephones, and the towns along the road notified. Three quarters of an hour later the car came back. The driver had obeyed his speeding instructions and made good time. He had travelled over 15 kilometers before being stopped and sent back.

While at Herpont there was some early confusion due to the handling of our baggage. It was absolutely necessary that the Regimental records be maintained. Of course these records were carefully filed in a locked strong-box. The keys to that box were missing.

I told the Sergeant Major I wanted to work on the records.

He produced the box. Then followed an embarrassing delay. The keys were still among the missing. I told the Sergeant Major to break the lock. He demurred, assuring me the keys were not lost—merely mislaid. But I was impatient. This time I insisted that the lock be broken. "But, suh, adjutant, suh," he protested, "that's the best box in this ahmy. We brought that all the way from Noo Yawk. We can't get no box like it over heah. I don't want to show no disrespect; but, suh, Adjutant, suh, befo' I breaks that lock I'd like the adjutant's permission to call in Corporal Hall of C. Company."

"What can Corporal Hall do?" I demanded.

"Why, suh, Adjutant, suh," was the answer, "you see, suh, Corporal Hall in civil life is a burglar."

And that box was opened.

When Colonel Hayward had embarked for France the first time, way back in November, 1917, his chauffeur, Sergeant Reese, had carried aboard the *Pocahontas*, and stowed away with great care in the Colonel's cabin, a large package in weather-proof wrappings, which, the Colonel confided to some of us, contained between 2500 and 3000 choice cigars from the Union League Club. When we had to disembark to go to Camp Merritt, while the machinery of the *Pocahontas* was being repaired, and through all our subsequent wanderings, and wonderings, this package in the particular charge of Sergeant Reese, had gone along as hand baggage. One day during our early association with the French, Cononel Hayward told General Le Gallais that he was going to give him a treat—he was going to present him with a box of real Havana cigars, such as it was very difficult to procure in France. General Le Gallais protested that it was too much—a cigar, or two cigars, perhaps, he would enjoy and be delighted to accept; but a whole box—the Colonel was too generous, it would not be right to accept so many.

"Pooh," said the Colonel, "I have many. I have so many cigars, a box from my stock will never be noticed."

And the Colonel, with beaming face, lifted the huge package

from the corner of his room, where Sergt. Reese had deposited it for safe keeping, and cut the strings. One by one the heavy wrappings were laid back. Then came lighter wrappings. After that came a layer of nice clean wooden boards, and when they came off, there were revealed to the astonished and agonized eyes of the French General and the American Colonel respectively, several score of carefully packed tent pins.

The Colonel sentenced Sergt. Reese to carry those tent pins all through the World War; but within a few weeks he relented.

We all became affectionately attached to our orderlies. And our orderlies (in majority of cases) were models of fidelity in their personal devotion to the officers whom they served. The men knew which men could be trusted and which men could not be trusted as to honesty, and, in many instances, orderlies of officers occupying adjacent quarters would combine and voluntarily form reliefs to guard their masters from loss of their effects through theft.

I was particularly fortunate in having orderlies of high character. Cookson, to whom I have referred a number of times, had his eccentricities as a soldier, but he had no eccentricities as to honesty. He came to me one day and handed me a roll of notes for several hundred francs, which I had carelessly left upon my table before going out to some formation. As he handed me the money, he scolded me like a younger brother, and said it wasn't fair to him; that if the money had been stolen he would have been under suspicion, etc., etc. And I allowed that Cookson was probably right and promised to try to do better.

My other orderly, Joe, came as near to the personification of the word comfort in the personal service line as I can picture in my imagination. In trenches or in billets Joe always turned me out with clean and apparently pressed clothes. I almost always had hot water with which to shave. If a barber was not available, Joe would say, "Excuse me," as I would finish shaving, and take the razor from my hand. Then he would trim my hair with the razor down upon the sides and my neck, and whisper—

"There, Sir Major Sir, that will look better until we can get Corporal Jackson over from 'B' Company to cut your hair."

Joe would sometimes make me take off a shirt which I would have half on, in favor of a clean shirt, murmuring words about the necessity of setting a good example.

If, upon a hike, I happened to be billeted in a house where there were other occupants of whose reliability Joe was not entirely confident, nothing could induce Joe to seek quarters of his own for sleeping. He would spread his blankets across my door sill, upon the side of the door towards which it opened, and there easy in mind as to the security of the life and property of his chief, he would, apparently, sleep in comfort.

With me, breakfast has always been my most important meal. To the confusion of any of my old friends who may have already recognized in that sentence an opportunity for a comeback of sarcasm, I hasten to admit that, under favorable conditions I have been known to enjoy, also, luncheon, dinner, and mid-night supper. But, with me, breakfast is an essential. With a good breakfast, I can go without the other meals and suffer no disabling discomfort.

Joe would waken me every morning by quietly shaking my knee and purring:—"Now, Sir Major Sir, just try to eat a little of this breakfast while it's hot."

I trust that the incongruity of this coaxing with the state of breakfast hunger of which I have hinted, and its revelation of tactfulness and spirit of service upon the part of Joe, may furnish the excuse for the introduction into this story of a regiment of so personal a note as that of a description of my gastronomic appetites.

I have rambled at some length over these incidents of devotional intimacy upon the part of my orderlies, as such incidents were more or less typical of the relations between all of the original officers of the regiment and their attendants. Such service breeds indulgence, and although undue familiarity upon the part of the men was almost never known, still there is no doubt of the fact that, in many instances, officers upon their own part let down the bars a bit, and encouraged their men to talk of personal matters. And sometimes, too, officers would wink at regulations, in giving their men some little privilege of a forbidden fruit.

The object of this introduction is to open the way to a good story on Colonel Hayward, a story which without some such introduction and explanation, might draw upon him criticism on account of having offered a soldier forbidden alcoholic beverage.

The Colonel had an orderly named Owens. Owens was at times a bit mischievous. At times, even, his deportment verged upon the disorderly—such as, for example, when he borrowed the Colonel's revolver on the way to Spartanburg, and shot up a southern town from a car window, as the troop train rolled through at night.

But there was something kind of irresistible about Owens. He was always laughing, and frequently, he was making other people laugh. For such people there are always good berths in this world. For Owens, in spite of the many occasions upon which he excited the Colonel's wrath, there was always a welcome home in the Colonel's entourage after each period of banishment and disgrace.

Now, one morning, according to the story of the camp, the Colonel turned to Owens as he finished dressing and said:

"Owens, there's a bottle of cognac upon that table that's very bad. I don't want it, and I'm ashamed to offer it to any of our guests. Now, if I were to give it to you, would you promise me not to make a fool of yourself and drink it so fast as to get into trouble again? Would you be decent and sensible about it, and give some to the other boys outside, and make it last a couple of days so that none of you would get soused?"

"Yas suh, Kunnel suh. I shore would, thank yer suh."

A couple of days later the Colonel asked Owens if he had finished the cognac, and how it had tasted.

"Yas suh, Kunnel suh, we dun finished et; an' et wus jes' raght—jes' ezzactly raght—jes' raght is der word, suh Kunnel suh. Ef et had been eny better you wouldn't hev gev et ter us; ef et had been eny worse we couldn't hev drunk et."

Early in April I was assigned to command the 1st Battalion, Major Dayton, at his own request, having been transferred to another regiment. On one of the first days of that new command I retired to my quarters to study; heavy of heart with the appreciation of unfamiliar responsibilities.

Cookson was fussing about the room. He gave one or two preparatory coughs, and then he spoke:

"Suh Cap'n Suh, Ah'm sure glad dat yoo all is er-sleepin' in yoo own cot in dis yer room, and not in dat baid in der alcove dere."

"Why," said I, "do you think it would be hard to make up the bed in the alcove?"

"Et ain't dat, Suh Cap'n Suh, et ain't dat; but dat baid in der alcove is hornted. Der landlady tells one uv our fellers dat talks French."

I laughed at Cookson, and asked if he believed in ghosts.

"Nah Suh Cap'n Suh, Ah doan guess Ah do *believe* in ghosts. Nah Suh, Ah doan believe in dem; but Ah kin tell yoo, Suh, Ah sure am maghty much afreerd uv 'em."

I laughed. Cookson was making me begin to forget my blues. And then he went on:

"Nah Suh, Ah doan never want ter go near ter no daid pusson. Why Suh Cap'n Suh, mah sister, who Ah wuz er-holdin in mah arms once, w'en she'd er been daid eight days, jes' cum out uv er trance an' looked at me. Ah doan never want not'n lak dat ter happen ter me ergin. Mah sister used ter have trances, and mah mudder tranced too; but dat wuz der wurst one she ever had. An der doctors thought bah dat tahm she must be reely daid."

I asked Cookson if his sister had lived any length of time after she came out of the trance.

"Why Suh Cap'n Suh," hissed Cookson, "she livin' yet!"

I asked Cookson what he did when his sister woke up while he was holding her—whether he dropped her.

"Yes *Suh*," said Cookson, "Ah jes' let her fall raght back on der baid."

"Did you scream?" I asked.

"Ah did wurse 'an *dat*, Suh Cap'n Suh."

"Did you run away?"

"Ah did wurse 'an DAT!"

"What did you do?" I persisted.

"Well Suh Cap'n Suh, Ah doan tink Ah ought ter tell yer. Et wouldn't be r'specful."

REVIEW, MAFFRECOURT, MAY 5, 1918

TWO BATTALIONS EN REPOS AT MAFFRECOURT, MAY 5, 1918, PARADING IN
REGIMENTAL FORMATION, BY COMMAND OF GEN. PERSHING

THE COMMANDING OFFICER RIDING ALONE WAS THE AUTHOR (THEN CAPT. ARTHUR W. LITTLE) WHO HAD
THE GOOD FORTUNE THAT DAY TO BE THE RANKING OFFICER PRESENT FOR DUTY.

*1907*

A PART OF THE PARADE IN REGIMENTAL FORMATION, MAFFRECOURT,
MAY 5, 1918

MACHINE GUNS ON THE ROAD, MAY 5, 1918 AT MAFFRECOURT

# XXII

# MY FIRST ANNIVERSARY
*April 13, 1918*

UPON the morning of April 13th, 1918, the regiment less the 2nd Battalion which had preceded it by a week, marched out of its billeting towns, Herpont and Herpine, travelling to the north.

After a march of some four or five miles, we reached a small town named Auve, where an important advanced zone hospital was located. Our orders of march provided that upon the northern boundary of Auve, after marching through the town, where the road would be found to be split into two branches, the regiment was to divide its forces. The main body was to travel to the East and North East to the town of Maffrecourt, there to establish a regimental base, for supplies and for the billeting of troops *en repos*. The 1st Battalion was to move directly to the north, to proceed through the town of Hans, to a camp in the plains some two or three kilometers farther on—Camp des Peupliers. There we were to establish ourselves and await orders from the Division General as to further movements.

As the regiment approached Auve, a halt was made. A staff officer rode down the line to inform me the Commanding Officer would turn out in front of the hospital gate to take a marching review of the 1st Battalion, as it made its farewell to the regiment.

The bugles sounded *Attention!* The march was resumed. Our formation was column of squads, in normal distances. The Band turned out in an open space and facing the reviewing party

159

played a march which Europe had come to look upon as my favorite. The 3rd Battalion, which had preceded us in column, was lined up upon the right of the road, standing stiffly at *Present Arms.*

I had made hundreds of reviews in my life, but I never experienced such a thrill in passing as I did upon that beautiful sunny morning in France, for the first time at the head of my own battalion—marching on to war.

After passing, myself, I turned out, as per regulations, and joined the Colonel in watching the companies march by. How those steel helmets did snap in the sun-light, in response to the command—*"Eyes Right!"*

The 13th of April! Just one year to the day from the date of my assignment to duty, when I had travelled over Brooklyn, to a dismal and dilapidated old dance hall used as an Armory, to take command of a struggling unorganized company of the National Guard!

What a change in a year! What a triumph!

No word was spoken between us; but, as those steady, colored soldier boys filed by, I sensed that Colonel Hayward's and my own mind and heart were in attune.

When the last man had passed, the Commanding Officer of New York's 15th Infantry and the Commanding Officer of its 1st Battalion leaned over in their saddles, shook hands, and said—"Good Bye."

# XXIII

# DEATH VALLEY—OUR FIRST SHELLING

*April 14, 1918*

I RODE rapidly to overtake my battalion, and to the head of the column, got out my map, adjusted it in my despatch case under the transparent coverings, and directed my march through the beautiful country—with spring in the air. The maps furnished us by the French were excellent, and the finding of the way was easy—a fortunate thing for the 1st Battalion, as the French aide serving with me had preceded us by several hours with a billeting detail.

At the end of an hour we halted for dinner. Dinner was good, and the men were very much refreshed by the food and the rest. For the first time we used our rolling kitchens, issued to us with other French equipment and rolling stock. The sandwich meal during a hike had become a thing of the past.

While at dinner, we witnessed a fight between a German plane and a French captive observation balloon. The anti-air craft guns made a regular Fourth of July of it with their day fireworks bursting hundreds of feet in the air. The German plane got away; but it is doubtful if any pictures of us were secured, as the plane never got very near to where the battalion was spread out and resting.

After dinner we had to change our formation for marching. We had arrived in the danger zone. Gas masks had to be worn at the "Alert," and men and vehicles had to be marched in small groups with great distances between. Two purposes were to be served by this extended column of marching order—the avoidance of observation, and the saving of casualties in case of attack by shelling. Our distances were so ordered that the dispersion of one shell could do damage to no more than one group. The battalion column spread out to a depth of almost three miles, with the 42 vehicles of our wagon train included.

At about four o'clock in the afternoon we reached our destination, Camp des Peupliers, upon the outskirts of the town of Hans and to the North.

To the South of Hans, just before marching through that town, we passed a camp of an American hospital unit. A great United States flag hung across the road like an election banner; and our tired soldiers snapped into attention as they marched beneath. Some of the ambulance boys ran out to ask me the name of our regiment. When I had told them, they came right back with another question— "Where is Jim Europe's Band?" Our fame (at that time our only recognized qualification for fame) had preceded us.

A half hour after our arrival at Camp des Peupliers, the Division Commander, General Le Gallais, rode in. Our French Generals were to me one of the most astonishing revelations of the spirit of service and patriotism that I have ever seen. Our division generals were as persistent in their personal touch with the activities of troops as we Americans usually like to think of a battalion commander as being. I have known American company commanders who demonstrated less interest in the welfare of their men than was shown continually by the French generals under whom we had the honor to serve.

General Le Gallais was cordial in his greeting, and, as usual, asked what he could do for us. I had noticed, as we marched through Hans, an extensive bath house plant. I suggested that, if we could have the bath house put into commission for our use, it would be a help.

"*Attendez!*" The Aide-de-camp clicked his heels together. Just one hour later, I received a polite note from the *Major du Cantonement de Hans* to the effect that bath accommodations could be offered the officers of the *Bataillon Americain* that evening and that at eight o'clock the next morning full service would be open to the men. It was a good bath—one of the best we ever had the privilege of enjoying. Hot water was plentiful.

The General, after a brief chat upon minor matters, proceeded to tell me of the work he had planned for my battalion. It was pretty wonderful—or so it seemed to me—intended as practical training, no doubt, but so very practical that I was to have my own little sector to defend and to command.

He explained it all to me; and wound up by saying: "And so—the responsibility will be with you and your officers." Then he smiled (Le Gallais had a wonderful, laughing smile) and said: *"Alors mon Commandant,* prepare for tomorrow."

General Le Gallais had said that our neighbors in the adjoining sector were of a so-called territorial regiment, with enlisted personnel of men averaging over forty years of age. The General suggested that when we learned how, thoroughly, our raids would probably go much faster and farther than those of our associates.

I laughed and said: *"Mon General,* I am 43 years old."

"Perhaps," said the General, "but you are the commandant, and you will not be permitted to go on raids."

It was one o'clock in the morning as I crawled into bed. The big guns were playing a lively and noisy tune. I reflected upon the trait of human nature which admits of men of normal capacity becoming so readily accustomed to new surroundings.

Of course, we were not under attack in our camp. Trenches well in front of us were being shelled, and towns to our rear were under bombardment. We could hear the shells go shrieking high up over our heads. They sounded to me like trolley cars coming fast over the Hackensack Meadows, and I knew they were "arrivals" because the "departures" were still being fired from points well in advance of us. The coming day was to change that.

The following day, Sunday April 14th, we marched in the afternoon the few miles between us and the sectors of the front.

We proceeded through Donmartin-sous-Hans, Courtemont, and Vienne-la-Ville, to the Camp des Haut Batis, a shelter for reserve troops behind the Secteur Citadelle de St. Thomas, where we were to spend the night, and from which position we were to send small groups to take post in the trenches, the following day.

This Camp des Haut Batis was located in a beautifully wooded ravine. High hills (almost mountains) form the northern boundary, and, incidentally, protection from the shells of the enemy. Along the southern boundary runs one of the great national highways of France. A national highway is the kind of thoroughfare which, in America, is called a state road. This road leads straight to the East, to St. Menehould, and beyond.

The beautiful ravine in which we were to make ourselves comfortable for the night bore the encouraging unofficial name —Death Valley.

The men had barracks, built in close to the hillside and comparatively safe from shelling. The officers had little huts built of rough boards.

Upon arrival at our camp in Death Valley I directed each captain to have his squad leaders choose bomb shelters for their men, and report in writing. The officers obeyed, of course; but I could see some of them wagging their heads over the idea of my officiousness, in trying to show off by making extra and unnecessary work for them to do.

An hour later, while the odor of a cooking meal was cheering our olfactory senses, I was seated with Adjutant Landon upon a pile of lumber, studying out our French orders for the movement of the next day. The guns had been playing, of course, all the afternoon, but nothing had come near us. Suddenly came the screech of an arrival, directly over Landon's and my head. It seemed to be about four feet above us; and, from the measurements made the next day with an estimated ordinate, it probably was about twenty to twenty-five feet over our heads. The shell struck in a brook just thirty paces beyond us, exploding as it struck, and making a great splash of mud and water.

Instantly, the orders were given and repeated down the line to seek bomb shelters, and after the arrival of one more shell all hands were under cover—and safe.

Some thirty shells found their way into our little camp within the next quarter of an hour; but nobody was hit, and no military property was damaged.

The next morning, while lunching with the French colonel who commanded the *sous secteur*, I expressed a wonder as to whether the Boche knew that Americans were there or whether the shelling of our camp in the woods was, in a sense, merely an accident.

"But certainly they knew," said the Colonel de Villiers, "they know everything and so do we. Tomorrow, I will show you my information bulletin that comes every day, and gives the gist of all the news, important to our sector, which has been gathered by our spies. Certainly they knew you were there; and so they gave you a welcome. They have not shelled that camp for many, many months."

We had experienced our first shelling.

I was delighted with the manner in which the men behaved and with the spirit which they showed. They laughed and screamed in gleeful excitement, as do pleasure seekers at Coney Island when being rushed over one of those great coasting "Dips of Death." But they were never the least bit out of hand, or really scared; and they took to their respective covers in good order and promptly.

Of course there were amusing incidents.

When the bombardment was about half over, I saw, from my bombproof on the top of my little hillock, two young officers, Webb and Sherman, strolling down the central roadway of the camp, arm in arm. These splendid youngsters, twenty-three and twenty-one years of age respectively, explained afterwards that when the shelling had come, they had found themselves at the end of the camp, away from their own company's quarters, and that they had considered it their duty to go to their own area, to make sure that the men were properly placed.

As I saw these boys out in the open, I rushed out of my hole in the rock to try and gain their attention. Every few seconds a warning screech would come, and prompt me to duck back into shelter until the arrival had functioned. Several times I played with myself this game of "Pop in—Pop out" and, once or twice, had to jump quickly, to clear in time to avoid the dispersion. Then, I suppose I must have become excited. I know I was in earnest. I jumped up high on a rock, made a megaphone of my hands, and shouted:—"Mr. Webb, what in hell do you think you are doing—trying to show off? With such an example to the men you'll have half the battalion out in a minute. Get under cover!"

Lieutenant Webb clicked his heels together, snapped his hand to his helmet, and shouted back—"I beg your pardon, Sir!" Then he and Sherman ducked into a hole.

Some of the men thought it might be a gas attack, and they put on their masks. In one shelter was a man who had disobeyed orders and gone about without having his mask looped from his shoulder.

He set up a howl: "Hes enybody got two masks?"

"Wait a minute, broather," said one of the boys, "wait till Ah gits mahne on, an' Ah'll put mah hand over yoo mouth."

Late that night the Officer of the Day stumbled upon a cabin full of men, all sleeping with their boots on, and the heavy booted feet sticking out from under their blankets. The O. D. expressed surprise to one of the men, who seemed to be wide awake, and asked why the men had not made themselves comfortable. The man explained that early in the evening a cat had knocked over a tin basin, and the men (then in stocking feet) thinking that shells were coming again, had rushed into a trench and gotten their feet wet and muddy. So they had changed their socks and put their shoes on—to be ready.

"I'm afraid you won't sleep very well," said the officer.

"Well Suh," said the man, "Ah doan know so much 'bout ef we all is gwine ter sleep much—but we'se here."

Our first shelling, from a military viewpoint, was of no great importance; but to us in those early days of our front line work, it appeared to mark our graduation from the ranks of tin soldiers to those of participants in the art of slaughter. Our morale was high. Our *esprit de corps* was marked. From colonel to cook we were sentimentalists, and by no means ashamed of the fact.

## OUR FIRST TOUR IN THE TRENCHES

*April 15–May 1, 1918*

AFTER one night at the Camp des Haut Batis we moved, upon the morning of April 15th, into the trenches of the front line of defense.

Just as we had broken camp and commenced our march of about six kilometers, a French officer approached me and reported as Lieutenant Drubay. Drubay presented orders of assignment to my staff. Lieutenant Herrengh was, by the same communication, transferred to other duty.

In a text book of instructions, issued by the French Army, entitled *Manual of Chief of Platoon*, which in time came to supersede with us most of the books on field service and combat regulations which we had studied, was to be read a simple little line which reflection has made me believe had much to do with the magnificent combination of spirit and efficiency of the French Army. The line was, in effect, a definition reading as follows:

*"Discipline is the art of compelling individuals to do what they do not wish to do."*

It has always been a source of regret to me that Lieutenant Drubay was transferred from our regiment to other duty (I believe with other American troops, less experienced than we had become), just before we got into action which offered opportunities for the citation of some of our officers and men. Drubay went through all the discouraging days of learning with us; and we reaped the rewards. For a very, very large share of whatever credit in the command of my battalion was given me by my superior officers, both French and American, I gratefully acknowledge my obligations to this gallant French officer, Lieutenant Drubay.

Upon that morning of the 15th of April, the meeting with Lieutenant Drubay was but the beginning of a series of interesting meetings along the road.

Just before we arrived at the bridge to the East of Vienne la Ville an elderly gentleman saluted me and said in perfectly delightful and cultured English: *"Mon Commandant*, I am Captain de Beaumont, and I have the honor to report to you as attaché, to make liaison between you and my colonel, the Lieutenant Colonel Adam de Villiers, commander of the 131st Regiment of Infantry Territorial, and commander of the sou-sector Afrique, of which garrison your battalion is to become a part. My colonel asks the honor of the company of yourself and your staff at lunch; and we have taken the liberty of sending out some officers and soldiers who speak English, to act as guides for your line officers and men, who will, of course, from this point go in very small detachments to their posts."

As I demurred, Captain (subsequently commandant) Paul Giblain of the 131st French Infantry arrived and introduced himself. Captain Giblain was in command of the group of English speaking guides to whom Captain de Beaumont had referred. Giblain showed me upon a map where provision had been made for the parking of our wagon train, and suggested that he be permitted to send some of his men along with ours to make sure that no misunderstanding should occur.

Then Captain Giblain joined with Captain de Beaumont in making clear to me that there would be nothing for me to do for a number of hours; and de Beaumont concluded the matter by saying:—"So you see, Sir, there's nothing for you to do anyway, and the Colonel de Villiers will be waiting for lunch."

We walked a short distance farther, then got onto a small flat car pulled by a mule, on a railroad line, and rode in state to the headquarters of the French colonel.

This mule-power railroad which subsequently became the

charge of the 15th New York has been described by Irvin Cobb in his story "Young Black Joe" published in the Saturday Evening Post; and I believe I'll allow the description to stand in the language of Mr. Cobb. My war experience may have taught me some things that I, perhaps, think I can do now, better than Irvin Cobb; but language isn't one of them.

We had barely been seated at the table when my first report was handed to me. It was from Lieutenant Webb, who was acting as Trainmaster. I was informed that one of our rolling kitchens had been wrecked. The four horses pulling the kitchen had run away and dumped the vehicle over an embankment. The horses were uninjured and no men had been hurt; but the kitchen was beyond road-repairs.

Col. de Villiers inquired if my news was favorable. I handed him the report to read.

"It is nothing," said the Colonel, with a comforting smile, "we must expect such accidents. I will send you one of our spare kitchens at once." And he gave the necessary directions.

It was at this luncheon that I met Commandant Josse, who was to be our immediate commanding officer.

Commandant Josse asked the honor of escorting me through the trenches, for the discipline of which we were now jointly responsible.

For about a mile we walked through the swamp-woods— walking almost always upon a duck board (a board walk just wide enough for one). To our right were breastworks founded upon gabians. In the swamp regular trenches were impossible. All about us were acres upon acres of barbed wire entanglements. In many places where we walked our heads were well above the top of the defense works, and all along the line, out in front, the enemy lines, similarly constructed, were to be seen. Artillery fire of a desultory character was constant, but the day was accounted a quiet one in the professional reports of strong point commanders, and there was no rifle fire. As I walked in trace of the Commandant Josse with our steel helmeted heads presenting tempting targets, I expected that the rifle fire would soon commence. The Commandant was taller than I and he did not stoop to cover as he passed or stood at the low spots; so I walked erect too—but I made no straining of my neck muscles in an attempt to make myself appear taller than I really was.

Suddenly the Commandant halted. "There," said he, "this is the most advanced post of our sector." I looked and exclaimed: —"Why it appears to be no more than 200 yards to the enemy line."

"Yes," said my host, "it appears to be so near, but it is really just 400 meters—we have measured." And rifles are fired with flat sights up to 600 meters! Comforting reassurance!

The commandant took a rifle from one of his men and handed it to me. *Mon Commandant,* said he, "will you fire the first American shot from this center of resistance of our sector?" When I had fired, the Commandant fired a shot.

"Gentlemen!" It was Commandant Josse who addressed his little group of officers, gathered about us in that most advanced combat group of our first-line trenches. "Gentlemen! For many months we have toasted the Americans as our friends. Tonight we may pledge to them our love, and toast them as allies!"

Then all the officers present, of both our battalions, shook hands with me in congratulation.

# XXV

# OUR FIRST EXPERIENCE IN NO-MAN'S LAND
## April 17, 1918

UPON the night of April 17th we functioned our first excursion into No-Man's Land.

During the day it had been discovered that some of our barbed wire entanglements had been cut. It was thought possible that a raiding patrol might be planning a descent upon one of our advanced combat groups. It was decided to try to ambuscade the party if it should come.

Company "C" happened to be stationed in the strong point upon which the attack was expected, and it was decided to pick our ambuscading party from that company. The Command was made up half of French, half of Americans. Grant, Webb, and Sherman, the three lieutenants of "C" company, quarreled for an hour over their respective claims to the honor of going upon the first patrol. Finally, Captain MacClinton invited them to spare him the difficulty of making the decision, by drawing lots. Webb won the honor.

The party was rehearsed in the respective duties of the men over and over again. There was one French soldier, who wore a patch over his left eye, who was a scream in the rehearsal. He would crouch and move along, catlike without a sound. Then he would flatten out, face down. Stealthily the head would come up again, the one good eye would sweep the plain, then the advance would be resumed. Suddenly he would turn half about, put finger to lips for silence, reach for a dummy grenade, go through the motions of throwing it, flatten out again for a few seconds, and then, with bayonet fixed, rush forward with blood curdling yells.

Presently, all the men caught the spirit of this poilu's leadership and the pantomime that was enacted made me wish that Sothern might have been there to see. If the Germans had been encountered that night by our mixed patrol, there surely would have been some rough work.

Our men picked for that patrol were just bursting with pride and excitement.

Mr. Webb, in giving final instructions, tried to impress upon the men the importance of silence, and the importance, too, of holding fire until the signal might be given. After his little lecture, Webb followed our invariable practice, and asked if there were any questions.

"Suh L'tenant Suh," spoke up one of the men, "Suh L'tenant Suh, ef we all meets one o' them Bush Germans, an' he rares up, Ah hopes yoo won' o'der me ter bring him in alive. Why! Ef he rares up—rares up, raght up in front of me, ah jes' cain't say jes' what ah'll do!"

A few minutes before darkness, our little party crept out to take position. After they had been gone half an hour, I just felt that I couldn't stand it another minute if I couldn't get to them to see what they were doing. Josse and I had gone with the patrol to the advanced point from which they had crawled over the top. Josse saw and appreciated my nervousness. We had spoken that afternoon of the remark of General Le Gallais to the effect that battalion commanders were not permitted to go on raids or patrols. Josse had joined in by saying that, except in rare emergencies, commanders must not go in front of their lines.

Then someone had contributed one of the jokes of the army —that 2nd lieutenants were the best officers for patrol work, because 2nd lieutenants were expendable, and the subject had been dismissed with a laugh.

But Josse was a real human man. As we lay there in the dark,

173

behind the breastworks of that combat group, he seemed to sense my feelings. He leaned over and whispered:

"Would you like to go out now, just for a few minutes, to see how the men are placed? I think it will be excusable for this once. It is a matter of education by experience for you. I take the responsibility. But please be very quiet, and crawl very low. If you should be killed, my career would—ah well, who can say? Come, shall we go?"

Step by step, half creeping, half walking, we advanced about two hundred and fifty yards, to the south bank of the Tourbe River. And there, we came upon our men.

They were about a hundred and fifty yards inside the Boche entanglements, but still over fifty yards from their actual trenches. A plank, serving as a bridge for the little river, had been drawn up on the German side. Our men just had to wait and see if an enemy party would come. The men were well hidden, and a covering barrage from our own machine guns would play, upon signal. Josse and I crept along the entire line of our ambuscade, speaking in whispers to each of the men. The confident grins with which we were welcomed were reassuring. Everything was all right.

We went back to the lines and waited until the hour for recall.

When the time was up, our party came in—wet and cold, but otherwise in good shape.

It was a disappointing affair, as nothing came of it—especially disappointing as one of the lieutenants of the 2nd battalion (Marshall Johnson) had that very afternoon been decorated with a *Croix de Guerre*, for bringing in a German prisoner taken in a raid, in which he had accompanied the French command to which he had been attached.

The following morning when the news of that medal-winning was circulated throughout our lines, the ambition of our boys from Harlem became spurred well-nigh to the bursting point.

All along the line, colored soldiers, alone, or in couples, or in

1908

BAND RETURNING TO QUARTERS, MAFFRECOURT, MAY 5, 1918

1/902

THE ONE-MULE-POWER RAILROAD, MAY 4, 1918. THE BUILDING WAS A
STATION ON THE PARIS-BERLIN LINE——USED AS A QUARTER-SECTOR HEAD-
QUARTERS

groups of three or four, climbed over the parapets of their trenches, took hitches in their belts, and started deliberately to walk out into No Man's Land—towards the trenches of the enemy. The officers, of course, called them back and demanded explanations. The explanations were all the same:

"Suh L'tenant Suh, Ah was jes' ergoin' over ter git one er them Bush Germans, so's ter git one er them qua di gairs fo' mah gal."

175

# XXVI

# THE TECHNICAL SIDE OF TRENCH WARFARE

WHILE I have chosen the narrative form for the record of my adventures with the 15th New York, I feel that, perhaps, the introduction of some technical matter * may serve to make my stories more readily understood. I have learned in conversation with friends that no general comprehension exists among civilians as to the plan and scope of trench warfare. In fact, I have found that the ignorance is by no means limited to civilians. Very few soldiers, relatively, who have not actually served as infantrymen or machine gun men, in the trenches, really know what the game is all about. And I have even known infantry officers of fairly high rank with weeks of experience to their credit, to be discouragingly bewildered as to their duties and responsibilities in the sectors of defense under their command.

I am free to confess that, in the beginning, I was as ignorant as the veriest tyro of the army. I was fortunate, however, in my teachers.

Gradually, the scheme dawned upon me. Before many weeks had passed I found myself actually planning alterations of our established groups—always with a view, of course, to greater possibilities of killing, with less danger to our own men.

Before going into the trenches my conception of their use was as a straight line fortification, of the order of breast-works, with the soldiers of defense placed with intervals of two or three yards, in order to admit of meeting attack with a solid line or wall of fire by rifle or by grenade.

I found, instead of straight lines of trenches, lines of very

* See Appendix A.

pronounced curves and angular irregularities. The soldiers, instead of being placed shoulder to shoulder, were placed in small groups, ranging in size from half a squad to half a platoon. With the exception of small posts established chiefly for purposes of observation or listening, these so-called "combat groups" were always established at points upon the irregular line which commanded a clear view of field of fire of that portion of the line which lay between it and the next combat group. The trench would be continuous, so as to admit of communication under cover between all the combat groups; but frequently, there would be a quarter of a mile between groups and sometimes as much as a third of a mile or more, where no soldiers at all would be posted. The open areas between combat groups, formed by these great horseshoes and angles of trenches, were filled in with barbed wire entanglements. It was extremely difficult for a body of troops of any size to work its way through such areas to the empty trenches, without discovery. As soon as discovered, any enemy troops would be subjected to flanking fire by light machine guns from the two combat groups commanding that area; and, upon signal from the officers commanding those combat groups, the unfortunate discovered enemy would also be put in peril of the searching and grazing fire of the heavy machine guns, placed in well hidden and strongly protected positions, far back from the parallel of survey, or line of observation.

All of this defense would be made practically without exposure or danger to the men operating our guns. Without enemy artillery to assist in attack, a sector of defense properly organized and faithfully served, would be impregnable against the attack of a body of twenty-five or thirty times the strength of its garrison. Two groups and a machine gun section, with a total personnel of no more than twenty-five men, could hold a quarter of a mile of front against a battalion—if the ammunition held out, against a regiment.

So well recognized was the futility of unsupported attack upon an organized section that, outside of small patrols with prisoner-seeking or information-seeking missions, any movement against our entrenched position, unaccompanied by artillery co-operation, came to be practically unheard of.

In attacks accompanied by artillery the men of the combat groups of the parallel of survey were in positions of peril nearly as great as those of the attacking units. The enemy artillery would shell the trenches and either kill the soldiers of the defense or drive them into bombproof shelters. The enemy would follow their barrage (line of artillery fire) as closely as it was safe to do so, and try to jump into the trenches and locate the garrison while the men were penned up in the dug-outs. Then it was a question of surrender or be blown to pieces by grenades thrown to explode in a narrow underground chamber.

Of course, just before the enemy could reach our trenches and scramble over the parapets, that artillery fire would have to be stopped, as a German shell could kill a German soldier in our trenches just as readily as it would kill a Frenchman or an American. In taking advantage of those few seconds of quiet and safety lay the secret of a successful defense of a sector.

The first duty of a combat group commander, when shelled, was to send up his rocket signal; and then follow his men to cover. That signal would be caught by the observers at the company (strong point) P. C. (post of command) and at battalion (center of resistance) headquarters. The battalion commander would order his machine guns into action, and telephone to his supporting artillery for a counter barrage. Usually, in less than a minute from the time of the explosion of the rocket signal the counter fire would be on, the soldiers of the attacking force would be subjected to destruction from the fire of our machine guns, and they would be locked into the area in front of our trenches by the so-called "box-barrage" of our artillery.

In the meantime, it was the duty of our men in the combat groups to rush out of their shelters at the instant of recognition of the suspension of the enemy shelling of our trenches, jump to their posts, and, if possible by firearms and grenades, prevent the

178

enemy from entering our lines. If unsuccessful in such a purpose —then, it was hand to hand, with a bayonet and knife.

Such was the general plan of defensive trench warfare as I came to understand it.

It is a matter of official record that the 15th New York Infantry (369th U. S. Infantry) 191 days under fire in both defensive and offensive action, never lost a foot of ground, and never had a man taken away as a prisoner. There were at least two occasions upon which men of our regiment were taken prisoners; but they were rescued, and the German raiding parties destroyed or put to rout—but they are complete stories in themselves, to be told at the proper time.

## XXVII

# ON OUR OWN
*April 20, 1918*

AFTER three days of our service in the trenches with the
French under a joint responsibility, General Le Gallais
called upon me at our little home in the woods, and advised me
that he was issuing orders to the effect that upon April 20th the
Center of Resistance, Melzicourt (adjoining Josse's Montplaisir)
was to be turned over to the 1st Battalion of the 369th Regiment,
completely. Our French associates and mentors would, upon that
day, leave us. We were to be alone. Metaphorically, we should
have to sink or swim.

I was frightened.

I suppose a wise man and a wise soldier should never plead
guilty to a sense of fear or fright.

I am, however, making no claims to great wisdom, either as a
man or as a soldier. I am middle aged. I have neither expectations nor hopes of great preferment in this world, either of military, political, social, or business endeavor. This war experience
of mine was the great public adventure of my career. In recording my experiences and observations, I realize that, if my narrative is to be of any value whatsoever, it must stand the test of
truth. The truth, and nothing but the truth, is what I am writing.
The whole truth (that other element of the oath of a witness) I
make no pretence of presenting. In a record of almost two years
continuous service with one organization, there could not have
failed to be many regrettable incidents of personal character
which, in the telling, would give pain to individuals without serving any purpose of public welfare by warning, and without con-

180

tributing in any important degree to the picture which I am trying to make of the development of the remarkable colored regiment with which I had the honor to serve.

When the General Le Gallais had left me, to study the orders for our new responsibilities, and to prepare for the acceptance of them, I was, as I have admitted—frightened. In addition to the emotion, however, I thrilled with another emotion, one demonstrating, perhaps, no more pronounced trait of worthiness or of greatness than the sense of fright; but, I believe, an emotion of perfectly natural human quality, for all that—the emotion of exultation and pride.

The 1st Battalion was the first unit of our regiment to occupy, alone, a sector of the defense line of the allies. I was the first officer of our regiment (not even excepting Colonel Hayward) to command a front line position. I believe I was the first officer of the United States Army to command a sector of any kind of the French line.

The first tour in the trenches of the 1st Battalion, 369th U. S. Infantry, was without highly dramatic incident. The sector to which we had been sent was a quiet one. We had patrols out, and ambuscades, almost every night; but we made no contact with the enemy, we took no prisoners, we suffered no casualties.

The right of our sector was bounded by the Aisne River. The Bois d'Hauzy, in which the C. R. Melzicourt was located, is a part of the Argonne Forest. I understand that it was, before the war, the hunting preserve of a great nobleman. It was a beautiful place for a summer home. When we entered the *bois*, in April, trees were bare, and the touch of winter still lingered. Before we completed our first tour, the buds were forming on the trees. When, after ten days *en repos*, we returned upon the 12th of May, to spend the balance of the month, we saw the wonderful spring break, in the woods, and develop into summer. The post of command of the battalion chief, and a number of the P. C.'s of company captains had tiny vegetable and flower gardens at their dooryards. I had, in my civilian days, frequently paid extravagant rentals for summer homes far less ideal than the two which I occupied alternately as the stamping ground of war, during April, May, and June of the year 1918—the quarter sectors Melzicourt and Montplaisir, in the Bois d'Hauzy.

Upon May 1st, the 1st Battalion was relieved by the 3rd Battalion. The relief was accomplished without difficulty, and my battalion marched some seven miles to Maffrecourt, the regimental supply base, for ten days *en repos*.

In accordance with the standing rule of our French Army, I remained, with the relieving troops, twenty-four hours in command of the sector, and as instructor to the incoming battalion commander.

As a starting point for instructions, in the realization that the 3rd Battalion chief probably knew very little more than I had known when I first found myself in command of the sector, I had prepared for him a detailed paper, in which I had covered everything that I had learned or believed I had learned.*

* See Appendix B.

New
Sjune
Called

Z
7164
M2
F35

Family counseling... [1981]  (Card 2)

1. Marriage counseling--
Bibliography--United States.  2.
Family psychotherapy--Bibliography--
United States.  I. Brown, Kristi.
II. University Research Corporation.

Z7164.M2F35                    016.3628'286
[HQ10]

                                    81-9644
                                    AACR2 CIP

Library of Congress
6654      35      893898      © THE BAKER & TAYLOR CO.      2079

## XXVIII

## COLOR SERGEANT COX
## DIPS THE STARS AND STRIPES

### April, 1918

WHEN our regiment, the 15th New York Infantry, first entered the Zone of the Advance we had to learn quickly a number of general regulations applicable only to troops occupying that area of danger. One of these regulations was that, whenever airplanes were sighted, all troops must take cover if possible. If troops were on the march, where cover was not accessible, then the men must spread out and lie down. This standing order was, of course, of importance (if the planes should prove to be of the Boche) as a means of preventing the enemy from counting our men or photographing them, or of succeeding in extensive execution by bombing.

Now, it so happened that upon the very first day of the regiment's advent in that country, as Major Dayton's battalion was marching from Givry-en-Argonne to Remicourt planes were sighted in the distance.

The order was given to halt, fall out, and lie down. Within a few seconds the entire command was prone—with the exception of one man, Sergeant Cox, the Color Bearer.

Major Dayton called to Sergeant Cox, and asked if he had heard the order.

"Yassuh Major Suh," answered the Sergeant, "Ah heered d'oder."

"Well then, why don't you obey it? Promptly now!"

"Suh Major Suh, Ah's ver' sorry, but Ah cain't jes' raghtly erbey dat o'der jes' now." The Sergeant, a magnificent physical

183

specimen of his race, six feet or more of height, a hundred and ninety pounds of bone and muscle, broad of shoulders, deep of chest, and tapering waist—his deep black face very serious, with hard set jaws and great round eyes staring straight to the front, added, as if in afterthought to his response—"Ah's ver' sorry, Suh Major Suh."

"Why can't you obey my order?" Major Dayton demanded.

"Suh Major Suh," the answer came back promptly, "Ah'll jes' tell yoo. Er long tahm ergo, more'an er year, mebbe er year an' er 'alf, way back at home in Noo York, raght out on 5th Av'noo, down en front of der Union League Club, Guvnor Whitman, der Guvnor of Noo York State, dun handed me dese colors. An' der Guvnor, he saiz ter me, 'Sergean', doan' yoo never let dis flag 'ere touch der groun'.' An' Suh, Major Suh, so long's mah old laigs is stiff 'nough ter hol' me up straight, and so long's mah han's is strong 'nough to hol' dis staff, dis flag, Suh Major Suh, dis 'ere flag ain't never ergoan' ter touch der ground'!"

Six weeks later, Sergeant Cox, in a sense, reversed his determination; and while the colors in his keeping were not exactly permitted to touch the ground, still he did lower the Stars and Stripes. It seemed to me, then, and I trust that my readers may agree with me, now, that Sergeant Cox, in lowering the United States Flag, demonstrated even a greater love for it and a greater appreciation of the significance of its meaning than he did upon the day when he decided he could not reconcile the orders of his Governor and his Major.

It was during the last week of April 1918, and a great review of troops was being made, incidental to the presentation of war medals to a number of soldiers of the French Army. The battalion *en repos* of each regiment of the 16th (French) Division was paraded. With the reserve battalion of the 369th U. S. Infantry, which represented our regiment at the ceremonies, paraded the Band and—the Colors.

There were three French Generals making the review.

The first: General Gouraud, the magnificent leader and hero

of the Fourth Army of France, a soldier who had lost his right arm in the Gallipoli Campaign and who had also been wounded in the leg, so that he had to walk with a limp, a leader, whom the *poilus* always cheered whenever he appeared before them, our General, affectionately spoken of by his men as "The Lion of France."

The second: General Helie d'Oiselle, Commander of the 8th Army Corps, of which our Division was a part.

The third: General Le Gallais, our own division chief.

As these three distinguished officers and war veterans passed down the lines, during that part of the ceremony which in our country is known as the standing review, and as they came opposite our colors, drawn up on a line with the front rank of our mass formation, instead of saluting and passing by (as is customary in the ceremony) these Generals of France halted, faced the colors, uncovered, and bowed very low.

As they stood there in an attitude of solemn adoration, down the cheeks of the great Gouraud—tears coursed.

In order to make my readers appreciate the significance of the compliment paid to our nation by those three French Generals, I must go back five or six months to the time of our arrival in France during the closing days of the year 1917.

When we first landed in France we found the morale of the country at very low ebb. France was bled white. The cry for help which for months, even for years, had been going out to the sister republic across the seas, had given way to a cry of despair.

France was beaten. And she was so sick of body and at heart that the common people of the towns and the soldiers of the ranks not only sensed defeat but admitted it.

Our first words of welcome from the population of the humble classes were words of protest at our coming. Why had we come? We could do nothing, now, but prolong the suffering of the nation! Germany was too strong. It was not to be beaten. If we had come sooner—perhaps; but now, it was too late. If we had kept out of the war, it would have been over by now; and

185

while of course the Germans would be the masters, still no suffering could equal that which had been endured for three years.

Of course the higher, the prouder classes and the officers of exalted rank did not talk that way; but undoubtedly they knew. Their faces were grave.

But during the six or eight months which had passed since the coming of American troops, a wonderful change of material conditions had been brought about. The miracles of the American Engineer Corps had commenced to take definite shape. The great projects of the American Service of Supply were changing the pinch of privation to the perk of plenty.

Millions of men of America were in the camps, being trained as soldiers and as sailors.

Stupendous issues of war bonds not only were being sold, but bought—bought with the cheers of the populace, with fêtes of enthusiasm, with singing and dancing, on the streets.

The spirit of America was enlisted—almost one hundred per cent strong. America would spend its last dollar and shed its last drop of male blood, if necessary.

Changes in morale for the better, like changes in morale for the decline, usually have their beginnings at the top. Long before the man on the street of France or the *poilu* of the ranks could realize the meaning of the great developments which had been taking place since the entrance of America into the war, the officers at the top knew, if the lines could be made to hold for the year 1918, that the doom of the German War machine was written on the walls. Already they could see not only the possibility of victory, but the probability of victory, and victory soon to come.

"And it would be a beautiful day for France!"

And so, upon that sunny April morning of 1918, when our three French Generals reviewed their troops, as they came to the lines of the American battalion of colored volunteer infantrymen from New York, their hearts beat with hope. As they marched down the line, the beautiful Star Spangled Banner, waving in the breeze, caught their eyes—the emblem of America! And through that emblem they could commence to see the dawn of a beautiful day (*"Une belle journée"*), as the French, with their poetic expressions, so loved to say.

The three Generals, Gouraud, Helie d'Oiselle, and Le Gallais, halted, faced the colors, uncovered, and bowed very low.

Color-Sergeant Cox stood fast, erect and stiff—a splendid bronze statue! For a long time, so it seemed, he stood so; and then, a shudder of emotion could have been seen momentarily to convulse his giant frame; his head was tossed back, as if in token of a weighty determination.

Sergeant Cox bowed low, as gracefully and with the same reverence as marked the attitude of the three Generals standing before him. And as the Color-Sergeant bowed, down went the National Flag of the United States dipping in salute, almost until it touched the ground.

When the review was over, Colonel Hayward addressed the Color-Bearer, saying:

"Sergeant Cox, don't you know the Manual of the Color? Don't you know, that in ceremonies where honors are paid to officers of rank high enough to be entitled to a dipping of the color, that it is always the state flag or the regimental flag that is lowered, and never the National Color, the Flag of the United States?"

And Sergeant Cox answered:

"Yassuh, Kunnel Suh, Ah knows all 'bout doze reg'lations; Ah knows 'bout der Manual of der Color; Ah knows et's all writ en der book—jes' 's yoo saiz. But, Suh Kunnel Suh, w'en Ah sees doze t'ree wonderful French Generals er bowin' down befo' me, an' partic'larly dat great General w'der beard, der one 'at only has one arm, and der one 'at the French soldiers alwuz cheers when de sees 'em; when Ah sees doze French Generals er bowin' down and er movin' of dere lips lahk as ef dey wuz er prayin' ter Old Glory, an' w'en Ah sees dat Lion O'France General er cryen tears of love fo' der Stars and Stripes, Ah jes' saiz ter mahse'f, Suh Kunnel Suh, Ah jes' saiz ter mahse'f, Sergean' Cox —'Der man dat done wrote doze reg'lations, he never knowed not'en 'bout no such 'casion such as dis!' "

# XXIX

# EN REPOS AT MAFFRECOURT
## May 1–May 11, 1918

AS stated, upon the morning of May 2nd, I turned over command of the C. R. Melzicourt to Captain Chandler, temporarily commanding the 3rd Battalion, and reported myself out of sector on the way to join my own battalion.

Upon the second full day of our stop at Maffrecourt, we took up some work of drill and training. We found some steep hills at one end of a clear plain, against which we managed to set up targets; and there, upon a primitive kind of rifle range, we practiced marksmanship with Labelle rifles and Hotchkiss machine guns, and Chau Chat automatics.

I spent the greater part of my own day at a camp in the Charmeresse woods, some five miles from Maffrecourt, observing the special training of a body of picked men of our battalion, in preparation for a *coup de main,* projected for some night of the week May 5th to 12th.

Lieutenant Hoyt Sherman was the officer whom I picked for the command in this important expedition. Sherman picked his own men. It was a proud detachment that left our battalion, with the mysterious air bred of secret orders, to go and live in the Camp of the Charmeresse with the 5th Battalion of the 334th Infantry of France, to prepare and to be trained for this delicate service, to which Colonel Belhumeur had done the 1st Battalion the honor of assignment.

Sherman and his men worked faithfully. By day they practiced their positions and duties under cover, in the woods. By night they rehearsed in the dark—feeling their way over ground and through imaginary trenches, marked by stakes, and laid out so as to conform to the positions of the enemy trenches to be invaded. The plans of enemy trenches were worked out from photographs taken by air planes.

This *coup de main* was never executed. The men were ready; but upon several nights for which the operation was set, the weather turned out to be unfavorable. Finally, Colonel Belhumeur and his regiment were ordered away to other duty, the personnel of the projected expedition was thus broken up, and the plan abandoned.

Upon the departure of Colonel Belhumeur, Colonel Hayward came into command of the *Sous-Secteur Afrique;* and the name was changed to *Sous-Secteur U. S.*

Shortly after my return from Charmeresse one afternoon during that first week *en repos*, as I was changing to fresh clothes, a note came down from the Regimental Adjutant's office on the hill, by which Captain Hinton begged me to come right up, to do the polite to a distinguished visitor. Colonel Hayward was up at the front at the headquarters of *Sous-Secteur U. S.*, at Vienne la Ville; and I was in command at Maffrecourt, not only of the 1st Battalion, but also of the supply station and all the units quartered therein, which included some 500 replacement troops.

I found at the Headquarters House, Colonel Roberts of the U. S. Cavalry, serving as an Aid to General Pershing. Colonel Roberts was cordial in his greeting, and stated that he had been sent by the General to look us over, informally, to see if we were happy and getting along all right, and to inquire if there was anything he could do for us.

Colonel Roberts exhibited great interest in our 18 days' tour in the trenches just complete. He asked me a lot of questions as to conditions up there, as to the bearing of the men, and, finally, as to my own feeling upon relief—was I tired, had I felt the strain, and had I kept well, physically?

I assured the Colonel that I was in robust health, that I had not been conscious of the strain until after being relieved; but that

I was a whole lot worried over the consciousness of my ignorance of which every day in the trenches had presented some new incident of proof.

"But you did well, I understand," said Colonel Roberts.

I answered that I was not at all satisfied with what we did, or with the way in which we did it.

Colonel Roberts then said: "I shouldn't be too downcast if I were you. Let me read you this letter of the French General to General Pershing."

Then he read.

I couldn't have wished for more praise for service where no great action had been fought.

Colonel Roberts folded up the letter, and returned it to his pocket. Then he smiled, and said: "So, my dear Captain, don't be too downhearted over your problems. I have never read more complimentary language in a military report. General Pershing wanted you to be able to let your men know that their efforts are being appreciated. Tomorrow, I shall visit Colonel Hayward in the sector, in order that he may be enabled to pass on the words of encouragement applicable to his whole regiment."

# THE BATTLE OF HENRY JOHNSON
# OUR SECOND TOUR IN THE TRENCHES
*May 11–May 31, 1918*

UPON May 11th, 1918, the 1st Battalion relieved the 2nd Battalion, in the C. R. Montplaisir. The 2nd Battalion went to Maffrecourt for its 10 days of rest and training.

Montplaisir was the center of resistance in which our 1st Battalion men had doubled for four or five days with the French Battalion Josse, during our first tour in the trenches. We were, therefore, more or less at home, we knew the terrain and the trenches. We also knew of weaknesses in the organization of the combat groups. This knowledge explained to us an uncomfortable experience of the first night of our second tour—by enemy sniping from the rear of the positions of our observation posts.

By daylight inspection we discovered points upon the front line at which entrance to the sector could be effected with comparative ease. We also found abandoned dugouts which showed signs of having been occupied by snipers.

The dugouts (and hiding places) we set about destroying. At the weak points in the line, we established ambuscades or rather, planned a series of ambuscades to be operated in rotation.

Upon the night of May 12th-13th, we had three parties out all night waiting for the enemy invaders. The entire battalion was keyed up to intense interest and hope. There seemed to us to be almost a certainty of contact, with excellent chances of success by the taking of prisoners. Captain MacClinton commanded one party. Lieutenant Webb commanded another. The third ambuscade, I, myself, commanded.

Slowly, the hours of the night wore away. The stillness was oppressive. A smothered cough or the snore of a dozing soldier, the whispered reproof of a non-com or the prod of a wide awake side partner, were sounds that seemed as if they must carry clear over the enemy trenches. Frequently, suspicious incoming sounds would cause us to strain eyes and ears. Such sounds were usually answered from our combat groups, stretched out to either side of us, over a long line of irregularity, by illuminating rockets—sometimes by the fire of automatic rifles and defensive grenades.

We saw the moon travel its complete course of the night, at first bringing out of pitch darkness sharply defined paths of beams and shadows, changing this great gridiron into a broad plain of beautifully soft but uncertain light, and sinking into the opposite side of the world from that upon which it had made its appearance—the light over the plain changing, through many shades of purple, once more into darkness to be awakened again after a few minutes of slumber by a gray lightening, followed quickly by the rays of the rising sun.

With each of the changes of the night we had our alarms, our thrills—our hopes; but that was all we had. We made no contact. We took no prisoners.

Just before broad daylight, while the troops of the entire battalion were "Standing-to" at their posts, through every line of the sector—observation, resistance, and redoubt—we crawled into the trenches, and wearily made our way back to quarters—and to sleep.

The next night, the night of the 13th-14th of May three other ambuscades were set—at other points and with other personnel.

At about half past two in the morning, at the point where my party had lain all the night before, the Germans came. There were no Americans there to meet them that night, however, and the Boche were able to make their way in peace, a hundred and fifty yards or more to the west, to the rear of Combat Group No. 29.

Number 29 was a tiny post, actually isolated, but theoretically a part of number 28, some fifty or sixty yards still farther to the West.

Number 28 was garrisoned by a strong force, of at least half a platoon, under command of an officer, Lieutenant Richardson Pratt of Brooklyn.

Number 29 was manned by four men and a corporal. The post was but little more than an islet of observation. Its armament had no automatic rifles. It was a part of the command of the officer stationed at Number 28.

As the enemy patrol made its way cautiously through the field of wire that protected the rear of Number 29 from rushing tactics, some slight sound (probably that of the functioning of a wire clipper) arrested the attention of Private Needham Roberts, on guard at the east side of the enclosure. Roberts slipped over to the other side, and, cautioning his partner of the relief, Private Henry Johnson, for silence, led him back to the spot where the noise had been heard.

Together the boys listened and peered. Presently that sound was repeated.

An illuminating rocket was discharged into the field from which the sound came; and, "Corporal of the Guard!" was shouted at the top of the voices of the two plucky little volunteers —Roberts of Trenton, N. J., and Johnson of Albany, N. Y.

The signal of discovery was the signal for attack—for the Germans. Quickly and without further caution the wire clippers worked. A volley of grenades was thrown into the little fortified area of Combat Group Number 29, and both Roberts and Johnson were wounded. The Corporal and the off relief of two men, sleeping in the dugout, were penned in.

Roberts, badly hurt and unable to rise, propped himself against the door of the dugout and threw grenades out into the darkness.

Johnson was back on his feet, rifle in hand, in time to meet the rush of Germans as they came piling into the enclosure.

The Labelle rifle carries a magazine clip of but three cartridges. Johnson fired his three shots—the last one almost muzzle to breast of the Boche bearing down upon him. As the German fell, a comrade jumped over his body, pistol in hand, to avenge his death.

There was no time for reloading. Johnson swung his rifle round his head, and brought it down with a thrown blow upon the head of the German. The German went down, crying, in perfectly good Bowery English, "The little black so and so has got me!"

"Yas, an' dis little black so and so'll git yer 'gin—ef yer git up!" went back the high pitched voice of Henry Johnson, in admirable repartee, as he varied, for a few seconds, the monotonous call for the Corporal of the Guard which he kept repeating, between the grunts of his exertions, all through the fight.

With the enemy in the front for the moment disposed of, Johnson glanced over his shoulder to the left, to see how things were going with his partner. Two Germans had lifted Roberts from the ground, one had him by the shoulders and one by the feet, and they were about to rise, to carry him away—a prisoner.

Our men were unanimous in the opinion that death was to be preferred to a German prison. But Johnson was of the opinion that victory was to be preferred to either.

With side spring, the active little soldier from Albany came down like a wildcat upon the shoulders of the German with the head of Roberts between his knees. As Johnson sprang, he unsheathed his bolo knife, and as his knees landed upon the shoulders of that ill-fated Boche, the blade of the knife was buried to the hilt through the crown of the German's head.

A bolo knife weighs no less than three pounds. The blade is at least eight or nine inches in length. The Germans upon patrol wear no helmets, presumably upon the theory that the danger of noise from the striking against them of wire is greater than the danger of wounds owing to lack of protection to the head. One of the war relics of the 16th Division of France, valued by General Le Gallais as a memento of the world-famous fight of his little American soldier, is the gray cloth, red bound round cap of that short-lived captor of Needham Roberts. Through the crown of the cap is a clean-cut slit about two and a half inches in width. Glued to the lining of the cap, glued by blood of its owner, is a thick lock of brown hair.

Johnson turned once more to the front. He was none too soon. The Boche who had been knocked down by clubbed rifle was up! He was up and mad—fighting mad. Down upon the plucky little Johnson he bore—his Lueger automatic pistol spitting a stream of fire as he charged. Johnson felt a burning, stinging pain. He cried out as if in despair; and dropped upon hands and knees. The German closed in. The next instant Johnson was up and under the guard of the German; and that terrible bolo knife was in the German's abdomen. Johnson showed no quarter. The knife was turned. The enemy soldier was disembowelled.

The enemy patrol was in a panic. The dead and wounded were piled upon stretchers and carried away.

When daylight came, we trailed the course of the enemy retreat (a roundabout course of at least a half mile through the woods) to the bank of the river, where they crossed. We trailed the course with the greatest of ease, by pools of blood, blood-soaked handkerchiefs and first aid bandages, and blood-smeared logs, where the routed party had rested.

Johnson was wounded in many places. He was almost exhausted. He seemed to know by instinct, however, that the mere turning point of a battle is not the time for the victor to suspend hostilities. The enemy was retreating. Certainty must be made that it should never come back.

As the Germans piled through the chicane which they had cut in our wire, Johnson pelted them with grenades. We found evidence that at least one man had been terribly torn by the iron of these explosions. At the narrowest point in the opening, where they could do no better than go in single file, was found a terrible mass of flesh and blood, and the cloth of a coat, and the pulped material of a first aid packet—blown open. Upon the ground, in this opening, was the shell hole blown by the grenade. The hole was of the size and shape of a five gallon punch bowl; and it was almost filled with thick, sticky blood. In the Champagne country, the soil is of a chalky clay, of a quality to hold water for very slow absorption. The blood of that grenade blown punch bowl was not wholly absorbed for more than a week.

As the relief-party, headed by Lieutenant Pratt, entered the enclosure of Combat Group Number 29, Henry Johnson fainted. As he passed out, he mumbled the words—"Corporal of the Guard!"

The first news that I received of "The Battle of Henry Johnson" was brought to me by Sergeant-Major Hooper, at about 3:30 in the morning.

Hooper entered my cabin and reported that there had been a fight in the left P.C. (*point d'apuis*); that no official report had as yet come down; but that two wounded men (probably dying) had just passed our headquarters upon a flat-car of the mule-power railroad line, to be taken to the sector dressing station, and to wait for an ambulance, which had been ordered.

A pair of rubber boots and a raincoat over my pajamas was the bill of dress in which I raced after that flat-car.

When I reached the dressing station, both men were conscious, and not only able but glad to talk. Captain MacClinton, in evacuating the men after the administering of first aid, had given to each a cup full of the rum which is always kept for emergencies at the company commander's P.C., in front line sectors.

Both Roberts and Johnson were remarkably coherent in their statements. It was the first fight we'd had in the regiment, and the first of our casualties. I feared that these men would die. They were wounded in so many places. I suppose my face must have shown emotional concern. I finished my note making and pocketed my book, just as the ambulance arrived.

Henry Johnson looked up at me and motioned that he had something more to say. I knelt at his side.

"Suh Cap'n Suh," said the wounded hero, in a low, husky voice, but with an indescribably gentle smile, "Suh Cap'n Suh, yoo all doan' want er worry 'bout me. Ah'm all raght. *Ah've ben shot beefo'!*"

One by one the witnesses either by sight or by hearing were examined and cross examined by me. Every foot of the ground of that fight and of the retreat was gone over by me, with others. I made notes as I examined. At the conclusion, I put aside as valueless every detail of which there was no corroborative testimony or evidence. The result was the story as I have told it. So I made my official report.

As the Germans gave their signal for retreat, they abandoned a considerable quantity of property, either in a spirit of panic, or in order to make themselves better prepared to carry the load of their dead and wounded. I cannot give off-hand the complete inventory; and, as I write, a copy of my report is not at hand. The abandoned property account included, however, the following items:

About 40 potato-masher grenades.

7 Long-arm wire cutters.

3 Caps (one of which was found in the state described above).

3 Lueger automatic pistols.

We found marks in the clay, outside the wire of the combat group, to show where two hospital corps stretchers had been set down during the fight.

From our knowledge that it was customary to equip no more than one man of every four with the heavy long-arm wire clipper we made the deduction that there were certainly no less than 24 men in that German patrol. The evidence of their having brought with them two stretchers was corroborative of such a deduction. Also, the fact that none of the dead or wounded were left in our hands, coupled with our knowledge that of the dead alone there were at least four, contributed convincingly to the conclusion that the enemy was of a minimum of 24 men.

And this attacking party was completely killed, wounded, or put to rout by one rather small of stature colored soldier, in civilian life a red-cap porter of the New York Central Railroad Station at Albany, N. Y.—by name, Henry Johnson.

By half past ten o'clock I had completed the examination and inspection of the witnesses and the scene of the fight, and dictated my official report, including the recommendation of both Johnson and Roberts for decorations of honor—for valor.

A few minutes later, an orderly reported that Colonel Hayward and three civilians were descending from the mule-car, just outside of my quarters. I hurried out to greet my visitors, and recognized Irvin Cobb, Martin Green of the Evening World, and Lincoln Eyre of the New York World.

Of course I just had to get those men out to Combat Group Number 29! It was a Heaven-sent opportunity for honorable publicity for our volunteer regiment from Harlem.

Cobb asked me if I could tell them of any interesting experience to include in the stories that they wanted to write of *"Les enfants perdu,"* whom they had just succeeded in finding after arduous and discouraging search.

I told them that things generally had been rather dull and quiet with us; but that amusing incidents, of course, were cropping up all the time.

"Have you had no fights, then?" chimed in Mr. Green.

"Why yes—we did have a little fight this morning, that was good while it lasted—if you're interested in that sort of thing," I answered. "Of course we get our shelling fairly constantly, and there's more or less sniping all the time; but, this morning a couple of our boys had a real pitched battle, for a few minutes. They did very well, too. I've just finished the report. I'm trying to get them the *Croix de Guerre*. Would you care to read it?"

"Yes indeed!" The three journalists answered, all at once.

As they read, the only sounds in that little room were strange grunts and exhalations, emphasizing their appreciation of having dropped in upon one of the really sensational incidents of America's part in the war.

"You win, Little!" exclaimed Cobb, when the reading had been finished. "You played your hand well. How about our looking over the grounds—to get the picture right?"

"Delighted to take you out there!" I answered. "But you may get sniped at. If you don't mind that, let's go."

It was a very warm day. Cobb said:

"The sniping part's all right. A wound stripe would make me just irresistible; but how about taking my coat off?"

Three times on the way out, Cobb stopped short, as he mopped and panted, and swore that he wouldn't go another step. I felt sympathetic. The sun beat down mercilessly upon the shadeless plain. I did want those writers, however, to see that grenade-blown punch bowl filled with blood. I coaxed and encouraged. After four periods, the objective, Combat Group Number 29, was reached. I believe those journalists were actually satisfied with the reward of their physical effort, in the material for local color gained by their visit to that exposed post.

When we returned to my P.C., lunch was ready.

Towards the end of our luncheon, Cobb looked over at me and said:

"Little, I know it's against your rules to talk shop at table; but, today, just for one question, I want you to indulge me. How much special training for this trench fighting had that chap Henry Johnson had before he licked those 24 Germans?"

"Just the same as the rest of the regiment," I answered. "No more than three weeks in theory. As a matter of actual practice, taking out our time for changing stations, and the ordinary routine of our early days with the French, I should say that the special training of our men has been equal to about one week of what I understand the draft men are now getting at the big cantonments over home."

"Well," said Irvin Cobb, "I've been thinking. It seems to

me that the performance of that young man was truly remarkable. Why, if he had had the normal training that our men at home are getting today, I believe that by tomorrow night Henry would have been storming Potsdam!"

A few days after the visit to our sector of Messrs. Cobb, Green, and Eyre, there appeared as a front page spread of the New York World, a signed article by the special staff correspondent, Lincoln Eyre, describing in detail "The Battle of Henry Johnson."

All the New York evening papers of that day carried quotations or reprints of the World beat. By the following morning the Associated Press had spread all over the United States the account of the prowess of America's first two colored soldiers to receive from the French Government the coveted *Croix de Guerre*. The 15th New York Infantry had passed out of the category of a merely unique organization of the American Army, a regiment with its chief bid for fame based upon the music of Jim Europe's Band.

Our colored volunteers from Harlem had become, in a day, one of the famous fighting regiments of the World War.

# XXXI

# BACK TO MAFFRECOURT

*June 1–June 10, 1918*

UPON May 31st, 1918, the 1st Battalion was once more relieved in sector by the 3rd Battalion. Nothing of extraordinary interest occurred in connection with the relief. I remained in sector, as commander, as I had done before, for 24 hours after my battalion left for Maffrecourt. This same rule was made applicable to the companies of the relief. Each retiring captain remained with the incoming captain for one full day.

Outside of the Johnson fight nothing of real importance had occurred during our twenty-day occupation of Montplaisir. We had had a number of interesting patrols and ambuscades, and at least one very heavy shelling of gas. No serious casualties had occurred.

One night we had received warning from Division Headquarters of the possibility of a general attack upon the sector, and I had had our machine gun voiturettes brought up from the supply base, with extra ammunition. Outside of a very satisfactory proving-up of the efficiency of the battalion stable sergeant, James H. Kelly, however, nothing came of the warning and scare.

Memorial Day (May 30th) had found us in the trenches preparing for relief. Our men had found the time, however, upon that day, to respect the spirit of America in paying honor to its soldier dead. In our sector were a number of little corners fenced off for protection against the tramping of marching feet—corners filled with graves marked with the simple wooden cross bearing the name of a soldier of France who had died for his country. With wild flowers gathered from the earth banks of our trenches and boyaux, our men had decorated these graves in reverence and in tenderness.

Upon arriving at Maffrecourt upon June 1st, to rejoin my battalion for rest and training, I found a command of very different spirit from that which had given me so much concern a month before.

Officers and men were on their toes, so to speak. The *esprit de corps* of the battalion was so strong that some of us older heads had to keep on watch constantly to make sure that it should not take the place of a proper love for the regiment.

The men were orderly in personal deportment, and ambitious in their attitude towards the program of military training mapped out for us by our French commanders.

Our town and billets, which were found in filthy disorder, were cleaned by our men, and kept clean. Our formations were prompt. Several times, after work hours were over, during the long twilight of the evenings, when I desired to experiment with formations to be used in manoeuvers for the following day, I asked for volunteers to make up a dummy battalion. The men never failed me. I always had more than double the number of volunteers asked for. And the officers—they were nearly one hundred percent, in their attitude of right-heartedness.

The command of the 1st Battalion had become a very real pleasure.

During that first week in June I was invited by an officer of high rank to accept promotion in another organization of the United States Army—to leave the colored soldiers. I responded that, of course, I should have to go where ordered, but that I was in love with my work, and desired no change in my command. With this splendid organization of military teamwork, I reported, upon the morning of June 4th at 7 o'clock, to our brigade commander, General Chabaud, for the first day of training in manoeuvers for open warfare. The battalion was reported upon a great plain at a designated position some 1200 meters S.W. of

Maffrecourt. A French battalion participated with us in the manoeuvers.

A detailed description of these manoeuvers, which covered a program of five half days, of course, can have no place in this narrative. The program covered everything from the mere group formations of the men, to co-operation with machine gun support, with artillery support, and with airplane scouts—all bearing upon the science of attack in open warfare.

General Chabaud was the best instructor in the higher branches of military training I ever met. Not only was he able to make his meaning clear to us, but he kept our interest enlisted during all of the many hours of hard work. He never gave way to impatience when we made mistakes. He never indulged in sarcasm, when foolish questions were asked. And he always was prompt with his praise, when the opportunity for praise was given by creditable performance.

An amusing incident, in which General Chabaud was prompt to acknowledge the joke on himself, occurred during the manoeuvers of the second day.

The manoeuver represented an attack upon a masked position. The march of approach was assumed to have been completed and the advance to attack was ordered with the 1st objective behind a hill some five or six hundred meters distant.

The advance upon the first position was to be made across open and cultivated fields with no cover or woodland or brush provided. The advance was to be made under hostile artillery fire. Upon arrival at first objective, the assault wave was to deploy and take protection in a natural trench formed by a hollow where the road ran parallel to the field over which the second advance was to be made.

The two platoons of the right column had to advance without any greater cover than long grass. The two platoons of the left column were able to advance on the far side slope of the hill running perpendicular to the first objective line until nearly up to the point of the line. The movement gave great opportunity to platoon leaders and squad leaders to exercise judgment in the choice of resting places and reforming places and to demonstrate control of their men. Each company executed the movement with great deliberation, but with great skill. Including the machine gun sections attached to each company there were approximately 700 men making the advance, but at no time could more than 15 or 20 men readily be seen even when observers were nearby with knowledge as to just where the men would be likely to appear. The movement was described professionally by the name "Advancing By Infiltration."

During the early period of this advance by infiltration, General Chabaud was standing by me, at my post of command, his eyes and ears alert in following the movements of our several units. General Le Gallais, our division commander, was observing from horseback, upon a little hillock some 25 yards in advance of us.

General Chabaud addressed me:

"You have given your orders for your left company to advance?"

"Yes, my General."

"Well, why don't they start?"

"They have started, more than ten minutes ago, my General."

"Then your first wave should be here by now."

"Yes, my General, it is just now a few meters in advance of where we stand."

"I do not see the men."

"No, my General, they crawl close to the ground, as you have instructed them. They hide in the long grass."

"Can you show me one now?"

"But certainly, my General. There is one at this minute crawling between the legs of the horse of the General."

"Splendid!" exclaimed General Chabaud. "You must lunch with me today!"

At the conclusion of this movement, General Le Gallais rode

205

over to us. Colonel Hayward had joined our group as an observer.

"It is good!" General Le Gallais expressed himself with enthusiasm, as he joined the group. "It is good! It is very good! It is so good it could not be better!" Then the General turned to me, and saluted me, saying—"Commandant, I felicitate you." Once more, he addressed the group in general:

"And now, having said something pleasant, I will wish you all good morning, and go away."

Our General of Division laughed gaily, touched his horse, waved his hand, and galloped off the field.

During our week of rest at Maffrecourt, I rode over to the hospital to call upon Henry Johnson and Needham Roberts. These brave boys had endured many operations, and they had progressed beyond the danger of fatality. They were both, however, doomed to be cripples for life.

They welcomed me, as I approached their beds, with those cordial grins which we had come to understand as more eloquent than words. Conversation, under such conditions, is a bit difficult. The officer wants to be so friendly and intimate. The well trained enlisted man struggles so hard with himself, to make sure the officer shall not feel that advantage is being taken of the situation of the moment.

For the want of something better to say, I asked Johnson how it had happened that he had been so proficient with a bolo knife. For answer, Johnson just grinned a little more broadly than before.

"Have you ever been mixed up before in a fight where you used a knife?" I persisted in my inquiry.

Henry Johnson looked across the room to where Roberts was propped up in bed. Their eyes met. Then back to my eyes flashed those of the single-handed conqueror of 24 Germans. Several times the lips moved as if in attempt at speech; but gave forth no sound. Then came a great effort at control: "Suh Capt'n Suh," the little hero gulped. "Yoo wants ter know ef Ah ever

SUPPLY TRAIN READY TO LEAVE FOR FRONT, MAFFRECOURT (SUPPLY BASE)

EN REPOS, MAFFRECOURT, MAY 5, 1918

had er faght wid er knahfe—oh Suh—!" The sound of a giggle came from that other bed. It was too much for Henry. He lost all control of his power of speech. A great guffaw finished his sentence. Tears of laughter rolled down his cheeks. My question had been too ridiculous! With a half turn of the body, that convulsed black face was buried in the pillow. The walls of that hospital ward echoed with the sounds of revelry, as we all joined in laughter—the Americans, in appreciation of the comedy of the moment—the French nurses and patients, in sheer contagion.

# XXXII

# PREPARING FOR A GERMAN OFFENSIVE

*June, 1918*

DURING the last week of May, another enemy offensive had been launched and pursued with success. A day or two after the 1st Battalion took station at Maffrecourt for its period of recess from the trenches, the circular quoted in full as follows was received by me.

4th Army       Annex to Intelligence Report No. 1,399
Hq. Staff

CONFIDENTIAL

2nd Bureau            German Offensive of May 27th, 1918.

1. *ENGAGED UNITS*

The front of attack on May 27 runs from Vauxaílion to Reims, that is on about 45 kilometers.

Before the attack, this front is held by 9 Divisions (from East to West: 14th D.R.—241 D.—13th D.L.—197th D.—231st D.—103rd D.—242nd D.—86th D.).

Most of those divisions have no great fighting value; they do not seem to have taken part in the first attack. The 13 D.L. and the 197th D., particularly, have been crossed by the 5th D. and 113th D. which have executed a passing through the lines.

On May 27, the first day of the attack, 9 new divisions are identified (6th D.—5 D.—37th D.—113th D.—36th D.—10th D.—213th D. —7th D.R.—6th D.R.B.).

On May 28th, 7 new divisions identified: (2d D.C.—33d D.—10th D.R.—5th D.G.—28th D.—50th D.—52d D.).

On May 29th, 2 new divisions identified: (1st D.C.—86th D.).

On May 30th, 2 new divisions identified: (9th D. and 51st D.R.).

On May 30th at evening, 19 new divisions are therefore identified on the front of attack, all of them good or very good divisions and trained to open warfare, many of them having already taken part in the offensive of March 21.

If we add to that number the 9 divisions which were holding the front before the attack, we come to a total of 28 divisions known on May 30th, at evening, not including a certain number of divisions in support not yet located up to this date.

An aviation officer captured during the battle has ascertained that a total of 45 divisions was anticipated for the offensive on the front of the Aisen; we can therefore estimate from 40 to 50 the number of the divisions which have directly or indirectly participated in the offensive.

Referring to German . . . . . . . . . . . . .

Not very encouraging, to be sure; but splendid as an instrument of morale maintenance! The great Gouraud looked upon us as his comrades and partners. Every success of the enemy in other territory of the long line of defense, brought nearer to us the day of assault upon the sectors of the 4th Army.

And probably at least ninety-nine percent of the men of that 4th Army awaited the day with eagerness and in confident determination that the leader who made of his men comrades and partners, should suffer no disappointment by defeat.

Upon the evening of June 7th, the officers and platoon chiefs of my battalion had practised until dark the movements which we expected to make upon the following day, in the concluding manoeuvers of our week of training. General Chabaud, in driving through the town the previous afternoon, had noticed our schooling activities. He was so pleased that he had offered his services as instructor or adviser, for the evening of our final preparation. He had left us at the conclusion of a reconnaissance of the terrain of our operations, expecting to meet within a few hours. We never met again.

Shortly after midnight I was awakened with an order to move at 5 A.M. upon the morning of the 8th of June. Our rest period was to be cut short. The general attack which had been awaited so long was believed to be imminent.

The 1st Battalion was ordered to establish itself at the *Cantonment de La Charmaresse;* and, immediately thereafter, to make a reconnaissance of the *C. R. du Poirier de Malmont,* the new position assigned to us for defense under the general order of plan of battle attached to the brief note directing us to move.

At Charmaresse we had two days of hard work. That is the officers and platoon chiefs had hard work. We made practically continuous reconnaissance of our new fighting position, in order to become so well acquainted with the lay of the land as to enable us to man the sector in the dark.

At the end of two days, we again received orders to move— this time back to our normal schedule of duty, in trenches.

Upon June 10th, the 1st Battalion relieved the 2nd Battalion in the C. R. Melzicourt and commenced our third and last tour of duty in the Bois d'Hauzy.

The general attack for which we had prepared, and for which Gouraud's Army had waited so long, had not come. It was to come, however, upon a later day—the day upon which France celebrates the Fall of the Bastille. When that day came, The Lion of France struck—struck a blow which turned the tide of the World War, a blow which broke the spirit of the German war machine, and which, under the subsequent nightly and daily blows of Foch, turned a four year old army of successful aggression into an army of defense—less than three months later to beg for terms of surrender.

# XXXIII

# OUR LAST MONTH IN BOIS D'HAUZY

*June 10–June 30, 1918*

D R. BRADNER became ill, and had to be transferred to duty of less severe physical strain than that of the trenches. While waiting for the arrival of the new surgeon assigned to the 1st Battalion, a surgeon was "loaned" to us. There was nothing the matter with the young man, in so far as I know. I never got to know him very well. He gave the impression, however, of being of the class frequently spoken of as "spoiled son of a rich father." His clothes—all right in their way; but I doubt if anyone would ever have mistaken him for Lord Kitchener.

I was seated in my bomb proof abri. I believe several officers were with me, and that we awaited the announcement of dinner. The early evening shelling of the sector was in progress. Thumping and thudding sounds were heard, sounds as of a heavy man running and jumping. Down the six or eight steps of my abri came those sounds. Without ceremony, the door was burst open, and the young surgeon who had been loaned to us landed, in panting confusion, in the middle of the room.

"My God, Captain!" The falsetto voice came in the shrill tones of unusual excitement. "My God, Captain! This is no place for troops! This is positively dangerous!"

It was upon the first evening of our return to the C. R. Melzicourt. The young surgeon had never before been under shell fire. Everybody else had had lots of it. We were blasé about it. Occasionally, a shell breaking near to a group would arouse a sufficient degree of interest to cause discussion as to whether the shell was a 77 or 155. Occasionally, a wager would be offered as to the location of an arrival. But that was about all. The harassing fire of the enemy, which occurred twice a day with clock-like regularity, was a matter of routine to the enemy. It came so to be looked upon by ourselves.

When the young surgeon had finished with the speaking of his piece, everybody laughed.

And yet, in a way, and certainly in the concluding portion of his exclamatory protest, the young man was right.

The *Bois d'Hauzy* had become positively dangerous.

In a corner of the church yard of Maffrecourt was a little plot, set aside for the dead of *les soldats Americains, les soldats negre,* the members of the 369 U. S. Infantry who had lost their lives during those early days of March, April, May and June, of the association of our regiment with the French.

Throughout the regiment, that little burial plot was known by the name "Sergeant's Hill." Many, I believe most, of the soldiers buried there were sergeants. According to my recollection, for the first 14 weeks of our service at the front we averaged one death a week; and none of these deaths occurred as the result of ordinary illness. By pistol or rifle bullet, or by knife wound, all of these first fourteen to be laid away to the salute of Taps in Sergeant's Hill, met their death. By no means were all these the victims of hate. Some were killed under suspicious circumstances, it is true. But others were the victims of carelessness upon the part of companions, or of foolishness upon their own part.

It was not until the month of June, I believe, that the enemy commenced to figure as rivals to our own men in the homicidal records of the old Fifteenth New York. It was not until the month of July had come that Germany forged ahead in the contest.

All through the month of June the shelling of both of our sectors became dirtier and dirtier, the use of gas more and more frequent; and even the dreaded Hyporite made its appearance.

Throughout the month of June the spirit of battle was in the air. Our drill and manoeuvers at Maffrecourt had all been along the line of preparation for the offensive to be launched at as early a date as practicable, dependent undoubtedly to a considerable extent, upon how soon America might be able to supply troops in sufficient force to admit of a steady advance upon Berlin.

Everyone was determined. No one overconfident. Not many, even unqualifiedly confident. Just determined to the stage of doggedness!

Reference has been made to a long-expected major attack on the frontage of the 4th Army, and to the overwhelming defeat, of that attack due to the genius of General Gouraud, when it did come on Bastille Day.

In brief, Gouraud's plan of defense was as follows:

Upon the launching of the general attack a secret code word was to be flashed from the 4th Army Headquarters through the channels, of army corps, divisions, brigades, regiments, battalions, and companies—right down to platoons. Upon receipt, through the proper channels of that combination of secret code words, the operations of preparation were to commence.

The first step of that preparation was the evacuation of all of the troops of defense from the sectors of the first lines!

Each battalion, however, in evacuating its quarter sector, was to leave a so-called "Holding Platoon" for the purpose of deceiving the enemy, and keeping from the assaulting troops the knowledge that their attack was to be made upon trenches practically empty.

The duty of this holding platoon, or "Camouflage Squad," as it came to be called, was to give semblance of a normal occupation and defense of each sector. To this end the members of the squad, no more than 30 men and 1 officer in all, stretched out so as to cover the entire front of our position (between a mile and a half and two miles of length), were to send up signal rockets and operate automatic rifles and other arms very freely, moving rapidly from post to post, so as to coax the enemy to make the final assault upon our trenches in as heavy strength as possible. At the last minute, just before the enemy should enter our lines the men of the camouflage squad were to run back to the line of resistance. There, the movement of a semblance of defense was to be repeated. After being driven out of that position the members of the camouflage squad were to make their way as best they could to a given point of rendezvous, after which the platoon or what might be left of it would rejoin the battalion, and the men would resume their normal duties.

In the meantime, the evacuating battalions would move into fortified positions some two miles to the rear of the trenches of the line of observation, and prepare to receive the attack of the enemy.

As soon as it became known by the signal rockets of the camouflage squads, and by the air scouts, that the enemy in force had entered our front line sectors, our artillery was to lock them in by box barrage, and other batteries of artillery were to play, with shrapnel, upon our own abandoned trenches from the rear.

Under the plan, the enemy troops would thus find themselves in a trap. If not wholly destroyed, they would be almost sure to be so terrifically smashed as to render them practically certain of defeat if they should succeed ever in reaching our intermediate positions manned by troops practically fresh and ready for combat.

It was a plan of strategy that appealed splendidly to the personnel of the units concerned. It smacked so much of the offensive in defense, and promised so well of success.

The evacuation of a sector rapidly and in secret, and in perfect order, to be followed immediately by the occupation of a new position for defense, and the practical certainty of the necessity of these movements being executed in the darkness of night, were operations calling for careful planning.

LIEUTENANT EUROPE CONDUCTING BAND HOSPITAL NUMBER 9,
PARIS, SEPTEMBER 4, 1918. OUR BAND WAS ORDERED TO PARIS
FOR A WEEK OF CONCERT DUTY

A DOUBLE INTEREST IS ENLISTED IN THE SIX NUMBERED PHOTOGRAPHS, OF WHICH THIS IS NUMBER ONE, ON ACCOUNT OF GEN. GOURAUD HAVING WRITTEN THE CAPTIONS AND SIGNED EACH PRINT. SEE APPENDIX, PAGE 371

( I )

"PHOTOGRAPHS I AND 2 SHOW YOUR SOLDIERS EQUIPPING THEMSELVES BEFORE LEAVING THE TRENCH WHERE THEY HAVE PASSED THE NIGHT."

(2)

"IN PHOTOGRAPH 3 THEY ARE GOING TO ASSEMBLING POINT TO JOIN THE ATTACKING TROOPS THAT HAVE BEEN ENGAGED IN THE BATTLE SINCE 5.25 O'CLOCK."

(3)

"AWAITING THE MARCH HOUR. THE COMMANDANT OF THE BATTALION . . .
(YOURSELF) (THE AUTHOR, SEATED AND READING) HAS JUST RECEIVED
HIS ORDERS FOR THE ATTACK."

(4)

IN NUMBER 5 "THE COMMANDANT . . . (YOURSELF) (THE AUTHOR, SEATED AND NOW WRITING) IS DRAWING HIS ORDERS FOR THE ATTACK."

(5)

"PHOTOGRAPH 6 SHOWS A GROUP OF SOLDIERS AT REST, AWAITING THE HOUR OF DEPARTURE."

(6)

21879

THE BAND ENTERTAINS HOSPITAL NUMBER 9, PARIS, SEPTEMBER 4, 1918

# XXXIV

# WAITING FOR THE GERMAN "VICTORY DRIVE"

*July 1–July 14, 1918*

UPON June 30th, the 1st Battalion proceeded to Cantonment de la Charmeresse, for rest, leaving the 3rd Battalion in the trenches of the C. R. Melzicourt and the 2nd Battalion in C. R. Montplaisir.

July 1, orders were received providing for the relief upon July 3rd of the 369th U. S. Infantry, from the S/Secteur Afrique, by a French regiment of cuirasseurs. The 1st Battalion was to give up its quarters in the woods of Charmeresse to the cuirasseur battalion *en repos* at 5 o'clock upon the morning of the 3rd—and establish itself with the rest of the regiment at Maffrecourt, there to await orders of disposition for the expected battle.

The 1st Battalion was nicely settled at Maffrecourt upon the 3rd of July, before the other battalions arrived from the trenches, during the afternoon.

Three months had elapsed since the three battalions had last been quartered together. The evening was spent in the pleasant reunion of old friends.

The regimental commander, after the relief from the trenches of his men, upon July 3rd, in accordance with the established custom which has been explained in foregoing chapters, had to remain over for a full day, until the new commander should get his hand in.

Word had come down from Division Headquarters that many signs pointed to a probability of the German attack being launched upon the night of the American Independence Day, upon the theory, presumably, that the day would be given up to debauchery, and that the night would find the armies of the Allies unfit to fight.

Poor Germany!

To German statesmen, America appeared to have grown fat and afraid, instead of strong, and forbearing.

So, I believe there is no doubt that the Germans, persisting in their misunderstanding of the spirit of America, did plan their "Victory Drive" for the evening of the 4th of July. Something happened to prevent. We do not know what.

The attack was put off for ten days, to the national independence day of France, in order, once more, to gain the advantage of attack over an army drunk in revelry.

The debauchery of the 369th U. S. Infantry at Maffrecourt, upon that 4th of July, 1918, the reckless revelry of our colored volunteers from Harlem, consisted of the following program:

In the morning, inter-company tournament of baseball, for the respective championship of each battalion.

In the afternoon, inter-battalion tournament of baseball, for the championship of the regiment.

In the evening, a vaudeville entertainment in the Y. M. C. A. hut preceded by an open air concert by the band of the 85th Infantry of the Republic of France, sent to us in compliment, and in thoughtful recognition of the fact that our own band of Jim Europe's famous players had gone to Chalons. As a part of the entertainment in the hut, and by way of patriotic exercises, each man in the regiment was handed a souvenir in the form of a booklet, printed by the Y. M. C. A. in colors and with appropriate illustrations.*

Our command went to fighting posts that night of the 4th of July, healthy in body, healthy in mind.

If the Boche had come, they would have found stout hearts under the black skins of the soldiers who waited in our trenches,

* See Appendix C.

hearts which had been touched by that prayer of the brave comrades who slept in Flanders Fields:

> Take up our quarrel with the foe.
> To you from falling hands we throw
> The torch. Be yours to bear it high.
> If ye break faith with us who die,
> We shall not sleep, though poppies blow
> In Flanders fields.

During the afternoon, as temporary commanding officer at Maffrecourt, I received word that at 6 o'clock, General Le Gallais would pay a call upon the officers of the regiment, as his mark of respect to our day.

General Le Gallais made us a little speech.

The General spoke of the significance of our Independence Day, and drew our attention to the fact that ten days from our day the French Independence Day would be celebrated.

He spoke with fine feeling of the bonds which united our two nations. He expressed his pride of command of the first American regiment ever to serve with a French Division.

Then he told us of the impending battle. He explained our plan of defense. He pointed out to us the strength of our preparation; and expressed confidence of the success, not only of our 16th Division, but of our 8th Army Corps, and of our 4th Army.

He warned us of the things which we must be prepared to meet in battle.

He advised us of the constant state of preparedness in which we must hold ourselves—ready to launch counter attack after the enemy attack should have failed.

He informed us that he had brought us back from the first line in which we had been for three months, and put us in the second line in which we had just been placed, because by so doing he could hold us at his personal disposition; and it was his desire to give us the honor of making the counter attack, and winning distinction.

He advised us that the attack was to be expected between the 4th of July, that very night, and the 14th, our two National Holidays.

He directed that we were to man our fighting positions every night, beginning that night, until the battle should be joined.

In conclusion, General Le Gallais laughingly indulged in what he characterized as a bit of American slang spoken in French. He said, if the Germans hit us they would get what was coming to them.

We felt quite excited and elated.

By 10:30 P.M. we were in our positions.

At about 3 o'clock of the morning of the 5th of July, we withdrew from our fortified positions and returned to billets. Each night for the succeeding ten days we went through a similar routine of duty.

The fighting positions were as follows:

1st Battalion upon the slope of a hill to the North of Courtemont, and covering the main turnpike leading from Hans, through Courtemont to Vienne-la-Ville and the front lines. It was a part of the mission of the 1st Battalion to defend the area in which was located Regimental Headquarters.

The 2nd Battalion occupied a hill to the right and rear of the 1st Battalion about half way between Maffrecourt and Courtemont.

The 3rd Battalion was at Bersieux, to the right of the 1st Battalion.

These defense positions were, of course, secret positions, or supposed to be. As a matter of fact it is not improbable that the enemy had a fairly complete set of photographs of our trenches in those positions as well as in most others.

We masked our operations as much as possible, however. The march, each evening, from billeting towns to stand-to positions was never commenced until darkness had come. Our stand-to positions were always evacuated almost an hour before broad daylight. By daylight our battalions were in the billeting towns, the horses unharnessed, and caissons and voiturettes hidden, and the men in barracks.

Our men were held in barracks all through the hours of daylight. Messing was accomplished by small groups—no more men at a time than could be accommodated under the sheds of the rolling kitchens.

There was, of course, work to be done all the time upon the trenches of our fighting positions. We assigned small parties in numerous reliefs to this work. Such parties could not be observed from afar. Upon the approach of airplanes, the men took cover.

The officers, in addition to participating with the men in all regular duties, had to make reconnaissances of neighboring positions, preparatory to the possibility of being thrown into new sectors during the progress of the battle.

We were all supposed to be left free to sleep each morning between the hours of about five, when breakfast would be finished, and noon.

A moderate epidemic of influenza broke out in the regiment, and not only thinned our ranks, but deprived us each day of the services of officers.

Upon July 7th, General Gouraud addressed his army in the order which I quote as follows:

Hq., July 7th, 1918.

4th Army
Staff— 3ᵈ B.
No. 6641/3

*ORDER*
TO THE FRENCH AND AMERICAN SOLDIERS OF
THE 4th ARMY

We may be attacked now at any moment.

You all feel that never a defensive battle was engaged under more favorable conditions.

We are informed and we are on the watch.

We are powerfully reinforced in Infantry and in Artillery.

219

We fight on a ground you have transformed by your persistent work into a formidable fortress—invincible fortress if all the passages are well guarded.

The bombardment will be terrible; you will stand it without losing courage.

The assault will be fierce, in a cloud of dust, of smoke and of gas.

But your position and your armament are formidable.

In your breasts beat brave and strong hearts of free men.

Nobody will look back, nobody will fall back one step.

Everybody will have only one thought—Kill, Kill many until they have enough of it.

And it is why your General tells you: That assault, you will break it and it will be a beautiful day.

GOURAUD,

General Commanding the 4th Army.

Gouraud was the idol of his men. That appeal, read to all units, had a splendid effect upon the morale of the 4th Army; but, as day after day wore on, and alarm after alarm proved to be false, everybody grew to be not only tired physically, with the strain of almost continuous duty, but bored and worn out mentally.

Each day, as we would go out in small groups to our fighting sectors, to work and to strengthen the defenses, we would notice new batteries of artillery, placed during the preceding night, and concealed from observation from above by clever camouflage.

As our officer groups would make the reconnaissances already referred to, we would almost stumble over hidden machine gun nests.

The words of Gouraud kept coming to us:

"We fight on a ground you have transformed into a formidable fortress—invincible fortress, if all the passages are well guarded."

*Our passages should be well guarded.*

Everybody was confident of victory. Everybody was eager

for the battle. The only cry of protest in the 4th Army was of the delay.

Upon the night of the 13th as we made the tenth consecutive stand-to in our trenches, we received a letter of advice as to the probability of attack which appeared to be more definite than any of the previous advices.

That advice was in the form of a secret communication. It told how German prisoners revealed the extensive changes in German troop locations. It assured us that the attack was set for midnight of that same date. It adjured us to do our duty and show our French comrades how Americans fight.

We had had so many warnings that this one found a rank and file that, instead of being from Harlem, might readily have hailed from Missouri.

# GOURAUD'S TRIUMPH

*July 14–July 16, 1918*

BASTILLE DAY, the Independence Day of the Republic of France! The Republic of France presents its compliments to her soldiers in the field, and begs the pleasure and the honor of a glass of wine with them! Such, in effect, was the message received by us as we met for luncheon at midday. The sentiment was reinforced by practical means.

For every four soldiers of the ranks, a bottle of champagne was presented. Each two officers of the line shared a bottle. Field officers were invited to help themselves.

International toasts were drunk. But that was about all. Once more, Germany had guessed wrong. There was no debauchery. There was no suspension of the activities of preparation for a winning battle. Gouraud had taken into partnership the personnel of his army of a quarter of a million men. He had explained his plan of defense—his expectations—his hopes. The final toast was "To our great General—God bless him!" He should not be disappointed.

At 11:15 P.M. Liaison Sergeant Reese aroused me from my bed upon the ground with stars for a canopy, and handed me a note from headquarters.

I read:
"Capt. Little—

Corps and Division advise attack expected at *midnight tonight.*
If it breaks, good luck to your battalion and to you.

Hold 'em!

W. A. P.

The note was handed over to Landon to read. We smiled and wondered—for a few minutes—then, once more, we pulled up to our shoulders the blanket which was serving us jointly, and—dropped off into sleep.

At five minutes before twelve a French gun was fired. That signal gun was followed instantly by hundreds of other guns. At midnight, exactly, the German guns opened. For the next six or seven hours we had to shout to make ourselves heard.

To the plan of defense which had been explained to us—the plan of evacuating the first line sectors, coaxing the enemy in, hammering them there with artillery, and making the first stand of infantry in the trenches of the intermediate positions—to that well understood plan Gouraud had added one more trick of strategy, apparently at the last minute.

When he became assured, through the medium of his splendid intelligence department, that the attack upon us was to be launched at midnight, General Gouraud just beat the enemy to it! He knew that their troops would be massed at the "jumping-off points," with definite orders to move at the zero hour. He knew that within five minutes the enemy orders could not be changed; but, by those five minutes of prior artillery pounding, he forced the assaulting troops to debouch from jumping off shelters too hot to hold them. The troops of the offensive had become, also, troops upon the defensive, and at the very beginning of the action.

The battle of Champagne-Marne, officially dated July 15-16, 1918, but which actually commenced during the final five minutes of Bastille Day, was fought upon a front of about 80 kilometers (50 miles). The area covered was practically all which was lying between Verdun on the East and Rheims on the West.

Thanks to the clever planning of General Gouraud, casualties upon the part of the French Army (of which the 369th U. S. Inf. was a part) were very light. There was nothing for infantrymen to do, during the artillery duel, but lie down in the trenches, and keep under cover. Under such circumstances, direct hits right in the trenches would be the only ones to do execution.

After the bombardment had been under way for half an hour or more, I became convinced that this must be the big attack, sure enough, for which we had waited. I sent runners to Maffre-court with written orders to Battalion Stable-Sergeant Kelly, and the company mess sergeants, to bring up rolling kitchens and conceal them in positions chosen in advance, and to be ready to serve breakfast at daybreak. I felt confident that we would not get back to our billeting town in time for the morning meal. *We never did get back at all.*

At about 4:30 A.M. I received a note by runner from the Lieutenant Colonel, commanding, advising me to try to get the kitchens brought right up as soon as possible, in preparation for an active day, and to serve the men immediately with coffee.

As I reached the end of the note, I looked up to receive the report of another orderly, who had stepped up while I had been reading. This orderly offered no salute; his hands were filled; in one he bore my cup, filled with coffee; in the other, my mess dish filled with stew. Behind him stood Sergeant-Major Hooper, at salute. "Sir," reported the Sergeant-Major, "All the companies are now being served with breakfast—in the trenches!"

Some service!

At 6 o'clock, upon the morning of July 15th, we received warning to prepare to move promptly upon orders of execution, and to be ready to form for counter attack.

Rumor had it that our army was winning. That was all we knew, except that, in our own sector, the line in front of us was holding.

At about 8 o'clock the orders came for us to move.

We moved by battalion to a point westward, some three miles or more away. We made rendezvous there as a regiment at the Camp Bravard.

Artillery fire was still heavy; but at Camp Bravard, there was a long shelf or table land close up under a steep hill which offered protection from the enemy. The men were disposed of along this shelf. At about 1 o'clock a hot meal was served. After that, the men stretched out under the warm afternoon sun and slept.

Most of the officers were called for conference or for reconnaissance to plan counter attack, and to be ready to move into a new position.

At about 2:30 in the afternoon Captain André de Fouquiers, Aide to the 8th Army Corps Commander General Helie d'Oiselle, came with news and with orders.

The news was a victory. All along our line of 80 kilometers the 4th Army of France had held. Upon more than three-fourths of that front the enemy had never gotten past the slaughter pits of our evacuated first line trenches. Over the balance of the front, the Boche had been successful in extricating themselves from the trap; and they had broken through the first line of infantry, only to be stopped short at the second line. The result was a number of deep toothlike salients biting into our lines, very dangerous to the Germans on account of our possibilities of flanking fire. The plan was to commence at once, by counter attack, to dislodge the enemy from the salients which they had gained—to drive them back that very night and the next day, before they should be able to find time to protect themselves by reversing the fronts of the French trenches which they were occupying.

The 369th R.I.U.S., in order to participate in this program of counter attack, was transferred from General Le Gallais's 16th Division to the 161st Division of General Lebouc. The 161st Division occupied the territory to the west of our former sectors. In front of Minaucourt, to the immediate west of the famous *Main de Massige*, and opposite the *Butte de Mesnil*, fighting grounds upon which two hundred thousand German and French soldiers had been killed during the first two years of the war, lay the *Sous Secteur Beausejour*. This sector had been

225

occupied by the Germans, forming one of those salients to which reference has been made. It was from this sector, Beausejour, that the 161st Division was going to drive the Germans. To assist in the enterprise, the Divisional strength had been augmented by the American regiment of Infantry, the 369th.

As Fouquiers gave us his splendid news, we were thrilled. There was, however, one anxiety which seemed to be shared by all of the French officer's audience, one point upon which we *all* wanted assurance to complete our happiness. We wanted to know how soon the great news could be known at home.

Shortly before evening, we moved—again to the west and the northwest. Always, it seemed to us, we were moving to the west. Jokes were beginning to be exchanged about bumping into Paris for breakfast.

Our new positions were uncomfortable and dangerous. The regimental headquarters was at P. C. Charlemagne, some three or four kilometers to the east of Laval. The battalions stretched out over a broad front to the north of this base, each in a quarter sector of its own, and all in the front line trenches of the new holding position. The French troops which had preceded us in these sectors of defense had now become troops of assault. They were driving the Germans back—out of the *Sous Secteur Beausejour*.

The 1st Battalion held our regimental left of line, the 3rd Battalion the right, the 2nd Battalion was in the center.

To our left, was a French regiment of "Blue Devils," *Chasseur Alpins*. To our right were the Moroccans. At least we were traveling in fast company. The comparative peace and quiet of the Bois d'Hauzy had passed into history.

With the coming of night the intensity of the shell fire had increased. The shelling had not actually ceased since that never-to-be-forgotten zero hour of five minutes before twelve of the night of the 14th of July; but, during the day there had been long stretches of comparative calm.

All through the night of July 15th–16th hell was at work. Casualties became more frequent. Our trenches were shallow. Now, not only did direct hits do execution, but the shrapnel from air bursts found frequent victims.

Our colored soldiers were tired, and, in a sense, hungry. They were being killed and wounded by an unseen enemy. They knew that their only immediate moves were to be forward, and that their only relief from the danger of the moment was to be by the greater danger of assault upon seen enemies.

There was no wavering. Not even one complaint did I hear, through all those days of exhaustion.

"God Damn, Le's Go!" was the slogan. Our boys from Harlem were straining to fight.

That night, about 60 of our horses and mules were killed. That meant difficulties in transportation of supplies in the immediate future—and real hunger to come.

It is a source of regret to me that I cannot write in detail of the activities of the personnel of the regiment other than that of the 1st Battalion. In writing so freely, however, and in so personal a way as that which I have adopted as the standard for my story, I have not felt at liberty to record matters with which I am familiar only by hearsay.

During the day of July 16th, rumors kept coming constantly, as is usually the way with soldier bodies. The rumors were all of victory, substantial victory, victory so extravagant in its proportions as to be unbelievable.

Late in the afternoon came something better than rumor. A letter from General Gouraud!

He had addressed us before the battle, telling us what he wanted.

Now, after the defensive stage of the battle, he addressed us again. This time to tell us the results.

Following is a quotation in full of Gouraud's address of praise and thanksgiving:

227

July 16th, 1918.

4th Army
Staff—5th B
No. 6954/3

During the day of July 15th, you have broken the effort of fifteen German Divisions supported by 10 others.

They were from their orders to reach the Marne in the evening; you have stopped them where we wanted to give and win the battle.

You have the right to be proud, heroic infantry men and machine gunners of the advanced posts who have signalled the attack and who have subdivided it, aviators who flew over it, battalions and batteries who have broken it, staffs who have so minutely prepared that battlefield.

It is a hard blow to the enemy. It is a beautiful day for France.

I rely upon you that it will always be the same each time they will dare to attack you and with all my heart of soldier I thank you.

GOURAUD.

The turning of the tide had come. After four years, all but three weeks, of successful aggression, the German had been stopped in his tracks. From that day on he was to be upon the defensive. Within less than three months he was to plead for mercy.

The "Lion of France" had struck a blow for the civilization of the world.

In his hour of triumph, "with all his heart of soldier," modestly he shared his honors with the officers and men of his command—who loved him.

# XXXVI

# THE BEGINNINGS OF
# THE WINNING OF THE WAR

### *July 17–August 1, 1918*

DURING the forenoon of July 17th, I received the following order:

*Major* Little:

You are directed to send one platoon commanded by an officer from your reserve company without delay to P.C. Charlemagne.

They will be met here by a guide who will conduct them to the P.C. of the 3rd Battalion which battalion they will reinforce.

The platoon will have to travel by day-light—using all available cover and proceeding by small fractions. If shelled en route officer commanding must use his discretion in taking cover until shelling ceases—but this platoon *must* reach 3rd Battalion *without delay*.

By order of LT. COL. PICKERING,
R. WHITTLESEY,
1st Lieut. 369th Inf.
Acting Adjutant.

You are now
*Major Little*

And so the news of my promotion first reached me.

Upon July 17th the three battalions of the regiment were widely separated—upon the third day of the big battle.

Regimental Headquarters was in a fourth separated position. And upon the day which marked the turning point of the Defensive Battle of the Champagne-Aisne into the Offensive Battle of the Aisne-Meuse, in the field and functioning as a part of that history-making activity I was notified of my promotion, in connection with an order to help out a sister battalion which was in some slight difficulty.

During the night of July 17-18th orders came for the 1st Battalion to prepare to move during the following night into a first line quarter-sector, the C. R. Balcon-Reverchon; and to make reconnaissance of the new position during the day, July 18th.

We started shortly after daybreak. Our party of reconnaissance consisted of one officer per company, one non-com. per platoon, the battalion interpreter, and the battalion commander.

We travelled by map, through a country entirely new to us, cross country a part of the way, and finally along the highway running through the towns Laval, Wagemoulin and Minaucourt. Care had to be exercised to avoid observation from sentry captive-balloons of the enemy, and from airplane scouts. Also, to avoid casualties from the shelling which, though light, was constant all over the terrain of our reconnaissance—particularly harassing along the way of the turnpike.

At P. C. Wilson, about a mile to the west of a point upon the highway half way between Wagemoulin and Minaucourt we found our guides from the 47th Battalion of Chasseurs, whom we were to relieve that night.

While the company commanders and platoon chiefs were being conducted by their guides through trenches, the chief of the Divisional Infantry of the 161st Division, Colonel Hatton (acting as Brigadier General) explained to me, through my interpreter, the situation into which we were about to be introduced.

The Centers of Resistance, Beausejour and Crochet, opposite the Germans' stronghold, Butte du Mesnil, were quarter-sectors which the Germans had entered under the evacuation ruse of General Gouraud, on July 15th. But, during July 16 and 17, instead of scuttling out and back to their own lines, as had been done in almost all of the territory of the battle, the Boche had attempted to settle down in these positions for permanent occupation.

General Lebouc, with his 161st Division, found himself put to the duty of retaking and occupying these sectors, and the attack was being made by the 163rd, 215th and 363rd regiments of infantry, backed, of course, by all the artillery of the division. A number of battalions of chasseurs were in support, and the support was now augmented by our American regiment, the 369th Infantry.

Colonel Hatton explained to me that the action of assault was, even as we conversed, in progress. He also advised me that my battalion was to be under his direct command, and that the two other battalions of our regiment would be disposed of as follows:

One battalion in support of the 163rd regiment in first line sector. The 3rd battalion was given this assignment.

One battalion under the orders of our own regimental commander, in the 2nd line position on the left of the Tourbe River, in the C. R. de l'Arbre R. The 2nd Battalion had this assignment.

As soon as darkness came, upon the evening of July 18th, we commenced our movement. The first three or four miles of the march of the 1st Battalion had to be made over a fine stone road along a ridge of the range of hills. Our orders for the march were specific, as to hour of departure, distances between units, and route. We obeyed our orders, of course; but, in obeying them, at least 1500 men suffered unnecessary danger of casualty and subsequent privation. As our units emerged from their shelters, to take up the march along the road, they ran into the units of one of the other battalions, travelling for several miles along the same route. Somebody had blundered in the matter of the timing of the progress of the units. The other battalion, from a starting point to our east, had been given a zero hour which, instead of providing for the clearing of our sector before the coming of the 1st Battalion zero hour, had managed to create a traffic jam alarming and perilous in its potentialities.

The road over which we had to pass was, as stated, along a ridge of a range of hills. Every figure moving along that road was, in daylight, a marked figure—marked by the sharp relief

of a silhouette against a skyline. During hours of daylight all
traffic along the road was forbidden. At night, supply trucks were
rushed over the road in endless procession. The road was under
constant daylight surveillance of enemy captive-balloon sentries,
and it was well registered by the Boche artillery. During former
nights, it had been well pounded by artillery, cut loose when the
roar of the great camion trains would give to the enemy a notice
of traffic on the road. On the night of July 18th-19th there was
little or no artillery fire directed against that road. If it had not
been for this fortunate circumstance, the losses of the 15th New
York would, I fear, have been hideous.

I must assume that the great majority of the men in that
traffic jam were to a large extent ignorant of the hideous danger
threatening them; but I was not ignorant of it, and I was not sure
that the men were ignorant of it.

My heart and mind functioned with trip-hammer fury, waiting momentarily for panic to break loose. I thought of every
manoeuver and military device that I had ever read about to put
into play to save the horrible carnage that was due and overdue.

After reviewing my store of military professional knowledge,
I commenced to go over the memories of historic crises. No results! Then, suddenly, came an inspiration of boyhood recollection—an inspiration prompted by despair.

I remembered how, at my mother's knee, I had been
taught that, when all else might fail, God had never failed when
appealed to in honesty and contrite spirit.

I stopped cursing for a few seconds. I stopped flaying about
with my cane. I prayed to God to help us in our emergency.
Within a matter of five or six seconds my prayer was answered.

Away off to the north three brilliant signal lights flashed
high in the air, and within a few seconds after those lights we
heard the whirr of aeroplanes faintly in the distance, coming
from the south.

A few minutes after that a German squadron of bombing
planes came within clear range, first of our hearing and later

232

of our vision, and flew on toward the German lines. An air raid
had been pulled down in the Chalons region and the hour for
the return had called for the signal direction lights marking the
path of return directly over that road along which we were pushing and stumbling our way. Of course, until that squadron was
safely behind the enemy lines, no artillery fire would be directed
down the path of their flight.

Some of our people were of the opinion that it was the hand
of God that saved our regiment that night. Some others seemed
to feel that it was merely coincidence that the Germans did not
shell the road on account of the squadron of airplanes over our
line. I believe that we owed our safety to the guiding hand of
God.

The 1st Battalion arrived at its destination between the hours
of two and three o'clock, upon the morning of the 19th. Just as
we reached the P. C. Wilson, the Boche laid down a lively shelling upon our sector.

Thanks to the energy and skill of officers and noncoms, we
suffered no casualties of death and but slight woundings. The men
were rushed into cover, and released in very small groups to
go forward to their posts under French guides. Our sixteen
machine gun voiturettes, laden with ammunition, and four ammunition caissons, were distributed with wide intervals through
a grove in front of the P. C., the horses and mules unhitched
and tied singly to trees, also with wide intervals between them.
Not an animal was destroyed. Not an ammunition cart was struck.

During the evening of July 20th I sent Company "B" under
Captain Fillmore, to reinforce a French battalion in the first line
trenches of the right center of resistance of our *sous secteur*. At
the same time I had to send Company "C" under Captain Mac-
Clinton to reinforce the French company holding the left strong
point of the left center of resistance—the *P. A. Christoferie* of
the *C. R. Crochet*.

Company "C" ran into some pretty rough weather. In order
to reach the post of its assignment, an open area of several hun-

dred yards had to be crossed. I made a daylight reconnaissance of the position with Captain MacClinton before the troops were moved in. We were accompanied by platoon chiefs, and we progressed with great caution. Outside of a steady shelling of the position, there was no effort made to get us. When it came time, however, for the company to get into Christoferie, MacClinton and his men were given a warm reception. They were under a concentration of fire all that night and all the following day. They suffered a number of casualties. Thanks to the cool-headed leadership of the company officers and non-coms, the casualty list was held down to moderate proportions. A group led by Lieutenant Webb had a miraculous escape from annihilation. A shell of heavy caliber made a direct hit in the boyau through which Webb and his men were marching. There was a sharp turn, or angle, in the trench between the men and the place where the shell exploded. That angle was all that saved the group, or at least the men marching near its head. As it was, several of the men, including Mr. Webb, were thrown violently to the ground from concussion.

During the night of July 20th-21st we suffered the first officer casualty of the regiment. It was a 1st Battalion officer who gained the distinction—1st Lieutenant Oscar H. Baker, of the Machine Gun Company. Baker was in command of two sections of guns covering the Company "C" position at Christoferie, and, with a number of his men, he was wounded by shrapnel.

The problem as to whether or not colored troops would do for combat units, was being solved by the volunteers of Harlem and Brooklyn—the colored national guardsmen of the 15th New York Infantry.

During July 20th and July 21st a considerable number of German prisoners passed through our positions on the way to the rear. Our men, always generous to a point of recklessness, divided with these prisoners of war, their scanty stocks of hardtack and chocolate and cigarettes. From the Boche prisoners we got our first direct confirmation of the rumors which had been coming, to the effect that the morale of the enemy army was cracking.

On July 19th the day of the arrival at P. C. Wilson of the 1st Battalion, I had reported our movement to regimental headquarters, by letter which I quote in full as follows:

HEADQUARTERS 1ST BATTALION

369TH U. S. INFANTRY, N. G.

July 19, 1918.

From: Commanding Officer 1st Battalion
To: Commanding Officer 369th U. S. Infantry
Subject: Report

1. The 1st Battalion has been placed during the night of July 18-19th. The kitchens were lost, but are finally located and will arrive after dusk and prepare the evening meal. With the permission of the Colonel Commanding the I.D. we have issued reserve rations consisting of canned corned beef, hard bread and chocolate for the noon day meal. Liaison with our flanking elements has either been established or is in process. This applies also to the 3rd Battalion.

ARTHUR W. LITTLE
Major, 369th U. S. Inf.

On July 21st by orders of the French colonel commanding the *Sous Secteur de Beausejour*, received at about two o'clock of the afternoon, the 1st Battalion or *"Le Bataillon Little"* as the French orders expressed it, was ordered into the C. R. Fortin, the east flank position of the reorganized new first line position of the *Sous-Secteur Beausejour*.

It was a custom of the French Army, in the publication of orders, to refer to organizations, particularly battalions, by the name of the respective commanding officers. In the order being referred to, the 5th Battalion of the 215th Infantry of France was mentioned as *Bataillon Salerou*, the 2nd Battalion of the 363rd Infantry of France was mentioned as *Bataillon Moretteau*, and the 1st Battalion of the 369th U. S. Infantry was mentioned as *Bataillon Little*.

235

The C. R. Fortin was to be occupied during the night of July 21st-22nd. Company "C" could not be spared at once from Christoferie, so the battalion was to hold Fortin with Companies "B" and "D" in the line, and, for the time being, without a reserve company. Of the Machine Gun Company, two sections remained with MacClinton at Christoferie. The main portion of the company under Captain Shether was to accompany me.

Reconnaisance of the new position had to be made during daylight. There was scant time for the accomplishment of all that had to be done.

At about four o'clock of the afternoon, Captain Favre of the 163rd French Infantry (my new attaché), Captain Shether and I set out to visit our new sector and to plan for the disposition of our troops. The position had been retaken from the Boche but a few hours before. In order to save time, we journeyed 'cross country, and eliminated several miles of travel by the road route. The route chosen was an open one, however, and under fairly constant observation by the captive-balloon sentries of the enemy. To meet this condition and to avoid as much observation as possible, we dispensed with orderlies and liaison detachments. If it should become necessary to send back a communication, we could borrow a messenger from the French command which had made the assault upon the position and which we were to relieve that night from occupation.

Orders for the troop movement had all been issued before we started upon our reconnaissance. We planned to remain at Fortin and meet the troops upon their arrival, Captain Fillmore with "B" Company had but a short distance to go, to the rendezvous of C. R. Fortin upon the Marson Road, from the post which he had occupied the previous night as a support company. Adjutant Landon, I designated as detachment commander to lead forward the main body of the Machine Gun Company and Company "D." Mr. Landon was the only officer with this detachment. The company officers and platoon chiefs preceded their companies by several hours for purposes of reconnaissance.

As Captains Favre and Shether and I crossed the range of bare hills between P. C. Wilson and C. R. Fortin, we were spotted by the enemy. The range was too great to admit of profitable rifle sniping; but the Boche made us dance with their 77s. They had had a number of days in the positions through which we were travelling, and their range cards appeared to be perfect. As we would pass one point of exposure, they would, apparently, time us to the next point. Then, as we would be due to arrive at a third point, they would drop a shell to welcome us.

Of course, with merely three officers in the party, and no troops to be handled, it was an easy matter to beat such a game as soon as we discovered what the game was. We merely varied our pace, when surely under cover. Sometimes, while out of sight, we would run and sometimes we would even sit down and smoke a cigarette. In the open places, we always walked with deliberate pace, easy for the watchers to count. The Boche wasted a lot of ammunition that afternoon; and, except for the first few shots, they never came near us.

At about six o'clock in the evening, while Shether and I were in the heart of the sector which we were to occupy, the enemy commenced to drench the communicating trenches with gas. When the gassing commenced, we were upon high, dry ground, and no great inconvenience was suffered. The gas could not have been one of the poisonous varieties. It had no effect upon me except to make my eyes water and to make me choke a bit, and vomit.

We worked our way down to the Marson Road and the point of rendezvous, with masks over our faces and darkness settling down over the masks.

The Marson Road was bounded on the south by a swamp; and from that swamp, the gas was rising in visible clouds. The road itself was built close in under a fairly high hill. In fact, in many places, it was cut out of the hill. Circulation along the road, therefore, was quite safe. To drop a shell down over that hill, close enough to the road to bring the men upon the road within the field of dispersion, was almost impossible. And, so

237

long as our masks functioned properly, the gas rolling up from the swamp, and being constantly replenished, could do us no injury.

We stepped into the *Poste de Secours* to seek a little treatment from the medical officers for our burning throats, and there we found all of the "D" Company officers and a number of the non-commissioned platoon chiefs in varying but fairly bad stages of knock-out from gas.

Presently, the detachments commenced to arrive. They came, of course, in very small squads with great distance between. We had, miraculously, escaped casualties during the advance along the Minaucourt Road, and in crossing the *Pont de Minaucourt* over the swamp to reach the Marson Road. There had been a fairly lively bombardment. The Boche, undoubtedly, had discovered that a relief was in progress. As quickly as the men could stretch out on the Marson Road they were safe; but the men didn't know that, and it was extremely difficult, under the circumstances of confusion and darkness and mask wearing, to make the men understand.

Our greatest danger that night lay in the possibilities of panic. Many of the men were having their first experience with a real gas attack. Most of the men were having their first experience with a shelling which they had to go through instead of taking it from a dugout. A considerable percentage of officers and men suffered from loss of morale. In their ignorance of the various kinds of gases, they assumed that the gas from which they were choking and crying was of one of the fatal varieties. A number of the men yielded to various forms of extravagances in expressions of distress. Some crawled into dugouts and tunnels and stretched themselves at full length on benches and floors, waiting to die. The rumor mill started to function along the line of orders to recall the movement, and abandon all thought of the relief of the French battalion for that night.

To meet this state of near-panic, and to beat it, a few officers adopted the plan of removing masks for a few seconds at a time while giving orders, so that the men would be under the reassurance or the fear (or whatever it is) of the personality that makes some men obey other men.

This practice caused some little sickness by nausea, but gradually orderliness returned to the command, and group after group was marched up into the sector. Presently, the relieved groups of French troops commenced to file out. Our men realized that the earlier groups had reached their posts in safety—and after that a state of normal discipline ruled.

The duty which fell to me of citing Captain Fillmore for conspicuous bravery and devotion to duty was a peculiarly welcome one. In the course of my command of the 1st Battalion, I had had occasion more than once to correct Captain Fillmore, for doing things which he ought not to have done, or for leaving undone things which he ought to have done. I had corrected many, if not most, of my officers as freely; but it may be that Captain Fillmore didn't know that. At any rate, I was perfectly conscious of the fact that Captain Fillmore did not accept my corrections as being made in good faith. I believe that Captain Fillmore was of the opinion that every correction ever offered him by me was offered on account of his being a colored man, and not on the merits of the good of the service.

Of course, no amount of explanation can remedy a situation like that. I never offered any explanation. In most cases, if a commanding officer plays fair, the subordinate officers will, in time, come to recognize the fairness. But I believe that Captain Fillmore never did get over his impression that he and all colored officers were victims of racial prejudice, in every development that did not operate to their advancement or personal satisfaction.

Upon the night of July 21st-22nd Captain Fillmore's assistance to me was of inestimable value. During the scenes of confusion and semi-panic along the Marson Road Captain Fillmore, with marked calmness and courage and persistency moved among the troops. In forming the groups to go forward to relieve French groups, the Captain performed the duties not only of captain,

239

but of lieutenant, sergeant, and corporal, as well. He demonstrated fine leadership, and set an inspiriting example.

I did not tell Captain Fillmore that I had cited him for conspicuous service. A week later, he left our regiment upon transfer. I felt that he was leaving with bitterness in his heart. Half a year later, while our regiment was at Le Mons, waiting for transportation home, Captain Fillmore called upon me, and showed me his *Croix de Guerre*. He asked if I had made the citation. I found a copy of my report and gave it to him. Captain Fillmore didn't say a word; but he held out his hand.

Vilquin (C. R. Fortin, after we moved in, was renamed C. R. Vilquin) was the roughest defensive sector ever occupied by our regiment. The Boche had been driven out unwillingly, and they had not gone far. They had a big reentrant flanking our salient on our left, upon which our trenches came at one point as close to the German trenches as fifteen yards. From this proximity we ran off to a distance of as much as half a mile at the right flank of our sector. The sharp-shooter sniping was constant and accurate. We suffered frequent casualties and we experienced numerous narrow escapes. From the German salient (our reentrant) we were subjected to enfilading fire along a considerable length of our trenches.

Our trenches and boyaux were filled with German equipment which had been abandoned when the enemy moved out. Some of the equipment was valuable. Some splendid vacuum food containers of from three to five gallons' capacity did service for the 1st Battalion from the day of our occupation of Vilquin to the end of the war. There were a lot of rifles and bayonets and helmets and belts, several machine gun spare barrels, a beautiful Goetz lens field glass, quantities of ammunition of every kind and a great supply of clothing, chiefly overcoats. There was quite a supply of emergency rations (canned food and very good), and a lot of solid alcohol for portable stoves. There were gas masks, packs, blankets, haversacks, shovels, picks, entrenching tools, and lanterns.

It was evident that as our men put it in their own slang, the enemy had "made up their train" in a hurry. To make a train was a slang for running away from a fight.

There were a number of excellent war maps, in which our positions were shown with nice accuracy. These maps explained to us the perfection of the enemy artillery fire upon our trenches. As we circulated through our trenches we were subjected constantly not only to rifle fire from snipers, but to artillery fire.

At Regimental Headquarters our report of "Sniping with 155s" was at first taken up as a joke. Later, it was recognized from the surgeons' evacuation lists that the sniping was not an invention of the brains of Shether and Shaw and myself. The term "Sniping with 155s" came into general and serious use.

In the sector Vilquin we found about twenty bodies of German soldiers lying at the posts at which they had been killed as they guarded the boyaux to protect the rear of their main body in retreat. These bodies we buried in excavations made in the sides of the trenches. In that sector it was impossible for a soldier to step out of a trench to seek, for any purpose, open ground between the arteries of communication, without drawing fire.

Upon July 23rd "C" Company, under Captain MacClinton was relieved from *Christoferie*, and rejoined the 1st Battalion at Vilquin, taking the position of reserve company.

The period of our occupation of Vilquin was one of strain and anxiety. Except for the sentinels and observers necessary for the safety of the position, and for officer reconnaissances, our entire command was kept under the protection of the dugouts all through the hours of daylight. Kitchen patrols, of course, had to work their way back and forth between the combat groups and the kitchens on the Marson Road, three times a day, to carry "Chow." The routes chosen for these patrols were through the best protected boyaux and trenches of the sector. In spite of all precautions, casualties were of daily occurrence.

At night our men worked over the rebuilding of the defenses of the sector, to prepare for attack if it should come. During the week of double assault and capture of this salient position great damage had been done to it. The wire entanglements about the fighting posts (the combat group positions) had, in a number of instances, been completely demolished. The sector had been under such heavy bombardment from both directions that, in many places, trenches had been caved in or so filled with earth as to render them impassable.

Our working parties were equipped with fighting arms, laid aside within easy reach.

During the nights, we practiced all through the sector with silent alarms in response to which the men dropped picks and shovels and sprang to combat posts.

Orders were received from "higher up" for the making of a series of night patrols under conditions of such impracticability as to render any chance of success in our mission quite out of reason. From the vantage point of knowledge of terrain and conditions available to me, but unavailable to students merely of maps read several kilometers in the rear of the theatre of operations, I ventured upon advices of protest, even while drawing orders to proceed with the program. My advices were rejected.

The third night's patrol (that of July 27th-28th) ran into a trap of machine gun fire, and returned to lines without gaining any information and without any evidence, by its report, of having made a zealous effort to accomplish its mission.

I ordered another attempt for the night of July 28th-29th to be executed by exactly the same personnel (officers and men) over the same field, and, of course, taking advantage of its knowledge of the approximate location of the enemy machine gun nest.

The result of that fourth patrol was demoralizing. No sooner had the enemy opened fire than a number of our men fell into a state of panic, threw away their rifles, and fled.

The officers kept their heads, and fully one-half of the men stood fast. Captain Shether (who had again come to my battalion that afternoon, to the temporary command of Company "B" upon the departure to another regiment of Captain Fillmore) was standing-to with his company in the rear of the position of sortie, and he stopped the winged-footed soldiers, and drove them back to their command. The abandoned rifles were recovered, and the patrol, reformed, returned to lines in order.

The incident was distressing. It was more than distressing. It was morale-cracking. Rumors and underground reports came to me that mutterings were being indulged in to the effect it was a pity that the officers of high rank couldn't be made to go upon some of these dirty missions which they seemed to be so fond of ordering for others.

Something had to be done—something spectacular and something prompt.

I submitted to Regimental Headquarters a plan for execution which would have served all the issues at one stroke. It would have produced enemy prisoners; and it would have jumped the battalion morale to a frenzy of enthusiasm.

I proposed to take Shether, Landon and Keenan, with a picked fighting orderly apiece, and sneak across No Man's Land well to the east of our sector, to the Boche side. Dr. Keenan and his attendant were to be equipped with field dressing supplies and a light stretcher.

We were to proceed very slowly, to take all night if necessary, and work our way, by creeping, west, along the front of the German lines, until we should reach the first of the three boyaux crossing No Man's Land in front of the quarter sector Vilquin.

At this point, three officers and three men were to spread out, to guard the fourth officer and his attendant from attack from the rear. This fourth couple was to crawl along the top of the bank of the boyaux until the enemy post was spotted, when fire, from very close quarters, was to be opened.

My troops in sector, behind the lines, were to keep up at a number of points the noises of clumsy patrols of large numbers, and thus hold the tense interest of the enemy watchers to their front.

If the first boyaux to be explored should yield no prisoners

243

and suffer no escaped soldiers of the enemy, then our patrol couple were to return to the look-out group, and establish them-selves as lookouts at that point, while the remaining three officers and three men should go on to the next boyaux.

This program was to be followed, if necessary, successively for the three boyaux, the surgeon and his attendant to act alone as look-outs at the end of the most westerly boyaux—the last one to be explored.

In the event of a small number of the surprised enemy sur-rendering to our unseen couple firing from the bank, such prisoners were to be disarmed and rushed across No Man's Land into our lines, and signals made for the rest of the party to come in.

By the combination of feint on the front, surprise attack from the rear, and very small but very select patrol, it was believed that the plan would carry a high probability of success.

The 29th of July afforded four officers and four men of the 1st Battalion a number of hours of suppressed excitement and high hopes of fame; and then, at four o'clock in the afternoon, came the note that smashed our hopes:—The plan was vetoed.

We sent out a regular patrol under the lieutenant whose turn it was for the duty. The patrol was executed creditably, but no prisoners were secured.

Upon July 30th orders were received for the relief of the 1st Battalion by the 2nd Battalion (under Captain Cobb). The relief was to be made during the night, July 30th, 31st.

Upon the morning of August 1st, I was seated in front of my quarters, with chair tipped back against a wall, basking in the sun and reading a New York newspaper. Across the road from me stood the ruins of a stone building, and under the shadow of its walls was a washing fount, of the general style to be seen in most small villages of France. The public bathing and laundry stand was undergoing the patronage of four men, as many as we permitted to assemble at any one place in the open

244

on account of the danger of wholesale casualties accruing from larger groups.

The world seemed to be a place of great natural beauty, of peace and of comfort. The warming sunlight was making me a bit drowsy. Suddenly, from above, came the sound which we knew so well how to interpret—the sound of a shell plowing its way through the air, the squeaking screech becoming louder and louder by each tenth of a second, nearer and nearer. Before I could bring down to its standing position my tipped-back chair, the shell had rushed past me. It had cleared the stone wall against which I had been leaning, a garden wall some eight or nine feet in height, but it had cleared it so narrowly that I had been sensitive to the air disturbance caused by the flight. And then it struck. That shell struck the corner of the stone ruin opposite me, no more than thirty feet away. Owing to the low ordinate of its flight the dispersion of the shell was all forward. I was not even sprinkled with the dust. Half a dozen shots were whipped in in quick succession, but before their arrival, everybody not caught by the first was under cover. The first shot, though, had fulfilled its mission. The four men who were washing themselves and their clothes were horribly wounded by the jagged, rusty fragments of that exploded shell.

Such incidents were accepted as part of the normal day's activities. They would arouse no excitement, and but a moderate degree of interest, much less interest than that aroused by the report of an arrival of mail from home.

Half an hour later, I was walking through the trenches of my battalion, inspecting and visiting. The men were all out—sunning. Each nook or bank that provided cover from observation was occupied—the men stripped to the waist, and busily engaged in the literary-sounding pastime of "Reading the shirt." In this reading of the shirt, the garment is held out taut, in the bright light, held out much after the practice in which a newspaper is held when being examined rapidly for striking headlines. In such manner are the seams pulled apart, and the "seam-squirrels," better known as "cooties," discovered.

As I passed one smiling boy of beautiful physique and skin like burnished copper, my attention was held by the great business which he appeared to be doing in his pursuit of slaughter.

"Finding plenty this morning, Corporal!" I inquired, as I motioned for him to remain seated.

"Nah Suh Major Suh," answered the soldier, "nah suh; Ah doan have ter find 'em dis mornin'. Ah doan even have ter look fer 'em. Ah jes' kills 'em."

# XXXVII

# LIEUTENANT WORSHAM KILLED IN ACTION

*Night of July 31–August 1, 1918*

DURING the night of July 31st-August 1st, the 369th suffered its first loss of an officer killed in action.

The statesmen of the world, the great financiers, the econo-
mists, the industrial engineers, the leaders of social and civic
reform—the pilots of progress in a hundred lines have preached
and taught, are preaching and teaching and will continue for all
time to preach and to teach of the problems of reconstruction
made necessary by the devastation of war.

There is one field of devastation, however, to which there
has been addressed little or no effort of reconstruction. It is the
unhumanizing of the fighting soldier's heart.

Perhaps it is on account of the hopelessness of successful effort
for regeneration that we find, in most channels, an ignorement of
the subject.

Perhaps it is because the men and women who serve as the
preachers and the teachers of the world—do not understand.

That the fighting soldier's mind and heart does suffer a loss
of its humanizing pulsation is, to my mind, evidenced by the
words of my opening paragraph of this chapter.

The new grief of the killing of an officer—our first officer to
die in action—inspired within me a new and tender emotion. And
yet, except from the viewpoint of the military economist and
strategist, there is nothing in the death of an officer to warrant
the writing of a special chapter, any more than there is in the
death of a private.

During the period of almost four months of front line defensive work, my heart had become hardened to the loss of human life in general. I had become accustomed to the reports and to the sights of men of God suffering and dying from wounds inflicted by other men of God.

I had become accustomed to the consideration and discussion of such human tragedies under the descriptive heading of the word "casualties."

I had become accustomed to considering reports of casualties from the viewpoint of the strategist. The vision of sorrowing mother, or wife, or child, or sweetheart, or sister, in far-off land —that vision, which in the early days had been such a heart-rending vision, had given away to a first consideration of replacements and how to get the replacement troops, quickly, to fill the places of their fallen comrades.

The day was to come when the abnormality of my mind and heart was to become normal in its new plane. The death of an officer came to affect me, emotionally, not at all. From the viewpoint of a weakening of the organization, a captain's death was more of a problem than that of a lieutenant; a lieutenant's death was a greater blow to the battalion than that of a sergeant; and the killing of a good sergeant represented a loss appearing to be, at times, almost irreparable.

As old General Franz Seigel of Civil War fame is credited with having remarked, "Strategy is no moore dan de problem of gitting der mostus men dere fustus." So I found a battalion commander's romance of the World War limited to a great extent to the problem of supplies for his command—supplies of food, ammunition, clothing, and—men.

Upon the morning of August 1st, 1918, however, when the body of Lieutenant Worsham was borne back by his men and laid away until darkness upon the floor of the ruins of a stable opposite my quarters, in the reserve position of our regimental sector, I had not yet become so professional of heart as I was later to become. I sensed a real emotion of brotherly love, of sympathy, and of admiration. I walked past the sentry at the door of the little broken down stable, which had become a temple, and there, uncovered, in an attitude of prayer, I looked upon the face of this young soldier who had given his life for humanity.

Two days before, I had met this officer for the first time, and but two days before that he had joined our regiment. Mr. Worsham had been assigned to duty with one of the rifle companies of the 2nd Battalion.

Late upon the afternoon of July 30th, while I was seated at the table placed upon the Marson Road, working over a mass of complicated orders, and reviewing the instructions with the officers and guides of my command, I noticed an officer leading a small group of men across the swamp bounding the Marson Road on the south. The officer approached me and saluted. He was a stranger to me. He reported himself as Lieutenant Worsham, in command of a reconnaisance party, preparing for the troop movement to come during the night.

After a very brief conversation bearing upon the matter of his mission, Mr. Worsham departed with his men. As he marched away, I remarked to an officer beside me: "There goes a fine young officer. He ought to develop into a great commander."

When Captain Cobb, the 2nd Battalion commander, arrived a few hours later, I asked him about young Worsham. Cobb said he had just joined, that he had made a good impression, but that he had as yet made no intimate friends. Cobb agreed that it ought to prove well worth while to watch the career of an officer of such promise.

The next night the career ended. One of those impracticable patrol orders, to proceed in force down a boyau known to be guarded by enemy machine guns, was put up to the 2nd Battalion.

Worsham was assigned to lead the patrol. He led it—bravely and truly. He must have known what he was in for. Anybody of any military experience must have known.

Worsham died of machine gun fire, at the head of his men leading them against the enemy. A number of his men (I believe the number was six) died with him.

As I stood, looking down upon the face of our first officer to make the supreme sacrifice, a surgeon entered the chamber, and kneeling, proceeded to remove and inventory the personal effects found in the pockets of the deceased.

In the breast pocket of his shirt was found a Testament, with his mother's loving message written upon the fly leaf.

When darkness came, the body of Lieutenant Worsham was carried upon a caisson to Valmy, our supply base some ten or twelve miles to the rear. In the cemetery of that quaint little village of France, upon August 3rd, the first officer of the 369th U. S. Infantry to be killed in action was laid to rest with full military honors.

The world-famed rag-time band of the 15th Heavy Foot played softly and solemnly that day; and the colored soldiers, gathered bareheaded about the grave, sang with exquisite sweetness and fervor.

The afternoon had been rainy and clouds were still darkening. Band Sergeant Frank De Broit, our leading cornet player, stood, until the prayers were finished and the grave filled, and then sounded the beautiful call of "Taps." An American officer had closed his eyes in his final sleep on earth.

A moment of silence—then, three volleys of rifle fire, in salute! As the last volley echoed away, the clouds parted and the bright Sun of an August afternoon shone forth its message of reawakening.

"The grave is but a covered way—leading from light to light, through a brief darkness."

# XXXVIII

# A LONG HIKE — TRAINING

### August 4–September 10, 1918

O N August 3rd I received word that I might start upon my first ten days' leave on the following day.

During the morning of August 17th, I rejoined my command, which had moved up, during my absence, to the second line sector of our regimental depth organization of defense.

I found Captain Bates, in temporary command of the battalion. Bates, during my absence, had been returned to the 1st Battalion as Commanding Officer of "B" Company, vice Fillmore, transferred to another regiment.

The battalion was in good shape and preparations were well under way for the relief to be made that night, by which we would go once more into the hateful quarter sector *Vilquin*.

Just before darkness, orders were received for the relief of the entire regiment from the *Minaucourt Sous Secteur*.

During the night, our positions were taken over by a French regiment, and the 369th took up stations *en repos* and *en alerte* for new orders at the small towns about the Regimental Headquarters at Somme-Bionne.

The 1st Battalion was quartered in Hans, a nice clean little town which had suffered comparatively little from enemy shelling. In the big park and chateau of the nabob of Hans was established the Headquarters of the 161st Division of France under General Lebouc.

We had been a part of the 161st Division for more than a month; but I met General Lebouc for the first time the day after our arrival at Hans, when I called to report my respects.

General Lebouc was like all other French officers of high rank—an inspiring example of friendliness, politeness, and genuine considerateness, coupled with a strict spirit of discipline in which he himself participated.

We were at Hans one week. During that time the routine for the several battalions was left to the judgment of battalion commanders for establishment. My battalion followed somewhat the schedules of a peace-time camp of instruction. We had been in the sector four months and ten days. In the school of the soldier, and in the military snap and swank so necessary to a crack organization, we had slumped badly. Such a slump was unavoidable on account of the character of the service through which we had passed—with men and officers all living together in mud and other physical discomfort, and in continuous peril. Besides, we had forty percent of our strength made up of replacement troops, many of whom came to us so green in their knowledge of soldierly bearing that we wondered what the officers of home training camps could be doing with their time.

During that week at Hans the First Battalion set about remedying this condition of sloppiness; and we profited in a marked manner. We had close order drills exclusively—company and battalion. We had ceremonies—Guard Mounting, and Battalion Parade. We then did Regimental Parade with two provisional battalions made up from our big war strength companies and with almost all officers and noncoms enjoying the opportunity to serve in high emergency acting grades. We had a regular inter-company baseball league, with games recognized officially as part of the daily schedule of training. And last but not least, we had a daily privilege of the Hans hot water shower baths and clothing sterilizing plant to which our platoons were marched upon the precise regularity of a railroad time-table.

Upon August 25th, orders arrived by which we were directed to hold ourselves in readiness to move at midnight upon a secret mission. The movement was to be made by *camion* (automobile truck) train.

Tense excitement prevailed. For ten days or more, rumors had been going the rounds of a great American offensive to be launched at the St. Mihiel salient, with final objective Metz. This mysterious order confirmed in many minds the conclusion which had been jumped at a week before, when our entire regiment had been withdrawn from sector, to the effect that our days with the French were drawing to a close—that we were to be returned to the American Army, made a part of an American division, and go into a victory drive under American generals.

The afternoon schedule of field exercises was cancelled. We cleaned house and town, packed up, established the necessary details to cover the service of a battalion movement, and then every man was given a couple of hours of time to himself.

At midnight of August 25th-26th, the regiment assembled at Somme-Bionne, to be carried off in the dark upon its mysterious mission.

A spooky movement, but interesting! With the 15th Foot, as with a sporting career, life was checkered, but rarely dull.

The platoons, widely separated, and in single file of extended distances, streaked along in silence and in darkness. Under commands uttered in undertones the platoons were divided into halves, and the sections, thus formed, were assigned to and loaded upon the great canvas-topped *camions*.

There were about 150 of those *camions* in the complete train; but, for purposes of mobility of movement, the train was divided into four sections—each battalion moving by itself; and the special units forming a fourth, provisional battalion.

The drivers of the *camions* were Singhalese.

Each battalion train had its train master, a French Army Captain. I was invited to take my adjutant with me and share with the train master his touring car.

This war was certainly like no war I had ever read about.

Our automobile dashed along the dark roads with no more apparent concern, upon the part of the French chauffeur, than if there had been light. We passed many *camions*, and ran several kilometers to a point of intersecting roads, where our train master ordered a halt, and invited us to get out and stretch our legs.

Presently the *camions* came along. The Captain directed them to the proper road, and after making certain by a count that the train was intact, once more we climbed into the touring car, and speeded to the head of the column, thence to run ahead again to the next cross roads, where we waited, as before, for the train.

Once, during the night, the count, at a passing point, showed a *camion* to be missing. The trainmaster hurried in the touring car, to the head of the column, and halted the train. Then we drove back along the traveled road until we found the missing car. The trouble was remedied and soon the train, once more complete, was on its way.

Our destination was still a mystery. Compasses showed that we were moving to the south and the southwest. That suggested no verification of the St. Mihiel rumor. At about three o'clock of the morning of August 26th, we arrived at the town named Courtisols, situated about 10 kilometers to the east of Chalons, and slightly to the north of that city.

At Courtisols we were billeted, and ordered to await further orders, and be ready to move early in the morning of the following day.

By daybreak we were all tucked away and asleep.

The first meal served upon August 26th was the midday meal, which did double duty as breakfast and dinner.

Upon August 27th, the regiment hiked southward, and billeted by battalions in the towns Sarry and Sogny—the distances averaging about 16 to 18 kilometers. By that time we had been advised that we were bound south for a training camp, where we might prepare for a month of drill and peaceful pursuits.

Upon August 28th we hiked again, this time to smaller villages, necessitating the division of battalions for billeting. The villages occupied were Vatry, Bussy-Lettree, Competz, Fontaine-sur-Coole, Versigneul-sur-Coole and Faux-sur-Coole. The marches that day averaged something over 20 kilometers.

Upon August 29th, we rested.

Upon August 30th we marched almost due south for from 22 to 30 kilometers (the distances varying for the several battalions according to the location of their respective starting points) passing through the towns Coole, Humbauville, le Meix-Tiercelin, and Dompret, to our destination, St. Ouen Camp.

During the greater part of the day we marched along a road bearing the name, *Ancien Chemin des Romains*. This road of the ancient Romans was, for the most, merely a well-cleared and leveled trail. There was no macadam. For some stretches, there was what we call "good, country dirt road." For much of the way, however, we marched on a surface of turf.

To my mind, the most interesting feature of that road, however, was its straightness and levelness. For almost 20 kilometers we marched south on the road, and the extreme latitudinal variation, over that entire distance from the point farthest west to the point farthest east was less than one and a half kilometers —about 1600 yards. There were no sharp turns, and there was one stretch of about 12 kilometers with scarcely even a bearing off of the straight line.

I believe the road must have been more of a military road than a commercial highway. We met not a single vehicle during a march of almost 7 hours.

St. Ouen Camp was, I believe, the best camp ever occupied by our regiment. In physical comforts and conveniences, both for officers and men, there was but little to be desired. In addition to all that, the surrounding country offered features almost ideal for drill grounds of every description, from parading plains to terrain appropriate for field exercises of major problems of combat.

The regiment was to be united for the first time in almost seven months—since the 12th of February. We settled down for a happy month (in prospect). There were acquaintances and

255

friendships to be made between old-timers and replacement officers and men. There was a great mass of paperwork to be cleared up. There were numerous court martial cases to be tried, of which the exigencies of the service had compelled postponement, in some instances, of many weeks. There were new uniforms and equipment to be drawn. Permanent promotions to non-commissioned grades were to be made to fit new tables of or-ganization which had just been published and made applicable to our command. Rifle practice and the science of musketry, of which a full forty percent of our enlarged command knew nothing was to be worked at upon an intensive basis. Drills and training, to cover everything from school of the soldier up, were to be made a basis of competition. Athletics were to be included in the curriculum. Requests for Y. M. C. A. entertainment groups were despatched to Paris for the attention of my friend Mr. Franklin S. Edmonds, of Aix-les-Bains, who had been promoted from his office of chief of the Leave Area of the Savoie to chief of the entire Leave Area work of the A.E.F. And, for the first time in months, the regiment as a whole was to be afforded the privilege of religious worship.

That splendid man, Chaplain William H. Brooks, of the original N.G. regiment, who had failed to pass the physical tests at the time of the federalization of the command in July, 1907, had been unreplaced for more than a year.

Shortly before the regiment started upon its hike for St. Ouen, however, two new chaplains had reported for duty—Benjamin C. Robeson, and Thomas W. Wallace. These officers, colored clergymen of high standards and of intelligent sympathy with our problems, valiantly set out upon their missions to move the hearts of men—who for months had been trained to do the business of the Devil—to the worship of God.

Everything seemed to be combining to promote the morale of the organization—and then, just as we were settling down into a solid comfort of enjoyment of our new life, like a bolt out of the blue—came orders to move.

256

Upon the afternoon of September 7th a French courier, covered with the dust of a long and hard ride, dashed through our camp, and brought his motorcycle to a stop before the door of Regimental Headquarters. Half an hour later and the battalions had warning orders to prepare for detailed orders for a move at daylight.

Early upon the morning of September 8th, the 1st Battalion led the regiment out of Camp St. Ouen, and commenced a long day's hike to the north.

There was a large prison stockade upon the northern border of the camp; and, as we filed by, the German soldiers lined the criss-crossed wired fence, and silently speeded us on our way. We little knew that within three weeks our ranks would be thinned and our morale shattered by casualties of battle to cost us almost thirteen hundred of our men and about fifty officers, killed and wounded. I have many times wondered if those German prisoners guessed.

We made a long, hard march that day. We were unfortunate in being forced to make a number of detours on account of roads under repair. We marched between 32 and 33 kilometers. Our men, however, were in good condition; and they marched through the large city of Vitry-le-Francois (within 6 or 7 kilometers of the end of the day's tramp) at attention, and with inspiriting snappy swing—chanting their marching songs.

The regiment billeted that night in a number of towns near Vitry-le-Francois—Couvrot, Loisy-sur-Marne, Maisons-en-Champagne, and Coole.

Upon the evening of September 9th as soon as darkness came, the regiment moved once more by *camions* to the north. We ran well into the middle of the night through Chalons, and to la Croix-en-Champagne, where we detrained; and the 1st Battalion marched over a cross country road to three camps near Somme-Bionne.

After getting the men put to bed in barracks, the officers paid for the privilege of having their blankets and cots carried as baggage for them, by sleeping in wet clothes, on the floor of a barrack room, without bedding of any kind. After two hours of sleep, orders were received to prepare to go into a defensive sector the following night. That meant immediate reconnaissance for all officers.

We found that we were to relieve a battalion of the 215th Infantry Regiment of France, in the quarter sector known as Crochet. This quarter sector was a part of the *Sous Secteur Beausejour*, situated immediately to the left of our old hated Vilquin.

The Company officer groups were sent out with guides to look over their respective positions, with permission to proceed, by company group, back to camp, as soon as their reconnaissance had been finished.

The Machine Gun C.O., 1st Lieutenant Delafield, and I, however, had to go over the entire sector. By the time that we had completed our rounds and walked back to camp, we felt that we had done a day's work. Between the time of detraining at la Croix-en-Champagne the night before, and of our arrival back in camp after reconnaissance, we had walked more than 32 miles. The full elapsed time was about 21 hours. Of that time I had spent about 2 hours in sleep. For food, I had had two sandwiches, two drinks of rum, one cup of coffee, and a slice of bread.

As I entered our barracks I found that my wonderful orderly, Joe Rantes, had unpacked my things and made my room look homelike. Within five minutes I was between the soft blankets of my own bed.

That is all I can remember of September 10th, 1918.

# XXXIX

# THE LOCAL INFANTRY ATTACK

*September 12, 1918*

O UR day of September 11th was one of rest, and of simple preparations for going into sector as soon as darkness should come.

We, the 1st Battalion, made the relief early that night, the relief of the *5th Battalion, 215 E.R.I.* in the *Quartier Secteur Crochet*, the first line of trenches of the *Sous Secteur Beausejour*. The sector was accounted a dangerous and difficult one; but we never made an easier relief.

The Commandant Salerou and his Adjutant, Captain O'Byrne, favored me with a set of instructions and position maps that were the clearest and most readily understood of any which I had had in all my experience.

The sector was of unusual length of frontage, owing to the fact that its left boundary formed one side of a great horseshoe of trench, running back from the normal front line of trench for the best part of half a mile. Thus, we had to serve a main parallel of trench upon two fronts, instead of upon one only as was usual when battalions made liaison with their right hand and left hand neighbors practically upon a common line. To meet the situation, the 3rd Battalion Machine Gun Company under Captain Lewis Edward Shaw was assigned to me for additional strength. Also, the Division Commander placed under my command a French trench mortar platoon. In the sector there was also a special post served by a pneumatic gun for throwing grenades. The officer sent to me for command of the gun, however, demonstrated, by killing a man in practice, that he didn't

259

know how to use the pneumatic. I didn't understand the gun myself, and I had no other officer who claimed to; so I locked up the ammunition and served the position by other means.

Thanks to the efficient guide service of the French battalion, the relief of the sector was completed well before midnight of September 11th, and we at Headquarters had the unusual privilege of going to bed upon the first night of a relief and enjoying a good night's rest.

Early upon the morning of September 12th, the Commandant Salerau conducted me, sector-map in hand, all through the quarter. Each post of each combat group was visited. By the noon hour we had returned to Headquarters. Immediately after lunch, the Commandant Salerou asked if I should object if he were to retire out of sector that afternoon instead of completing a full twenty-four hours as adviser. I felt well acquainted with the sector and confident of my battalion in its ability to carry on. I readily consented to the departure of the Commandant; but requested the services of his *Adjoint* (corresponding to our adjutant), Captain O'Byrne, through the second night.

That request was a fortunate one for me and my reputation. That afternoon, the 1st Battalion gained fame, and, according to the ways of the world, its commander was accorded the dignity of being made the recipient of a distinction of honor. I have always believed, and so stated in my official report, that to Captain O'Byrne and his official service of advice belonged the true credit for the success achieved that day by the *1er. Bataillon 369eme. R.I.U.S.*

A warning communication was received at Battalion Headquarters during the afternoon of September 12th, advising us that reliable information had been obtained to the effect that an attack was to be made upon our sector during the night of September 12th-13th.

With the *Captaine* O'Byrne in attendance I set out at once to make personal liaison with the commandant of the sector on our right, in order to assure perfect understanding of cooperation between our border (or mixed) posts. The French commandant met me by appointment at the border post, and we agreed upon our program of defense.

Then O'Bryne and I tramped and splashed through the mud of the entire sector, from right extreme to left. We visited every post, and, by small groups, spoke to every man in the battalion. We told the men of our warning; and reviewed with them the orders of defense. There was to be no falling back to a line of support; and, in this sector, there was no redoubt position. The sector was a half salient and it had to be held without the compromise of a foot. The support position for that sector was the second line sector, held by the 2nd Battalion under Captain Frederick W. Cobb. The reserve troops for our sector were the troops of the 2nd Battalion in the second line. Our 1st Battalion troops were disposed all in the front line. No units were held in reserve.

We completed our rounds shortly before six o'clock, at the post of command of Company "D." We were tired. Two complete inspections of a sector like that in one day is no easy bit to do. With mud throughout from two to six inches in depth, a full fifty percent was added to the load of exertion.

The "D" Company P.C. was upon the Marson Road, at the rear curve of the big horseshoe running westward to a sector held by a regiment of Blue Devils.

The 1st Battalion P.C. was on a parallel with "D" Company P.C.—also, of course, upon the Marson Road—and about a third of a mile to the east.

Shortly before 6:15 P.M. *Captaine* O'Byrne and I took our departure from Mr. Seibel's *abri*, and started to walk along the open ground above the communicating trench leading to Headquarters. There was no danger of observation at this point, and no firing was going on.

We had progressed a couple of hundred yards or less when, without the slightest warning, we were startled by the sound of terrific explosions. Two or three hundred close range mortars had been fired simultaneously with shells containing gas, trained upon the full length of our front line trench.

We were experiencing for our first and only time the plan of fire known as a "Projector Attack."

The scheme is, I believe, to endeavor to catch almost all the men of a defense garrison out of the dugouts, lolling at ease along the sides of the trenches—taking them wholly unawares—and gassing so large a proportion as to cause disorganization in the combat groups.

The "projector" volley is followed instantly by a regular barrage to cover the advance of attacking infantry.

Theoretically, this form of attack is one of assured success for an assaulting party the mission of which is to take a salient position of size sufficiently moderate to lend itself to the plan of concentration of fire.

Upon the afternoon of September 12, 1918, however, it didn't work, in so far as its success was to be measured by the attack upon the *C.R. Crochet*. I do not know why it did not work. From the viewpoint of timing and intensity of fire, and of other professional considerations of the science of slaughter, the effort was perfect. It may be that it was the sheer ignorance of our tyro soldiers in refusing to be subdued by the gas, that caused the failure of the German plan. Whatever the cause, or where-ever the blame, the action resulted in complete success to our arms. No German soldier succeeded even in getting over the parapets into our trenches; and, naturally under such circum-stances, none succeeded in staying in our trenches. We had carried out our orders, and given to the enemy, "not a foot of ground."

Our losses were sixteen killed and wounded, three of the wounded being officers of whom one was a French Lieutenant, whose name I regret I cannot report.

The Artillery action covering the attack was the most inter-esting action from the viewpoint of thoroughness that I had ever seen.

There appeared to be three complete zones of fire.

The first, the barrage on the trenches to cover the advance of the assault troops.

The second, a complete covering of the trenches of approach all through the sector.

The third, a heavy fire upon the second line sector to force the men of the 2nd Battalion to keep cover, and to prevent any successful counter attack by them.

At the sound of the "project" volley, *Captaine* O'Byrne and I started to run for cover.

A few seconds later a heavy caliber shell rushed over my head, in low ordinate, and struck upon the far side of me, with dispersion away from me. The shock of explosion was sufficient to topple me over, slightly unsteady as I must have been in running. I rolled down a steep little embankment, and for an instant, was stunned.

The action started at 6:15 P.M. and continued in full intensity for one hour and twenty minutes.

Battalion Headquarters transmitted signals with a promptitude which gave us the support of a well directed artillery defense from the French batteries in our rear, within less than three minutes after the commencement of the attack.

For an hour and a quarter, there were some fireworks in the air!

Speaking of fireworks, I am reminded of an incident of some little human interest that occurred during the engagement. Our men always had lots of trouble in using the skyrocket signals exactly correctly. There were standing jokes in the regiment, of the grotesque errors that had occurred at times, when it had seemed to be necessary to signal from front line posts to rear.

*"We have taken our second objective and are going forward"*
*"We are being attacked by tanks"*
*"Covering barrage is too short, lengthen range"*

Such are fair examples of some of the startling messages which would sometimes be read by our observers when our knowledge of the situation in general made us realize that the signals were just nonsense, or perhaps, fired in mere error for an ordinary illuminating flare intended to show up some suspicious-sounding party working in front of the wire in No Man's Land on an otherwise perfectly quiet night.

While Captain O'Byrne and I were striving from our retreat of cover, to keep in touch with the situation as well as we could by peeking out between shell arrivals and noting everything possible, we observed at one time a magnificent display of rockets, all along the line. Of course I did not have the signal code with me, and many of the signals we could not read. Presently there appeared one that caused O'Byrne a great convulsion of excitement.

"There, the enemy is in our trenches! God help us!" Exclaimed O'Byrne in perfectly good English, thanks to his grandfather having been a British subject resident upon the Emerald Isle. "If it's true," said I, "God help the enemy! Our men, I admit, don't know so much about this game of sector warfare. And an artillery barrage which kills, without giving a man a chance to strike back, is, to say the least, puzzling to amateur soldiers; but, if the Boche ever gets inside our trenches, then you'll find our boys from Harlem will be at home. Bayonets and knives will be the order, and there won't be anybody there, when that happens, who'll take any interest in sending up a skyrocket.

"My dear O'Byrne," I continued, "I think you'll find the real meaning of those rockets to be celebration. I believe the fight on the front line is over, and soon we'll be able to get out of this cave, and count noses."

And so it turned out to be. I ordered a patrol out at once from "D" Company, with a mission to explore No Man's Land over the entire front of our sector, and secure information of every kind, by salvaging abandoned property of the enemy, by taking prisoners if stragglers should be found, or by bringing in the enemy dead if they had not been carried away.

Lieutenant Ernest A. McNish was put in command of the patrol.

Within a short time a report of the main features of the action was codified and wired back to Regimental Headquarters.

Within less than half an hour, 1st Lieutenant Tessier, General Lebouc's Aide, and another officer of the Division Staff, whose name I cannot recall, called upon me. "By command of the General Lebouc, to felicitate the Commandant Little and his brave men, and to thank them for their fine service." You can't beat these French officers for the psychology of leadership!

The wounded had commenced to arrive at Dr. Keenan's little dressing station. Keenan was very shorthanded of assistants trained in matters of surgery. I wasn't trained, but my rank seemed to give me some poise in the *Poste de Secours*, and I helped the doctor by handling basins and bandages, jumping about at his orders with all the alacrity I was accustomed to exact from others outside of that little shop of suffering. It was well past ten-thirty in the evening when the last man had been evacuated.

As the doctor was rolling down his sleeves preparing to call it a day, I asked him if he had some liniment. He asked me what I wanted it for. I told him I had bruised myself when I had rolled down that embankment, and that I had a sore chest.

"Let me see it," ordered the doctor.

So I rolled up my shirt.

Keenan felt around a bit; then he got out the stethoscope, and applied it, then he felt some more. "Yes sir, I guess you're perfectly right about having a sore chest," he said, with a grin on his face. "It's going to be sore for some little time, too. You've just got two fractured ribs, with a nice little wound stripe coming to you, Major; and I'd just like to congratulate you, if you don't mind, and then I'll get to work and fix you up."

And dear "Old Doc. Keenan" stuck his tongue in his cheek, and offered me his right hand.

Half an hour later Lieutenant Webb entered my room.

265

I had just gone to bed. Suddenly, the realization had come to me that I was very tired. I had had neither time nor appetite for supper. The close binding splint of adhesive tape with which Keenan had strapped up my chest, afforded me some little discomfort.

Webb spoke apparently under some stress of excitement. "Major, there's one of our men bringing some prisoners down the boyau from 'D' Company P.C. A runner just came in with warning. What do you wish to do with them, Sir?"

"I'd like to see them," I answered. "Send them in here when they arrive, and later, pick a good reliable guard and send them back with a report to Regimental Headquarters. And," I called after him, as he was disappearing through my bedroom door, "just see that the man in charge gets a receipt for the prisoners."

A few minutes later, the sound of shuffling footsteps came to me through the door from my office, and I looked up to see two German soldiers come grinning into my room, and stand beside my bed.

They were very large men, and, as they stood towering above me, as I lay upon my low cot, they appeared to me to be giants. One of them had his arm in an improvised sling, and he was quite bloody from the wound which he was nursing. They had been smoking, and they held lighted cigarettes in their hands as they stood in silence before me. But, upon the faces of the Germans were broad grins. It was difficult to believe that they could be newly made prisoners of an enemy of war.

I was startled. My brain worked rapidly; and through it ran a review of most of the tricks of the Germans of which I had ever heard. I pictured to myself the *coup*, by which our sector, successfully defended against open attack only a few hours before, had fallen ignominiously for a trick. I pictured myself a prisoner, taken away in disgrace without the giving of a blow. My eyes jumped to my pistol, hanging in its holster from a nail near the foot of my bed. And I was strapped up so tight in the body, that it was a matter of a long drawn out system of movements for me to be able even to change from a lying to a sitting posture. I was helpless—and, with bitterness, I realized it.

Just then I heard a sound from behind the German who stood farthest from me; and I looked quickly, to recognize one of our own men—about the smallest soldier who ever passed the physical examination for the U. S. Army.

This little "D" Company lad had no grin upon his face. He appeared to be taking his mission very seriously. Standing in half crouching attitude, he held his rifle in the position of charge bayonets, with the muzzle placed against the small of the back of the prisoner directly in front of him.

I was glad to see that boy! And I told him so.

Then I asked him to tell me what had happened, where he had gotten his prisoners, how he had gotten them, had there been a fight, how many were there—all about it?

"Well, Suh Major Suh," the little fellow commenced. "Well, Suh Major Suh, Ah'll jes' tell yoo der truth." And when I knew that we were going to get something good, even though we might be expected to swallow a bit of exaggeration.

"You see, Suh Major Suh, Ah was sent out on a patrol with L'tenant McNish. An' pretty soon, out in front er where dose 'C' Company fellers is, we sees a patrol er comin' towards us. Et wuz pretty dark, an' der L'tenant he motions fer us all ter keep quiet an' ter lay down. At odder patrol et jes' keeps er comin' an' pretty soon we all sees daiz Bush Germans. N' den der L'tenant gives der motion to fire; an' we all lets em hev it—good. Some uv 'em wuz hit—we all could see et. And some run away. N' den we closed in and took some pris'ners. Ah doan' raghtly know, Suh, jes' how many day wuz—all to-gedder. Der L'tenant jes' tells me to bring in der prisoners an' Ah came. W'en Ah started, day wuz five uv 'em; but day wuz such big fellers 'at Ah jes' thought Ah'd better clean 'em out er bit."

# OUR PART IN
# THE BATTLE OF THE MEUSE-ARGONNE

*September 25–October 6, 1918*

THE 1st Battalion filed out in column of half platoon, single file groups, with distances of fifty paces. The night was moderately dark and an order of greater distances would have been accompanied by risk of loss of liaison between the groups.

The hour of our departure was about 6:30 in the evening. The 2nd and 3rd Battalions had started earlier. They had farther to go and they could not wait for darkness.

We commenced our march to the front along the highway. The route was, Somme-Bionne—Somme-Tourbe—LaSalle—St. Jean-sur-Tourbe—Laval—Wargemoulin—Minaucourt. We were to take station for the night upon the protected slope of the *Ravin des Pins*, a mile or so to the east of Minaucourt. At Minaucourt, at the P.C. René, were the Headquarters of the Division. It is to be recalled that under the orders received that afternoon the 1st Battalion was attached to the Headquarters forces of the Division, under direct orders of the Commanding General Lebouc.

Before the head of our column had gotten half-way to Somme-Tourbe, I came to a realization that, with the great traffic jam upon the road, it would be impossible for the battalion to reach its destination on time, unless we could find some other route.

I sent for 1st Lieutenant Siebel, relieving him temporarily from command of Company "D," and inviting him to march with me at the head of the column, and to serve as guide.

I had had Mr. Siebel make reconnaissance that afternoon, on horseback, in order to be prepared for the possible necessity of travelling 'cross-country that night. Siebel had a kind of super-sense of direction and location.

We struck off the road immediately, and for the next three hours the stars were our guide-posts, and the only sounds to break the stillness of our march were the occasional clatterings of tin cups or canteens carelessly used by some hapless soldier due for an instant correction of violent language from his non-commissioned immediate superior.

Once, we believed ourselves to be lost. The column was halted, and Siebel disappeared into the darkness. Within ten minutes he was back with the advice of absolute confidence to change our direction sharply to the right. With anxiety in my heart I moved off in the new direction; but there was no real occasion for the anxiety. Siebel was right. He had called that super-sense of his into play, and within a few minutes more we had found the trail which we had been seeking and which led us in time to the main road, a few hundred yards to the north of Wargemoulin. Along this road we picked our way, dodging in and out between a great variety of war vehicles of traffic, until we came to the trail leading into the *Ravin des Pins*.

Our orders required us to be in position by ten o'clock. We arrived at 9:39 P.M.

A few minutes later, two groups of messengers were despatched with reports.

The 1st Battalion of the 369th U. S. Infantry awaited orders for battle.

The slope of the *Ravin des Pins* upon which we disposed our troops for shelter provided emplacements, also, for a number of batteries of field artillery.

At eleven o'clock the great guns spoke. THE BATTLE OF THE MEUSE-ARGONNE was on!

Six o'clock news bulletin!

The artillery engagement had proceeded in perfect order, as

269

planned, and at 5 o'clock the first assaulting wave of infantry had gone over the top. The first and second objectives had been taken with astonishing despatch, and prisoners estimated at 18,-000 were already in the hands of our division, and marching to the rear. The infantry of our division had gone over the German lines in a path of about 1,500 metres, just about midway between the two widely known strongholds, *Butte du Mesnil* and *Mt. Tetu*. They were now going through the district known as *Maisons de Champagne Farm* in a generally northerly direction, with a left boundary at Ripont.

My first orders came shortly after 10 o'clock.

We went forward into the *secteur Vilquin* to await our further orders. How we hated that sector, Vilquin! Two months had passed since we had lived there under the horrible conditions of discomfort and danger. I doubt, however, if a span to the extent of a hundred times two months could have caused us to forget our way about that labyrinth of trenches.

We took our new position without casualty, and without incident of unusualness.

There was one incident, however, that I deem worthy of recording. I am not sure of its unusualness; but to my mind it was interesting by way of demonstration of the cracked morale of the German Army.

The 1st Battalion was filing across the Marson Road, and the men, divided into small groups, were disappearing down the arteries of the sector. A steady stream of prisoners, bound in the opposite direction, were marching past us. One of our men, in violation of orders, chided a group of Germans as they passed:

"Well, what do you think of the Kaiser, now?" a lad from Harlem jeered.

"God damn the Kaiser!" came the response of a German officer.

About midnight, a messenger from the 3rd Battalion came to my P.C., looking for Colonel Hayward.

The messenger informed me that the battalion commander

and his adjutant, Lieutenant Walton, had been badly (probably fatally) wounded, and that Captain David A. L'Esperance had assumed battalion command, and was reporting his position to the regimental Commander.

At about 2 o'clock of the morning of September 27th, as we crossed the *Ravin d'Hebuterne*, and later went over the Trenches Jacquinot and Bourrasset, the garrisons of which had caused us so much distress during the month of July, we indulged expressions of reminiscence. The chief sights of interest to us, however, throughout that advance during the hours of gray dawn, were the activities of the artillery. The day before, when we had moved forward, we saw long lines of field guns, almost hub to hub, in their firing positions. Now, we saw these scores of guns being moved forward, in order to cover the rapid advance of our infantry in pursuit of the enemy.

The work of moving those guns over the mutilated surfaces of the sectors was a work of tremendous physical effort. The four-horse teams of two and sometimes three gun carriages would be hitched to one gun. Then, three men would man each wheel of the carriage. At a given word, all drivers would crack their whips and swear together, and all men other than drivers would strain at the wheels, and push from the rear of the carriages. And so, by brute force, foot by foot, and sometimes, as it appeared, inch by inch, these engines of death delivery were trundled through the thick, sticky mud of the Champagne, over trenches and dugouts, through broken wire, over dead bodies of horses and human beings, up the steep inclines of small mountains, to take position for a new range—to smash a way for the advance of the Allies to victory.

In the position recently vacated by the 2nd Battalion, we found about ten or twelve dead bodies of 2nd Battalion men. The Germans had discovered Captain Cobb's command the afternoon before, and had shelled them out of their reversed trenches.

In shelling its own evacuated trenches, the enemy, of course, has two great advantages. It has the benefit of range cards made and verified at leisure over its own terrain. And the trenches upon which it fires are trenches with the good protection only on the new rear of the position.

Cobb had saved his command from heavier losses by moving off during the night to the right flank and taking cover behind a hill. Something had gone wrong, however, with his liaison with Regimental Headquarters; and the order whereby he was to attack at 5:15 upon the morning of the 27th, the trench *de Ripont en Zig Zag*, had not reached him.

Shortly after we moved into the abandoned 2nd Battalion position, some minor action took place in front of us upon the other side of the Dormoise River. Our men recklessly perched themselves upon the parapets of their trenches and waved and shouted in excited interest as they would have done at home at a ball game. Within a matter of seconds, accurate shell fire had been drawn upon our trenches; but within those seconds the officers of our battalion had gotten to work. The voice could not be heard clearly; but a number of us did fairly fast seventy-five yard dashes along the tops of those parapets, and, with each stride, a cane cracked a surprised colored soldier into a position of safety, prone at the bottom of his trench.

We had no casualties in that position.

At about ten o'clock we all enjoyed an excellent meal. We cooked by squads over cans of solid alcohol; and we made a hearty stew with boiling water, soup cubes, "iron ration bully beef," and hard tack. As a result, everybody was cheerful and keen to go.

During the morning, Captain Shether and 1st Lieutenant Landon came through our lines, separately, to work their way forward to search for the 2nd Battalion.

At about one o'clock, Shether came back through our lines, on the way to Regimental Headquarters, to report that he had found the 2nd Battalion.

From our position on the hill upon the south of the Dormoise valley we had an excellent opportunity to watch the infantry manoeuvers of the division.

The 163rd (French) was already upon the north side of the Dormoise River. Our own 3rd Battalion was also over. These elements had been held all the morning close up against a steep hill bounding a highway along the north bank of the river. From the crest of this hill, a great plain spread out as far as the eye could reach. While in that position they were, of course, under perfect cover from artillery fire; and the enemy paid no attention to them. As soon as the advance started, however, the music of the artillery and machine guns broke out.

We saw the men of the first line drag themselves up that steep hill, and deploy, under fire, on to the plain. The movement was beautifully executed. Apparently, there was no excitement. All hands took their time, and alignments and intervals were well maintained.

A few minutes later, the 2nd Battalion appeared from around a hill to our right. They had to cross the Dormoise on two or three frail foot bridges, in single file. It was a ticklish piece of business, with shells dropping all about, and, occasionally, getting a victim. But the unusualness of the manoeuver enlisted so great a degree of interest upon the part of the men, apparently, as to over-balance the sense of fear. As I watched the groups, through my glasses, going over one of the plank bridges, I could recognize individuals. Many of the men behaved as if they were out on a lark, playing a game of "Follow my leader." Every now and then a clumsy man would fall off the plank and get a ducking. Then, how those men would scream with laughter!

A third of a mile to the left of our position was a fine stone bridge. I calculated that there would be time for three of my companies to work their way down to that point, cross the river at ease, and get back to the trace of the column, by the time the 2nd Battalion could make its crossing, take formation, and gain its distance. Just after the operations of the afternoon started, we received orders to extend the 500 metres distance between battalions provided for in the written order to 800 meters.

I sent the Machine Gun Company and Companies "B" and "C" the long way by the stone bridge. They were able to keep cover all the way down and back; and were exposed only for the few seconds necessary to dash across the bridge in very small groups. Company "D" and our Headquarters Group took the short course and crossed on the single plank bridges.

The rendezvous, upon the Northern side, was in a long roadside cemetery. Some of our men found something to appeal to their sense of humor in the cemetery situation. With a laugh all along the line, we climbed the hill and spread out on the plain.

Being third wave in a movement of that kind is a curious kind of position to be in. You get a lot of fire, but you don't get any chance to return fire. The advantage is, of course, that good cover can be taken. The plain had been and was being heavily shelled, and there were lots of shell holes, which offered good protection against everything but direct hits and spent bullets or pieces of shrapnel.

We advanced easily and with very slight casualties, maintaining our position in relation to the 2nd Battalion, as directed.

Shortly after five o'clock, the first line apparently ran into a determined resistance, and we were all held up.

With the coming of darkness, the sounds of battle diminished. Presently, there was nothing but the desultory firing of artillery, punctuated very rarely with the *rat tat tat tat tat* of a machine gun.

At seven o'clock I sent permission to Company commanders to arrange reliefs on the line for watching through the night, but to have the men spread their blankets and secure as much rest and sleep as possible.

At the first glimmer of daylight we were all up and astir.

During the night contact with Regimental Headquarters had been broken. I set out to re-establish it.

Acting Regimental Adjutant Whittlesey recognized me at

some distance, and came forward to greet me. "What is the news?" I inquired.

"The 2nd Battalion was shot to hell in the dark early this morning, trying to take the ridge at Bellevue Signal," Whittlesey answered.

"Where are they now?"

"Up there, what's left of them," the adjutant responded, "Maury's French Battalion attacked with them, and Favre's battalion in support, was thrown in too, before the thing was finished. The thing's all right now. The hill's held all right. We'll probably rest here today to clean up the casualties a bit, and then tomorrow you'll get *your* chance. Come on up and see the Colonel."

As I approached, the Colonel's back was half to me, and he was speaking earnestly to 1st Lieutenant Landon, who had just come up from the right and reported that the 1st Battalion was moving into the Battery 0254 position.

"Harold, my boy, I'm awfully sorry," Colonel Hayward was saying, "I'm awfully sorry to make you go out again. I can see that you're about all in; but the necessity is desperate. You're the only man who can find Little right now, in a hurry, and he's got to be found in a hurry——!" At that instant, Colonel Hayward's eyes left Landon's and glanced back over his right shoulder. He recognized me: "Thank God!" Colonel Hayward exclaimed, "Thank God—here is Little now!"

"Little, where are your men?"

"My two right platoons are on this road with their right at battery position 0254, the other platoons are coming down the hill at hundred pace distances, to take position on their left."

"Listen, Little, that place your men are moving into is a death trap. It's perfectly registered. They may start any minute to shoot it up. That order for position 0254 was sent to you in error. Where it was really intended to send you was to the entrenched position on top of that hill back of those woods."

275

As the Colonel talked, he pointed with his cane, across the road to the south, and across a ravine.

"Who have you got with you, Little, who can get back quickly, and stop that movement? It may be a matter of minutes or seconds—or lives—who can you send—quick?"

"I'm going myself, Sir!"

"You can't do it fast enough with your strapped-up chest."

But I was off.

At five minutes past eight o'clock I dispatched a report as follows:

> 1st Batt.
> 9/28/18
> 8:05 A.M.
>
> To
> C. O. 369th Regt.
>
> The Battalion is in the trenches on crest of hill directly in rear of Regt. P. C. Center of line on P. C. Regt. Organized in depth, 3 companies in line, 2 platoons of ea. Co. in line.
>
> Batt. P. C. (Temporary) in old artillery emplacement just in front of trench at center of position.
>
> No casualties.
>
> This note is being sent by three (3) post relay.
>
> ARTHUR W. LITTLE
> Major.

I discovered later in the day that my report, "No casualties," was not quite accurate. The shelling, of the position being evacuated, as well as of the position being moved into, commenced almost immediately after I had left Colonel Hayward to change the movement. One of "D" Company's men got a slight shrapnel wound in the hand, and, I believe, there were two or three other mere scratches suffered—nothing serious, however. We were lucky.

A dismal, dreary day was September 28th. Rain fell in a steady drizzle. There were no dugouts or *abris* of any kind in the position which we occupied—nothing but shallow trenches. There were a number of abandoned battery positions with camouflaged roofs sufficiently compact to offer a fair protection from rain; and these shelters, of course, were all taken advantage of. The men, for the most part, however, had to try to keep dry by stretching canvas shelter-tent halves across the top of the narrow, shallow trenches, and crawling in under. It was always an inspiring revelation to me to witness the cheerful resourcefulness of our men in making the best of any situation of hardship that confronted them.

We were running short of food. We took a careful count of stock, and planned the use of our remaining "iron" rations so as to provide each squad with two good meals for that day, of the stew which I have described, having just enough for a breakfast to be served the following morning. We figured that mess would play but a small part in the schedule of service for the following day. A water detail was sent out under a clever sergeant (I believe it was Mess Sergeant McNamara of Company "C"), and all canteens were filled with fairly decent water from the Dormoise River.

At about ten o'clock in the morning I was out on the extreme right of our lines, inspecting the organized position of Company "D," when Dr. Keenan joined me.

Keenan handed me a little note, and asked me to read. The note was from Whittlesey and it was addressed to Keenan. It said that the wounded were being brought in to the regimental dressing station more rapidly than it was possible for them to be cared for. There was but one surgeon present and functioning— Major Shiels. He was working magnificently, like a man inspired; but the roll of sufferers was gaining on him. Did Dr. Keenan feel, in spite of the prospect of his having a terrific day before him, tomorrow, with his own battalion, that he could volunteer to help Shiels?

Dear old Shiels! How the fates and the hand of God do assert themselves at vital moments in the history of men and of organizations! It was owing to a series of mere accidents that Major Shiels was with us at all. And now, this accidental member of our medical staff was alone in the front line dressing station, saving the lives of hundreds, possibly saving the life of the regiment!

As I read Whittlesey's note to Keenan, all these strange incidents flashed through my mind. Then I looked at Keenan.

"Well," I said, "do you wish to go?"

"Major, I've got to go!"

"Yes," I said. We shook hands; and Keenan was off—to prove himself a hero.

I didn't see Keenan again until late upon the night of the following day. Even then I didn't exactly see him. He reported to me in the dark, in a place where to show a light meant death. But he found me; and he reported for duty. I have heard that Shiels and Keenan, during that dreadful day, September 28th, handled between three hundred and four hundred casualties, French soldiers as well as Americans. Their dressing station was under incidental shell fire all the time. I have heard that under such stress these two surgeons performed major operations to save life. Some doctor men!

That long day wore away; and the night passed without incident or interruption.

The morning of September 29th dawned clear and cool. There was expectancy in the air. Our last remaining rations were eaten. Then the one or two razors remaining amongst the officers were used, in order of rank, at Battalion headquarters, after which they were passed along the line for the company officers to shave if they wished to. It is a curious record of occurrences that, from the two and a half day battle that ensued, every officer who shaved, that morning, came out on foot and on duty; and every officer who did not shave, was either killed or so severely wounded as to require evacuation.

At about a quarter past eight, I received the following note:

29 Sept., 18.
8 hr. 15

Major Little:

Come to Regt. Hqrs. at once.

Leave instructions so that 1st Battn. will be ready to move at moment's notice.

By order of COL. HAYWARD
R. WHITTLESEY
1st Lieutenant, Actg. Adjut.

When I reported a few minutes later, I received our orders for attack.

The orders were in French, and the French Aide, Lieutenant Maxwell, read them aloud translating as he read. There was no time to make a perfect translation or to rewrite. As Maxwell read, the Colonel, and a number of members of his staff, and I marked our maps, to show the path of the advance to be made; and the successive objectives, for pauses and reorganization, were noted.

# SECHAULT

*September 29–30, 1918*

THE 1st Battalion was to advance in a north-easterly direction to Bellevue Signal, a distance of something over 3 kilometers. There, we were to relieve the French Battalion Favre, which was organized in trenches upon the north front and crest of the hill. At as early an hour as practicable after making the relief we were to go over the top from these trenches, descend the hill, cross the plain with the Bussy Farm on our left, and the foothills of Mt. Cuvelet on our right, and advance something over a kilometer, to the town Sechault, which town we were to take by storm and occupy. When Sechault should be wholly ours, mopped up, and rendered safe as a new base of advance, the 1st Battalion was to go forward for another jump of between two and a half and three kilometers, clearing the woods to the northeast of Sechault and taking *Les Rosiers Ferme*. The Rosiers Farm was to be our final objective for that movement. That objective, when reached, was to serve as a new base. We were to dig in there, reorganize, and await further orders.

Presently, we commenced our advance. We moved forward in a long column of single files with five paces between the men. I had been given a French soldier from Favre's Battalion, as a guide. He and I led the column.

The guide furnished me was not much good. He could tell me no more about the location of Favre's battalion than my map could have told me. He did not, however, advise me of his ignorance until after he had led me and the battalion stupidly into what might have been a slaughter trap.

Liaison Sergeant Hannibal Davis posted a runner at every 200 paces to form a chain of communication from Regimental Headquarters to me, wherever I might be. It was an expensive plan of liaison, in that by it a good many men were kept out of the firing line: but it worked. We never failed in prompt communication with Regimental Headquarters, and so the expensiveness of the plan was justified. In the course of our training for the campaign, one of the French generals had instructed us that: "Liaison is more important even than ammunition."

We advanced, quietly enough, to the southern edge of the plain of Bellevue Signal, and there the guide turned sharply to the right, making of our long column, in effect of visibility, a deployed line, extended along a skyline. No better target could be desired by an enemy. I protested in my poor pidgeon French; but the guide's only response was to take up a double time along the ridge. Within a few seconds, the shelling commenced. I ordered a lie down and take cover at once, and sent back directions to infiltrate the rear elements of our column into the trench cut just below the rear edge of our plain.

Then Webb and I dashed off in pursuit of that guide. We found him resting under the shelter of a wrecked German artillery position, at the extreme south-eastern corner of the Bellevue Signal plain.

We discovered that he didn't know where Favre was.

My liaison group had followed me in to where I had come up to the guide. I must hand it to those boys. Nothing but the hand of God ever got them through the two hundred yards and more of that skyline target bombardment in safety. I opened my map-case, took these liaison boys to an opening of our shelter, and showed them where we were. We matched up the map points with the locations of the real terrain. Then we sent out the boys by twos, to go through the several lines of trenches opening near us, and leading off—we knew not where. Their mission was to find Commandant Favre.

We had not to wait long. Within a very few minutes one of

the couples was back, ready to guide me to the Commandant's dugout.

A battery of "Whiz-Bangs" had opened up on us. It was our first acquaintance with "Whiz-Bangs" and we didn't like them. A "Whiz-Bang" is an Austrian "88," named "Whiz-Bang," according to the principles of onomatopoeia, on account of the sounds of the shell in arriving. The German "77s" or "155s," or in fact any calibre, sounded warnings of long-drawn-out screeches, during the entire course of projection, by which the experienced soldier could judge with fair accuracy of the direction of flight and the probable point of landing. The Austrian "88" offers no such courtesy of warning. It's all over in a second.

"Whiz-Bang!" The shell has arrived and exploded. If you are within the zone of dispersion, you are (as our men used to say) "a poor boy." There is no possibility of avoiding the penalties of that dispersion by dodging temporarily into cover.

In due course, full understanding with Commandant Favre as to the details of relief, was reached.

By small groups, and with great care and patience the men of my battalion, under the leadership of Bates, MacClinton and Seibel, successfully relieved the men of the 361st and 363rd French Infantry—in broad daylight, under heavy fire, and with less than ten casualties. It should be understood that the battalion Machine Gun Company attached one section of two guns to each rifle company. The balance of the company, consisting of three sections of two guns each, remained in the rear with the one platoon from each company held back as support, subject to the direct orders of the battalion commander.

Our first company went over the top shortly before three o'clock. We moved from the left ("B" Company) with "C" and "D" starting successively at fifteen-minute intervals, so as to admit of the long flanking turns to the right (after a straight northerly descent from the hill) necessary to form a straight line of advance in a north-easterly direction.

From my post of command on the hill-top I watched the men

work their way down the sharp descent of the hill, through a foliage growth of considerable thickness, and deploy upon the open plain beyond, into a well organized line. I cannot find words to speak too warmly in praise of the work of the officers and platoon sergeants, in leading the men across that open plain of shell-fire and hell-fire, and in holding them under splendid military control.

When the hands of my watch advised me that the right company ("D") had started its descent to join the line being formed out in front, I signalled to my liaison group, and commenced to pick my way down the hill.

Near the foot of the hill, under cover of dense shrubbery, I was advancing quietly. Suddenly, from around a sharp turn in the path, I heard voices, speaking in German.

With automatic pistol at "ready," I sneaked up to the turn and peeped through a cut in the foliage. A group of our men had surrounded a German soldier, and 1st Lieutenant Seibel was questioning him in German.

As I stepped out into the open path Mr. Seibel saluted and reported: "Sir, I congratulate you and report a prisoner."

The prisoner was a thick-set private soldier, of about 5 ft. 8 inches in height, with his face masked in a very full and very unkempt red beard. He wore, as head gear, the round gray cap with red band. It was a curious thing about the Germans, how seldom they wore their steel helmets when on special duty, alone or in small groups.

The red-bearded prisoner took one look at me, and in that look he recognized a superior officer, carrying a pistol at "ready." He let loose a perfect flood of German language. Of the words I could not understand a syllable; but his intonation was one of supplication for mercy. I asked Seibel to interpret.

"He begs you not to shoot him, Major," Mr. Seibel explained. "He says he did only what he was ordered and compelled to do."

"And what did he do?" I inquired.

"Private William Haynie found him concealed in one of the dugouts of the Northern slope of the hill here, Sir; and he admits that he signaled directions for the barrage that is covering the plain there, through which we must advance."

"Send him back to Regimental Headquarters, under guard of two reliable men; and have your men report back to you on the southern edge of the town. Proceed with your advance."

Shortly after I reached the southern edge of the town, Sergeant Vidito of Machine Gun Company rushed up to me and reported that he had just killed a sniper concealed in a clump of bushes about 40 yards away. I commended the Sergeant. Then he wanted me to go with him to examine the remains of his victim; but I declined the invitation. The bodies of dead men in those days offered to us no interest of curiosity. I directed Sergeant Vidito to remain with his section, take cover and await orders.

Company "C" had gone into and was working its way through the middle sections of the town. Company "D" was advancing through the right border streets. Both of these companies were meeting with resistance. Company "B" was entrenched near the Southern edge of the left end of the town. There was no fighting being offered in their front; and Bates reported to me that he was holding his company intact, so as to be available for a special reinforcement if one should be needed. The support elements were entrenched with me in a roadside ditch bounding the Southern edge of the town.

My liaison group, however, was missing. Corporal William H. Cooper of that group was the only man near me and ready for service. I assigned to Cooper the task of organizing and commanding a new group. He picked up two men from each company, and within a few minutes created for me a first class emergency service. Sergeant Major Marshall had been requisitioned by Regimental Headquarters to remain there as a kind of representative of the 1st Battalion. Corporal Cooper, in addition to acting as emergency liaison sergeant, did the work of sergeant-major. For three days he filled a number of gaps for me, and filled them well. I have always, since those days, felt for Cooper a full measure of gratitude and affection.

As we lay in our ditch that afternoon of the twenty-ninth of September, I could not keep my mind from marvelling at the contrast between the details of an actual experience of the so-called "storming of a town" and of the traditional activities.

According to all rules of the game that I had ever read, I should have been dashing madly in front of our troops, waving my hat to inspire them, and calling upon my soldiers to "Give 'em hell!" as we would rush into an entrenched line of fire-delivering defenders. According to actual experience, if I had deported myself in any such manner, no more than a score of men could possibly have seen or heard me. The front of our advancing line was nearly a half mile in width. There were no great numbers of enemy soldiers to be seen, and our own men for the most part took mighty good care to do their rushing in prone position, wriggling forward like a snake, or upon hands and knees, if there was sufficient cover to the front to warrant so bold an attitude. Most of the fire that impeded our progress (outside, of course, of the fire of artillery) was machine gun fire, directed, as a result of carefully drawn plans, down the avenues of the town, and from hidden islands of comparative safety well out on the plain to the north of the town.

And, while the men were performing deeds of heroism in undignified postures, I was lying in a ditch, as a rule, to the rear of these men, receiving and despatching letters at a rate which would have done justice to an efficiency expert directing the campaign of a mail order house one week after the publication of its fall catalogue.

But, while I was certainly not qualifying for the rôle of a Sheridan riding the Valley of Shenandoah, still I was gathering the news items of a great little drama.

As I lay in my ditch for almost an hour that afternoon the "copy boys" kept me busy.

Lieutenant Holden of the Machine Gun Company had captured a German machine gun, and turned it on the enemy.

A "77," mounted at the southern main entrance to the town and firing during our advance, had been captured by the first assault wave of "C" company. The final shot had been fired from a cellar a hundred feet away, by means of a long wire.

An ammunition dump filled with live shells, a few yards from this field gun, had had a bon-fire started in it; but a "C" company man (to our shame we did not get his name) had crawled into the dump and put out the fire.

Second Lieutenant Hundley of "B" Company had been wounded in the arm and sent to the rear.

A large grenade dump on east end of the middle of the town had been taken by "D" Company.

First Lieutenant Robb, in driving out a machine gun crew from a brick house on the north-east corner of town, had been wounded in the left side by a bullet, had used his first-aid packet for bandage and refused evacuation.

A detachment of the 372nd U. S. Infantry (apparently lost), 20 men under command of Captain Coleman, had reported through Captain MacClinton of "C" Company and been assigned to duty.

First Lieutenant Vaughn of "D" Company had been wounded and sent to the rear.

Second Lieutenant Page of "C" Company had located a nest of three enemy machine guns in a position on plain to the north of the church in town and requested reinforcements to attack the position.

First Lieutenant Robb had been wounded again, this time in the arm, by shrapnel, but insisted upon carrying on.

"D" Company had established "F.M." (automatic rifle) posts in the second story of the brick house cleared by Robb, and was firing upon machine gun nests upon the plain, to permit "C" and "D" companies to establish lines outside of town in ditches to the north.

At five o'clock I sent a report back to Regimental Headquarters:

1st Batt.
9/29/18
5 P.M.

No. 3
To C. O. 369th

The town (Sechault) is filled with M. G. snipers. We are cleaning slowly but surely. Cannot tell yet how soon we can go forward. Shall we halt when too dark to see?

My Hdqtrs Group seems to be lost. They were in rear of our Right in the trench position. Please try to send them up.

A. W. LITTLE
Major.

An enemy plane swooped down and flew swiftly along the full length of the ditch in which we lay, flying from north west to south east, and firing upon us with machine gun. This plane flew so low that we could see the features of the face of one of the Germans, as he leaned over the side of the ship to look at us.

Shortly before five o'clock, I was puzzled to see quite a big line of colored soldiers advancing across the plain, and coming towards Sechault. My men were all up—who could these men be? A few seconds later, Captain Eric Winston of "H" Company, 2nd Battalion, staggered up to where I was and threw himself in the ditch beside me.

"Cobb's killed!" Winston half gasped, half sobbed out his report. Cobb killed! What a loss! Captain Frederick H. Cobb, for fifteen months commander of Company "E," one of the crack organizations of the regiment, had been acting as major of the 2nd Battalion ever since Major Monson Morris had left us in June. Cobb was a sterling officer, and he had handled his battalion well; but his promotion had been withheld.

"How did it happen, Eric?" I inquired.

"Why, sir, the battalion was being held for your support, as you know, upon the rear slope of that eastern spur of Bellevue

Signal. We believed we were well sheltered there; but suddenly, they found us and opened up with heavy shell fire. Cobb got his right at the beginning—with almost a direct hit. A piece of the shell took off the entire back of his head. Of course he never suffered—that's one thing."

"Who are all these men coming across?"

"They're our men. We couldn't stay in that place. Clark took command and decided to move up to you."

Just then, Captain John Holley Clark arrived and reported the 2nd Battalion with a strength of about a hundred and fifty.

I was glad that he had come. A report had just arrived from "C" Company scouts of what appeared to be a counter attack forming to the north.

I turned over the final mopping up of the town to Clark and his 2nd Battalion, ordered "B" company and all my support platoons and machine gun sections forward, and set about the preparation for the meeting of a counter attack.

To the C. O. of Company "C" I sent the following note:

9/29/18
5:40 P.M.

Captain MacClinton

I am sending M.G. Co. to North end of town. Bates is in town now with his company.

I am coming forward myself.

A. W. L.

To Colonel Hayward, I sent my fourth report:

1st Batt.
5:45 P.M.

4th Message.

Scouts report appearance of a counter attack from North. Am forming on North East end of town to meet attack. 2nd Batt. is in town cleaning what is left.

A. W. LITTLE
Major.

To
C. O. 369th

The counter attack did not materialize. If it had come I believe we should have given a good account of ourselves. In the dusk of the evening that was gradually changing into darkness, we were able to dispose our troops in such manner as to yield to us the advantages in combat that accrue to defenders of an organized position. There were ditches all around the outside of Sechault. They were by no means all connecting, and some of them were in strangely irregular positions. They served us well, however, as trenches. We were fortunate in finding them, as our men had, for the most part, thrown away their entrenching tools as useless incumbrances.

Sechault was a small town set out in the center of a great plain. We established our trench lines upon three sides of the town. The fourth side (the south-east) we left open. We were confident that there was no enemy strength behind us. The trenches occupied were approximately a hundred yards beyond town street limits. Covering these trenches and the plains in front of them, from all sorts of strategic angles, we had our machine gun emplacements set. We were in good shape as to machine guns. In addition to our own twelve, we had one German gun. Also, we had a half dozen or more of the 2nd Battalion guns. And there was plenty of ammunition.

Battalion Headquarters was established in the wreck of an old stone house which had one room with a roof over it and but one window to mask. This house was near the north-west edge of the town and totally unsuited for the use of a P.C.—therefore we chose it. Fifty yards away from the P.C. was another wreck of a stone house which had many window openings. We named that house the "Block House," and planned it for use as a redoubt, in the event of our first lines outside the town being driven in.

1st Lieutenants Richardson Pratt and Hugh A. Page are entitled to the greatest of praise for their intelligent and courageous energy in personally establishing the infantry posts of resistance in the trenches outside the town.

Captain Coleman, and his men of the 372 U. S. Infantry are entitled to a word of appreciation for the cheerful and satisfactory manner in which they performed their duty under trying circumstances. A well disciplined extra unit, even of a half platoon, was a welcome reinforcement to us that night.

Circulation through the town was difficult and dangerous. Every avenue and most of the cross streets were covered by enemy machine guns.

To cross the street or to step out from the cover of a building was to invite a stream of machine gun bullets—and to have the invitation promptly accepted. We therefore adopted the habit of sending these invitations only by the exposure of one officer or man at a time. When it would be necessary to cross a street the person to cross would jump out from cover quickly and take it on the run. By such methods, after some practice, we rendered the German machine gun barrages as but little more than salutes.

At about seven o'clock, Captain Clarke reported to me with his men of the 2nd Battalion. He had combed the town, and believed that it was clear of enemy soldiers. We agreed that, in view of our depleted ranks, it would be well to handle the two battalions as one consolidated battalion, instead of as a two-battalion regiment. We sent the company "F" men, therefore, to Company "B," as a reinforcement platoon. "G" Company was made a part of "C." "H" Company was thrown into "D." There was no confusion or question as to seniority for command by this plan, as the only 2nd Battalion company commander who would have outranked his corresponding company commander in the 1st Battalion was Captain Winston of "H" in combination with 1st Lieutenant Seibel of "D." As this complication first presented itself, Captain Clark interrupted to show that there was no complication, as he had sent Winston to the rear for gas treatment.

Shortly before eight o'clock, I received the following communication from Colonel Hayward:

29 Sept. 18.

19 H 05

C. O. 1st 369th

You will hold the village of Sechault tonight assisted by the 2nd Bn.

The high command informed of your situation and will act accordingly; also informed of possibility of counter-attack and will provide for same.

2. The 363rd on your right and 163rd on your left have been positively ordered to establish liaison with you tonight and to establish their lines up to your village.

3. Established small outposts on enemy side of village to give warning of any attack.

4. Keep constant touch with 2nd Bn. Show them this order and each Bn. send into Regtl. P.C. four reliable runners under an officer or superior N. C. O.

Wm. Hayward
Col.

That communication confirmed the growing horrible suspicion that we were alone, a mile or more in advance of the rest of the division, out in an open plain, with a long night ahead of us, and subject to being surrounded and cut off.

According to our orders we had been supposed to form the point of a wedge in our advance that afternoon. The two French Infantry Regiments, the 363rd and 163rd, were to have been echeloned to our right and left rears respectively, at distances of 400 metres.

For more than two hours I had had scouting parties out in an endeavor to establish liaison with our supporting regiments, protecting our flanks; but reports were always the same—"No trace of any troops within sight or hearing of the points where they should have been."

Shortly after the receipt of the foregoing communication I received another note:

29 Sept. 18

C. O. 1st Battn.

Division believes counter-attack improbable but will prepare for same.

In case of heavy bombardment of your village or any special situation arising you will have to exercise your own best judgment on the spot.

The most effective way of meeting an enemy bombardment will probably be to move all the troops 150 or 200 metres ahead of the village where they should dig in and protect their line by outposts. Much is left to good judgment of two Bn. Cdrs. concerned.

By order of COLONEL HAYWARD
R. WHITTLESEY
1st Lieut. Actg. Adjt.

Pursuant to the order to send back more men and an officer to serve as additional liaison men at Regimental Headquarters, I had decided that the only officer I could spare was my adjutant. So, I informed 1st Lieutenant Webb that he would have to go. It was tough sledding, but I couldn't deplete my line voluntarily. The enemy was doing that rapidly enough.

Shortly after we had learned positively that we had no flanking support—that we were, in a sense, marooned—an officer came to me and urged me to withdraw from the town, and fall back to the line of the Division. When I refused his advice he became insistent, saying that I had no right to hold the command in such a position. I quoted my orders and told him that I had no right to do otherwise. The officer said it was suicidal, that we should be wiped out. I answered that even that extreme was covered by regulations providing for obedience to orders. The officer then said that I couldn't hold the men, that they would run out on me. I expressed my confidence that the officer was wrong in his prognostication; but allowed that we'd stay there anyway. Future events proved that the officer *was* wrong. Our men proved their title "good soldiers" that night.

As closely assembled as we were during that strenuous period it was not possible for that conversation about our probable predicament to go unheard. Equally it was our privilege to hear any conversation that took place between the men. So, a short time after that officer had retired, I overheard the following bit:— Said an unseen private to an invisible sergeant, "Sergeant, does you think we-all's goin' back? To which came the reply, "Hell no! We's only just got here!"

Good soldiers? I'll say so.

Dr. Keenan had come forward with his sanitary detachment, and established a dressing station in a building near the southern edge of the town, a building in which he had been able to rig up door and window covers so as to provide for lights. As I recognized the doctor's voice in the dark as he reported, I breathed a prayer of thankfulness for the devotion of that brave medical officer. Our casualties were hideous and continuous.

I remember that I commenced to suffer tremendously under the strain of the situation; and that I sought a few moments of solitude, to pull myself together. I paced up and down outside of my headquarters, with head bowed and hands clasped behind my back. Adjutant Webb found me there as he sought me to report himself on the way to Regimental Headquarters with his detail.

"Major," he said and his voice was pleading in earnestness, "Major, please don't stay out here; they'll get you, sure, if you do."

"My God," I answered (and I'm afraid there may have been a sob in my voice). "I believe that's what I want! What do I know about warfare? What have I done this afternoon? Lost half my battalion—driven hundreds of innocent men to their death. It would be a relief, my boy—a relief!"

Then Webb threw his arm about my shoulders, and spoke to me as a son might have spoken, in a tone of tenderness and of affection—this lad whose twenty-second birthday I had helped to celebrate a few months before.

"Please don't talk or feel that way, Major," the boy plead. "I can't see you give way to despair; we've been too close these past few weeks. It's no longer the superiority of the age or rank

293

that counts with me, Major. It's something deeper; and you've just got to come in." Half a minute more, and Webb had gone on his mission; but somehow or other, I felt a lot better.

Back in our P.C., we sat on the floor in darkness—Clark, MacClinton, Seibel and I believe some others besides Corporal Cooper and his liaison squad. Over in a corner, by himself and very quiet, sat 1st Lieutenant Robb. He was suffering from his wounds and quite weak; but he persistently refused to quit. He would be all right when the time for his relief should come, and he would be all right for the fight to come in the morning, too. He was just resting, that was all.

Out of the darkness came the voice of Sergeant-Major Marshall:

"Is the Major there? . . . Good! . . . Sir Major Sir, I've got a detail at the lower end of the town with bread. I thought you might be getting hungry. I knew you'd used the last of your rations this morning. Yes, sir, we've got 80 loaves—those big round French loaves. Yes, sir, I called for volunteers to help me, and got permission to bring them up. Yes, sir, I got all the volunteers I wanted. I could have gotten double the number if I'd needed them. And who do you think was one of them, Sir Major? Captain Fish! You know he's not on duty. He's just visiting as an observer, and he asked me to let him come along without rank. He's down there with the detail now, sir. Yes sir, the bread's carried in shelter halves. Bring it right up to you here, sir? Yes, sir, in a minute."

When that bread arrived I had a circle formed in the dark, a circle of officers sitting upon the floor, tailor fashion. Each officer was directed to take his knife and proceed to cut the loaves each into eight equal parts. An eighth of one of those big French loaves was a lot of bread. Then the platoon chiefs were called back, one after another, from their posts on the line, from left and right and working towards the middle, and sent back again each with a detail carrying exactly the right number of hunks of bread to provide a hunk for each man. And so, in stealth, and with patience, the men of the 1st and 2nd Battalions were fed—the only food that they had had for eighteen hours and the only food that they were to get for thirty hours more.

During the night, a messenger arrived with a note requiring a memorandum showing the co-ordinates of the position of our improvised trenches. The report was to be used as a guide for the French artillery the following morning, to clear the way for our advance. Now, to furnish that information was not the simplest of jobs. Two groups of men had to work at each of the openings to our room, the window and the door. One group upon the outside and one upon the inside—holding up blankets so as to block out (or rather, block in) all light from the single flash with which we were going to work. Before we flashed the light we got everything in readiness. The map was laid out flat on the floor and I was ready with writing pad and pencil. 1st Lieutenant Pratt, who, having personally placed most of the men in the trenches, was the best informed man we had as to their exact location, was called in to read to me the co-ordinates. As he read, I wrote. It was all done within a minute or two; but even that time had been too long for safety. There must have been some imperfection in our light shield. Just as we had concluded our report a shell came smashing in—too close for comfort. For a half hour or so, we moved our P.C. over to the "Block House."

I had given strict orders that our men were not to fire unless the enemy were to come upon our trench positions, so close as to be actually seen in the dark. These orders were strictly obeyed. All night long, the enemy tried to coax us into an exposure of our position by fire. From both sides and from the front we were fired upon constantly; and illuminating flares were thrown up. But our men held their peace, and the enemy, kept in ignorance of the positions and the strength of our outlying posts, made no rush upon us.

Between two and three o'clock of the morning of the 30th, a body of men, apparently about half a platoon, approached our lines from the north-west. Our men remained silent until the patrol was within less than fifteen paces. Then they challenged. A number of voices shouted back—"Kamerade—Kamerade!" Our men warned the approaching party, once more, to "Halt!" But no halt was made. Instead, the men of the patrol continued to advance upon our lines. The order "FIRE!" was given. Then the men of the patrol halted, grounded arms, and raised their hands. One of the party had been killed by our volley, and three had been wounded. The men actually *were* comrades—a patrol from the French 163rd Infantry. It was a sad incident, but one in which I believe the French were wholly to blame. Experience of nine months in front line work taught us of the 369th that the sentry is in fact as well as in theory the monarch of his post; and that the only safe plan of conduct after hearing a challenge in the dark is to halt and lie down—and then proceed with the conversation.

Just prior to the occurrence of this lamentable incident, we received a call from 1st Lieutenant Tessier, Aide-de-Camp to the General Lebouc. Tessier was guided to us, through the dark, by our own Adjutant Webb.

Tessier brought the compliments and encouragement of our General. That man was a true leader in his understanding of human nature. Lebouc never depressed his subsidiary commanders with complicated orders. He never indulged in mere fault finding. And he was always prompt with some graceful act or word of commendation, where he could see that the men of his command were doing the best they could.

The night wore on. There were many alarms, but no serious incidents other than the one of tragedy in which we fired upon the French patrol. Just before daybreak, a runner came in from the lines in the trenches with a startling report. There were evidences of activity all over the plain to our north. It looked like an attack in force to be launched at that favorite hour for raids— the hour when it is darkest just before dawn.

All company officers on relief rushed to their posts. Warnings were sent to the several machine gun groups. The Headquarters personnel was disposed at the windows and loop holes of the "Block House." The garrison of Sechault was *en alert!*

Some wag, kicking awake a delinquent group of sleepers or hiders, called out a warning order of assembly:—*"All out for Custer's last stand!"*

There was a half hour of tense waiting. The men who knew the true situation, and the officers, made remarks of comment upon the call of the wag for Custer's last stand, seeing in it a justification of that time honored adage of many a true word being at times spoken in jest.

There was no suggestion of any running out, though. If that threatened fight had occurred, it would have been a real fight. The boys from Harlem had loosened their knives in their sheaths.

While we waited, a lively shelling of artillery was smashed into the town. The flashes of light, and the noise of the explosions added to the realism of the picture of drama in which we were playing a part. And, then, true to the rules of melodrama, where each scene of tense excitement is followed quickly by one of relieving farce-comedy, one of our wonderful colored artists of humor made us all laugh.

We had all, without doubt, been thinking of home. When the volunteers of the Old 15th thought of home, they thought of the men who had waited to be drafted, and who, by waiting, had been able to enjoy the society of the girls of Harlem—the girls our boys had left behind them.

Out of the darkness and the quiet that followed the arrival of a number of shells near to where we were standing-to, a rich and penetrating voice arose, in clear tones of farce-pathos:—

"Mah Gaud, boys—how dose brayve draaft sojers must be sufferin'! Et mus' be a turrible naght at Yaphank!"

Morning dawned, and the activities of advance were resumed.

Just after daybreak, the following order was received:

30 Sept. 18
1 H 30

Order of Operations:—

Today continuation of the march towards Challerange the left in advance. The 162nd will march on Petits Rosiers, Challerange and west of Challerange. The 369th in echelon to the rear, and on the right, marching towards Ferme Les Rosiers by the east of the Parc; distance between the leading elements of the 163rd and the leading elements of the 369th —300 metres. The 363rd in echelon to the rear on the right in liaison with the Division L'Ardenel, distance between leading elements of 369th and leading elements of 363rd, 400 metres.

II. Attack will be preceded by artillery preparation—no rolling barrage. The artillery will execute before the hour H and each support group for regiment as a principle some concentration fire on the covers and assembly points of the enemy. From H the fire of the Field Artillery will jump from cover to cover and in successive bounds to be regulated by direct understanding between the regiment and the supporting group. Minimum distance between advanced elements of the infantry and field artillery fire 400 metres.

III. H = 7 h. Infantry goes forward under above described conditions each regiment marching by successive battalions in each assigned direction. Local resistance to be overwhelmed by outflanking. The 363rd will be largely echeloned in depth to the rear and the right in liaison with the Division L'Ardenel, insuring the protection of the flank of the Division.

IV. P.C. of D.I. Croissant. I.D. Shelter 0254—later on Bellevue Signal.

Lebouc

\*   \*   \*   \*   \*   \*   \*   \*   \*   \*

In order to form lines properly for the new advance and in order, also, to clear the terrain as well as possible for an artillery preparation, at 5 o'clock in the morning I drew back the men from the trenches (ditches). In order not to lose to the enemy the cover of the ditches, we left one holding squad for each company sector, and we left in place all of the machine gun sections except one on each extreme flank which we had established in the dark the night before, in order to be able to sweep the plain in front of our lines with direct grazing fire, if we should have been called upon to meet an attack in force.

In withdrawing from the trenches, we unfortunately, exposed ourselves liberally; and, within a few minutes, the enemy artillery made the town too hot to hold us. I ordered a second shift of position, therefore. And this time, the men managed to sneak back in small groups, without attracting the attention of the enemy observers, and take position in the ditch at the south edge of the town, which had served as a Support shelter the afternoon before.

In this position, the companies were properly organized. Before the Zero hour, 7 o'clock, we were ready and waiting for our guides to our left—the 163rd French Infantry.

At the Zero hour there was no sign of any French troops upon either flank, or, in fact (in so far as our observation was to be considered), anywheres in the world. And there was no artillery preparation that we could discover with the naked eye.

Finally, the French regiment to our left did come up, and pass us to go forward. The enemy shelling of Sechault and the terrain in front of it was continuous and heavy. We lost distance and time getting started; and the first waves of the 163rd disappeared into the woods of *Les Petite Rosiers*. I believe we were about half an hour (or a kilometer) too far in the rear of the movement. Well, the day before our flanking supports were 18 hours and several kilometers—behind us.

At twenty-three minutes past eight I sent back the following reports:

1st Batt.
9/3/18
8:23

C. O. 3rd Batt.

1st and 2nd Batt. are commencing advance. Compass 40° magnetic.

A. W. LITTLE
Major.

1st & 2nd Batt.
9/30/18
8:23 A.M.

*1st Message*
To
C. O. 369th Regt.

1st and 2nd Batt. consolidated are commencing advance.

Future reports will be made by relay to Center of Intelligence at Sechault.

I am short of men and must keep relay line as short as possible.

A. W. LITTLE
Major.

It should be borne in mind that the 3rd Battalion had become our support; and that 1st Lieutenant Landon had established an optic signal station in Sechault, referred to as "Center of Intelligence."

As soon as all elements of our line had been well started, I worked my way, accompanied by the Battalion Headquarters group, to the front, where we could study intelligently the progress of events. Captain Clark, as second in command, was of invaluable support. He was cool and collected. I advised with him constantly, and received the great moral encouragement of sensing from his expressions that we were doing the best we could. First Lieutenant Delafield as C. O. Machine Gun Company accompanied us to our observation post out in front of our lines, and remained with us until I sent him back to the base of his company. The liaison group stuck by me, too, in a fine spirit of fidelity and devotion to duty.

During the first hour after our start, I received numerous reports from the center and right companies ("C" and "D") advising me of machine gun obstacles, and of casualties. "B" company, on the left was having no trouble, and the 163rd French, to "B" Company's left, had, apparently, had clear sailing.

Clark and I studied the plain carefully, and we believed that

300

we had spotted the machine gun nests that were holding us up. At about 10 o'clock I sent word to Capt. Bates to attempt to surround the nests by working his way well to the front and sending a platoon or more off to the east, to attack the Boche from the rear. This movement we covered by having 1st Lieutenant John H. Connor take a section of machine guns out to our ditch line, and graze the plain with a general fire direction to the sharp North East.

The following report was sent to the rear:

*Landon*

We are trying to get behind the M.G. nests by going far out around our left (enemy right) flank. Also we are going to use one M.G. on the positions.

Do try to have Boche barrage stopped while we are working.

A. W. L.

Then came a long and anxious period of watchful waiting. Clark and I were lying down in the open, about 25 feet apart. The liaison group ranged behind us with distances and intervals of about ten paces between each man and his neighbor. Things were not going real well with us. I believe both Clark and I were depressed in spirits. Clark had been married while the regiment had been at Camp Whitman. His baby boy had been born while we were in the Bois d'Hauzy. As we lay out in front of Sechault that morning of September 30th, Holley Clark unbuttoned his blouse, and drew out from his breast pocket a photograph. He studied it earnestly for a long time and his face seemed to soften in expression. Then he looked over at me. He smiled. "Like to see my boy?" he said. And, as he spoke, he shied the bit of cardboard over to me. It was a lovely picture of a mother and her baby, with cheeks pressed together, and eyes looking straight out into the eyes of the soldier husband and father—in France.

"I'd like to see that boy, sometime." The young father spoke in a quiet tone, but with an expression of great wistfulness. And, as he spoke, there was a "WHIZ" and a "THUD"! A great

301

shell had struck midway between us where we lay, and half buried itself in the earth.

For an instant, I believe we each instinctively closed our eyes. And then, we opened them, looked first at that shell where it lay, unexploded, exactly as it had struck, and then into each other's eyes.

"A dud, by God! You're just shot full of luck, Major!" drawled Clark. "Thanks, yes, I think it's lovely, too," added my second in command, as he pocketed the photograph which I had shied back to him.

At about noon, Bates reported the accomplishment of his special mission. More than 20 Germans had run out from the shell holes in which they had been concealed with their machine guns and retired to the woods to our east, upon the approach of the "B" company men.

Upon the completion of liaison of all units of the consolidated Battalions, we proceeded, once more, to move forward.

Regimental Headquarters was advised in the following message.

12:33 P.M.

*Landon*

We are going forward. Bates got out and did as planned.

A. W. L.

Our men entered the woods at about one o'clock.

We met with determined resistance.

At 1.45 we reinforced the line by throwing in all supports.

At two o'clock I sent back a report:

2. P.M.<br>9/30/18

C. O. 369th

Battalion first line now in woods before the *Fme Roselle*.

Lots of M. G. and snipers.

Progress slow.

A. W. LITTLE<br>Major.

JUST BEFORE OUR COLORS WERE DECORATED. PLAINS OF MUN-
CHAUSEN, DEC. 13, 1918.

COL. HAYWARD     MAJ. LITTLE          LT. COL. PICKERING

35591

OUR COLORS AFTER DECORATION, PLAINS OF MUNCHAUSEN, DEC. 13, 1918

At about this time, a demure looking little colored boy approached me, reported that he came from Lieutenant Rice (Regimental Liaison Officer) and presented me with a pair of pigeons. It was too absurd! Our party had gotten almost to the hand to hand stage (including officers). For five days, not a word had we of constructive help from the department of modern methods of communications not a word except a constant cry for more and still more men to be taken from our fighting lines to serve as runners. And now, at this desperate period, to send me *birds*— without anybody to take care of them!

I fumed.

A shell ripped in, close to us.

"Well, Sir Major Sir," said the boy, in calm respectfulness, "I guess I'd better be going now."

"You take this damned bird cage back with you!" I thundered. And the incident was closed.

After an effort of almost two hours to get through those woods, I recognized that the time had come to apply a lesson covering an exactly similar situation in which we had been taught what to do, in the manoeuvers near Somme-Bionne, during the week preceding September 25th.

I sent out the following order:—

1st Batt.<br>2:55 P.M.

To

Cos B—C—D.

Draw your men out of the woods and *creep* back three hundred yards. I am asking for artillery to reduce M.Gs.

A. W. LITTLE<br>Major.

To Colonel Hayward I sent the following report:—

1st Batt.
9/30/18
3:00

To C. O. 369th Regt.

Cannot get through woods without artillery. About a dozen M. G. nests reported. Shrubs not high enough to afford cover for surrounding. I am withdrawing men to 300 meters in front of woods. Entire section mapped should be heavily shelled.

A. W. LITTLE
Major.

To this note I attached a tracing of my map, showing the area to be cleared by artillery.

The withdrawal was accomplished in good order. A well organized line was established in a little stream bed running across the plain. Then we commenced to tabulate our strength. The losses of the day had been heavy. The most sensational casualty report came from 1st Lieutenant Robb, shortly after we had settled in our position of withdrawal to wait for the artillery requested.

Robb reported by note that, a few minutes after my withdrawal order had been promulgated through Company "D," an enemy plane had flown low over their lines, and spotted the post of command, in a shell hole. A few minutes later an enemy shell plumped into the hole—a direct hit. The company commander, 1st Lieutenant George F. Seibel, was killed. Lieutenant Ernest A. McNish, also was killed; and a number of men were killed or wounded. Mr. Robb reported himself as wounded once more. He further reported that he had remained on duty in command of the company until the withdrawal had been completed, and the company properly organized in the new position; and that "now," he had turned the command over to the 1st Sergeant (there being no officer left) and was about to start to work his way back to the battalion dressing station.

In addition to Robb's three woundings, received one at a

time during those twenty-four hours, he had had the grip of his pistol shot away, and a hole had been shot through his helmet. In my report of the heroic conduct of 1st Lieutenant George S. Robb, I tried to do him justice. I am happy to be able to record the fact that, in recognition of Robb's services, he was decorated with the United States Congressional Medal of Honor—and thus became one of the select class of 78 Americans in the World War to be awarded our highest mark of distinction, for valor.

At about four o'clock I received a note from Captain David A. L'Esperance, in command of the 3rd Battalion, advising me that his command (cut to 137 men and 7 officers) was in the ditch at the south edge of Sechault, and ready and anxious to obey my orders to come forward and help—if I could use them. I acknowledged receipt with grateful and affectionate expressions, explained the meaning of our maneuver, and asked L'Esperance to remain where he was for the present.

Then I called the 1st and 2nd Battalion officers together, in conference.

Opinion was unanimous that our command was "all in" physically. The spirit of the survivors, however, was magnificent: It seemed to us that it would be a wrong to abuse that spirit.

Acting upon that unanimously expressed sense of the officers present, I directed Captain Clark to report to Colonel Hayward and, in my name, request a relief or a rest, for our consolidated command. I outlined the form in which Clark was to make his presentment, and expressed my belief that, on account of his personal intimacy with the Colonel (in civil life, Clark had been Public Service Commissioner Haywards' Secretary), our message would be better received that way, than in any other way.

Captain Clark answered that, of course, he was there to obey my orders, and that he would carry the message if I insisted; but that his relations to Colonel Hayward had always been strictly those of a follower, and that he couldn't conceive of the Colonel listening receptively to any such recommendations as we had in mind, if they were to come orally from himself.

So I said, "Well, let's wait a minute, then. I'll see if I can write it. If I can, we'll send a note."

A few minutes later I submitted my note (to be sent through Landon) for approval or criticism:

4:35 P.M.

Dear Harold:—

Please say to the Col. for me that in my opinion no attempt further should be made to go through those woods without either tanks or full demolition of concrete pill boxes by heavy artillery.

The 2nd Batt. has about 100 men and 3 officers.

The 1st Batt. has about 300 men and 9 or 10 officers.

The 3rd Batt. has about 137 men and 7 officers.

I believe every man will obey orders to go in those woods if orders are given; but, under present conditions, they will all stay there—and the 15th N. Y. will be a memory.

Our men are wonderful. Without 5% of normal food or sleep they are standing by; but great weakness is upon us all.

I hope that a relief can be made.

Also, that no unsupported advance by any soldiers be ordered through those woods.

A. W. LITTLE
Major.

The note was approved, and despatched. I had sacrificed my chance for the immortality of a fame of a Marco Bozzaris, or of a Custer—but, the three combat battalions of our regiment were saved.

By return runner, came the following two notes from Landon:—

Major Little—

This note just received from regimental headquarters. The French artillery you just heard, I suppose is what was referred to in the note attached.

Please send me another runner that knows your position, as one has been wounded.

LANDON

P. S. Your longer note just received, I am sending up to Colonel by runner.

The accompanying note was as follows:—

Sept. 30/18
16:15 o'clock

Major Little—

The artillery fire you asked for will be given. After its completion, continue your advance as before.

COLONEL HAYWARD
LT. COL. W. A. PICKERING

The French artillery fire referred to consisted of about half a dozen shots. I had no choice but to obey, and to trust that the written order, when found upon me, might fall into honest hands—to place the blame for the disaster about to occur, where it belonged.

We were about to start upon our renewal of attack, in fact our scouts had already gone forward, when a breathless runner handed me a note, marked *"Urgent."*

30 Sept. 18
17 h 30

To
C. O. 1st Battn. 369 R.I.U.S.

Latest orders from the I.D. is to the effect that the 363rd will relieve us and pass through your lines tonight.

Sit tight and hold on until the relief comes.

By order of COLONEL HAYWARD
R. WHITTLESEY
1st Lt. Acting Adjutant.

*God!*

I have heard, but I cannot vouch for the accuracy of the report, that when my request for relief reached Colonel Hayward, he expressed himself as thankful, and immediately went about getting into touch with Division Headquarters. According to the report, the Colonel had been asking for our relief for some time, without success; and, when my note came from the very front, he clutched at it as new and indisputable evidence of the seriousness of the situation, in corroboration of his views.

The 363rd Infantry of France relieved us at about 1 o'clock of the morning of October 1st. We doubled with them in the trenches for the balance of the night. At about 6 o'clock in the morning, the French artillery gave the woods that I had mapped a regular shelling; and shortly after 8 o'clock, our French comrades left us, to take up their advance. I understand that they passed through the woods and reached the objective, Rosiers Farm, without opposition. Our work and sacrifices of the day before had not been wholly in vain.

At about seven o'clock that morning, a detail had reached our lines with food. The food was welcome. After thirty hours or more of fasting, everybody needed something to eat; but we were all so cold that we couldn't really enjoy ourselves. There were no blankets left and our clothes were saturated with the moisture of the atmosphere.

Captain Clark had managed to get himself wetter than most of us. After the French had relieved us, we all gave way to the desire to sleep. We scooped out little shelves for ourselves to lie upon, in the sides of the brook bank. There was always danger, though, of rolling off the shelf, into the brook. Clark conceived and executed the fine idea of overcoming this danger by extending his shelf all the way across the brook into the other bank. He couldn't roll off. Fine! Soon he was tearing off a wonderful sleep. About an hour later he dreamed he was lying in cold water. He awoke, to find his dream come true. The shelf running all across the brook had, of course, functioned as a dam; and Clark's bed was covered with a full inch of water. One of the few comic pictures of that day was that of the commanding officer of the 2nd Battalion going about his business all morning, with his shirt tails hanging outside his trousers exposed to sun and wind—objective drying.

Just after the French regiment left us, I went back, with Captain MacClinton, to look through Keenan's emergency hospital.

The Doctor had done a wonderful work. With his faithful little sanitary squad, he had done everything that could be done for the comfort of the best part of two hundred wounded soldiers. Those who could walk had been tagged, and sent to the rear; but only a few of the men who had to be carried had been sent back as yet. The floors of two enormous rooms were covered with wounded men laid out, close together in rows. Upon the end of one row, about fifteen feet from the door, lay Robb. Mac-Clinton and I stood near the closed door talking to him. Doctor Keenan rushed forward and pulled me violently away from where I had stood.

"Don't you know better than that, Major?"

"What's the trouble?" I inquired.

At that instant a shell landed and smashed open the door.

"That's the trouble," said Keenan. "If I hadn't pulled you away you'd have gotten some of that."

As he finished speaking, we all got some of the next one— which was gas. That hospital chamber was suffocating in a few minutes. We all turned to, to help the ones who couldn't help themselves, to put on their masks. Fortunately, the gas was not one of the deadly varieties, and before very long the air in the chamber was refreshed! For a few minutes, though, there was an awful scene of choking and gasping and finally, of coughing, in that place. I had been slow in getting my own mask on. For a few minutes I was quite overcome.

Mr. Robb had both of his arms and hands bound up. I'm afraid MacClinton and I were awkward in adjusting his mask. The poor chap rounded out his three days' record of woundings with a good hard gassing. But he got through everything all right. He was in the hospital for a long time, and was not able to go home with the regiment. A report came through that he had died of his wounds; but the report turned out to be untrue. Today, I believe, George S. Robb is enjoying normal health, in his home in Kansas.

During the afternoon, all of our troops were ordered back

to the sheltered slope of Bellevue Signal, where, for a number of days, we did what was possible towards reorganization and re-equipment, with the salvaged arms to be found all over those plains of battle.

Dr. Keenan remained in Sechault for a couple of days, with a detail of 20 special men. He saved the life of every man who could be saved; and he took the record of every man who had given his life to his country—every man whose body could be found and identified.

Four days after our relief from the assaulting lines, Dr. Keenan was evacuated by order of Dr. Shiels. As four of his own devoted bearers lifted the 1st Battalion surgeon on a stretcher, to carry him out to an ambulance, I pressed his hand and looked into his eyes, as I spoke the words of farewell to a beloved friend.

Keenan's eyes gazed into mine, but they gave no sign of recognition.

A case of complete collapse from exhaustion, I believe, is the English for the medical record set opposite his name.

Seven months later, I heard that Willis H. Keenan, M.C., had just been discharged from hospital, convalescent.

I am thankful to be able to report that my recommendation of a Distinguished Service Cross—"For Valor"—to Doctor Keenan was favorably acted upon. He richly deserved the decoration.

One of the most sensational tragedies of the five days' battle of the 15th Heavy Foot, was the one in which 1st Lieutenant Charles S. Dean of Morristown, N. J., made the supreme sacrifice. Charley Dean was one of our original officers. He went through the early days of recruiting and organization, and through the camp days of Peekskill, Whitman, Dix, and Wadsworth, as a shavetail to Captain l'Esperance in "M" Company. Over in France he went to school, and learned the machine gun game. Then he got his promotion to 1st Lieutenant, and went into the big battle as a machine gun officer in the 2nd Battalion.

During the night of September 27th, when Cobb's battalion

was being so dreadfully cut up, Charley Dean attempted to gain a position of superiority with his platoon of machine gunners, in order to try to save the situation. Dean and his men advanced in extended line until they came to enemy wire. When they started to cut their way through the wire, the enemy heard them, and turned loose machine guns, already registered.

When the searching parties went out four days later, 1st Lieutenant Dean and his platoon were found all together in perfect alignment, with faces toward the enemy and with bodies hanging on the wire, all present—none to be accounted for—all present—dead!

Just before supper time upon the evening of October 4th, a French soldier rushed through our bivouac, with a bundle of newspapers under his arm. The *poilu* was shouting in great excitement (In French of course) the headlines of his papers:—"TURKEY, AUSTRIA AND GERMANY DEMAND AN ARMISTICE!"

We were so tired and discouraged! We wondered if it were possible that such news could be true?

Upon the evening of October 6th, the 161st Division of France was relieved from the offensive, and its American regiment the 369th Infantry—what was left of it—marched through most of the night to the rear, and went into bivouac encampments, by battalion, near Minaucourt—the place from which it had made its debut, some eleven or twelve days before, as an organization of shock troops, in the great victory drive of the Allies.

# THE VOSGES MOUNTAINS
## PREPARING FOR A NEW OFFENSIVE
### October 7–November 10, 1918

UPON October 2nd at 12 o'clock, noon, I submitted my report of operations covering the activities of September 29, 30th and October 1st.

A feature of this report not included in the narrative of the preceding chapter, was a rough inventory of enemy supplies taken by our men in the taking of Sechault. This list included:

1 "Seventy-seven" artillery piece.

A large quantity of ammunition for the captured gun.

3 Light machine guns with a lot of ammunition.

A well filled ammunition dump with generous supplies of ammunition for all arms.

Several thousand "Potato-Masher Grenades."

About two freight car loads of barbed wire on reels.

A considerable quantity of timber suitable for the building of dugouts.

A large quantity of concrete.

A lot of hospital supplies.

Material of all kinds including ammunition would have filled from 25 to 30 freight cars.

During the days that followed, I was busily engaged in preparing proper citations for all the men of my command who, by their performance of duty, merited a badge of special distinction, when I received an order to discontinue the work of preparation of such a list.

The direction was accompanied by an explanation that it had been decided to decorate, with a *Croix de Guerre*, every man whom I could vouch for as having actually remained on duty during our three-day operations. As I had made a list, personally, of the names of every man with me at the time of our relief from Sechault (written as the men filed past me and were identified by their company commanders at the time of our evacuation of the town), I naturally welcomed this order as a saving to me of an enormous amount of clerical labor, which was being performed under difficulties. I had no office machinery with me in the field—nothing but my note book and some sheets of carbon paper by which I was able to preserve for reference my record of reports and orders.

During the night of October 8th the regiment moved by *camions* to the south.

Regimental Headquarters was established in Arrigny, a town about 20 kilometers to the south-east of Vitry le François. The 1st Battalion was billeted in Ecoulment, a very small village three or four kilometers from Arrigny. The other two battalions were billeted separately, in small villages quite near to Arrigny.

We rested for several days in these little villages. Colonel Hayward rejoined the regiment. The country in which we were stationed was refreshingly pastoral. The weather was balmy. We bought of the farmers with whom we were billeted, fresh eggs, milk and poultry. The war had left no mark upon the farms of that area. We had four days of restfulness and a building up of morale.

Upon the afternoon and evening of October 13th we hiked to the railroad town of Chavanges. There, we loaded our 725 officers and men, 72 horses and mules, and 42 vehicles on to a special train; and, at about half past three upon the morning of October 14th, we started upon a long railroad ride to the south.

We had no idea where we were going; but we knew that we were on the way.

We travelled through the balance of that night, through all the day of the 14th, and at about ten o'clock of the morning of October 15th, we reached Belfort. At Belfort, a French General

Staff Officer gave me orders to cover the balance of our journey for that day.

Pursuant to those orders we went on by train to Vauthiermont where we detrained just before noon. Then we hiked, with a map for a guide, about ten or eleven kilometers, to a town named Roppe. Rain fell all day. We reached Roppe at about half past four in the afternoon, wet and cold. There we billeted for the night.

Early upon the morning of October 16th, we were moved by *camions*, into the heart of the Vosges Mountains, into the Valley of the Thur, in Alsace.

Our day's journey was one of real delight. The sun shone brightly, the atmosphere was clear. Our motors climbed over perfect roads, ranges of mountains of from 4500 to 6000 feet of altitude. Captain MacClinton rode with me in the touring car of the *camion* train chief. From the summits we enjoyed magnificent views of the Alps upon one hand, the Vosges upon the other, and between, lay a great, comparatively flat, country leading to the Rhine, with the Black Forest beyond.

The regiment was billeted in the towns St. Amarin, Moosch, Bitschwiller, Willers, and Thann.

The 1st Battalion moved into the Vosges from a day to three days ahead of the other units. We arrived at Bitschwiller at about noon upon October 16th, and there we were billeted for the night.

Pursuant to my orders, I reported upon arrival to Colonel Gastinel of the 84th Infantry of France.

Colonel Gastinel was in command of the *Sous Secteur A* of the *Secteur de la Thur*. From him, I received orders to move into the *Quartier Secteur Collardelle* the following day, to take command of that quarter sector, for defense, and to relieve the 1st Battalion of the 1st Regiment, Infantry of France.

Colonel Gastinel was most cordial in his reception. He had as his *adjoint*, a Captain Perrin, an officer who before the war had been a professor of languages in an American school. I, therefore,

314

had an unusually easy experience in understanding clearly the orders given me.

I was to start early in the morning of October 17th with my company commanders and platoon chiefs, and proceed with guides, into the *Secteur Collardelle*, by a short cut through narrow and steep trails. The main body of troops would start somewhat later and proceed by the road—a longer route, but an easier one as to grades. My advance party would arrive in sector about six hours ahead of the troops; and, during those six hours, we should make reconnaissance, and, in so far as possible, "learn the sector." A pack train of 40 mules would be placed at my disposal for the purpose of transporting baggage and rations. When our own supply train should arrive, within about ten days it would be possible for us to get our rations into the sector (which was about 4000 feet above sea level) each day, by means of our own ration carts with four or six horses hitched to each, instead of the normal two.

That was fine, and simple enough. "And now," I inquired, "where shall I draw my rations?"

"Didn't you bring them with you, enough to serve until your train arrives?"

"No," I had to respond. "When I asked for instructions as to supplies, I was told that they would be ready for me at Bitschwiller or Thann."

"Well, we have no· surplus supplies here," I was informed by Colonel Gastinel.

And there I was, in the heart of the Vosges mountains, with a family of more than 700 hungry black babies, and not a thing to eat even in prospect, for two or three days!

Captain Perrin did some telephoning, trying to locate our Regimental Headquarters. They were *en route*—somewhere, but not on call.

Then Colonel Gastinel got busy. At the end of about a half an hour, he turned to me, smiling, and said:

"Mon Commandant, it is all right. I have borrowed enough

315

food for you, from several regiments stationed near here, for you to take with you tomorrow morning. I have borrowed extra supply wagons for my own regiment, so that, when we send to the base for our new supplies tomorrow, we shall be able to draw some for you too.

"I am so happy, my dear Commandant."

That Colonel had nothing on me, about being glad!

Then Colonel Gastinel wanted me to dine with him. But he was in Thann, and I was quartered in Bitschwiller, six kilometers away. If I dined with him it meant three more walks over that road—and a daybreak start for our mountain climb in the morning! I started to beg off. The delightful old Colonel met me half way, assured me that I was quite right, and told me to go back to my quarters and go to bed early.

From the viewpoint of a health recuperation, our tour of duty in the Vosges mountains was a huge success.

Our food supply was uniformly poor, and until well on towards the end of our tour in sector, our men suffered for want of blankets. In spite of these handicaps, though, the men benefited from their life in the mountain air. We remained steadily in sector for a full month. When we left, the health and morale of the battalion as a whole was high.

During our tour in *Secteur Collardelle*, we had but one real affair of excitement. It is to be understood that we always had our two enemy shellings each day; but those periods of harassing fire came to be looked upon as matters of routine.

The report of our one serious action I quote as follows:

Document                                                    October 28th, 1918.
28-10-2

From: Commanding Officer 1st Battalion 369th U. S. Infantry
To:   Colonel Gastinel, Comdg S/Sector A.
Subject:   Report on attack upon C. R. Collardelle.

1. This morning at 5 o'clock, the enemy engaged this C.R. with intense artillery fire and machine gun fire over the entire area of the

front line positions. The action continued with vigor until 6:20 o'clock, then lightened, and by 6:30 ceased.

2. The action was marked by unusual accuracy of fire, most of the trenches and boyau in use being registered with direct hits, and in some cases practically destroyed. Four St. Etienne Machine Gun positions were registered, but the guns had been carried to abris, waiting for the barrage to cease. Three Abris—in Berliat and G.C. 9 and G.C. 8 were partially destroyed.

3. A heavy fog rested on the valley in front of our positions and it is impossible to say whether or not the engagement was a part of a raid by infantry.

Only in one G. C. was a report made of enemy soldiers seen. In G. C. No. 9 Sergeant Morris reports that immediately after commencement of action, he saw two Germans in front of G. C. No. 9 making their way towards G. C. 8.

The barrage was started to the rear of our front line positions and was rolled forward—which might suggest that no attack by infantry was in contemplation or attempted. Lieutenant Kooken of Company B and Sergeant Morris of Company B, report that last evening between hours of 18 and 19 sounds of revelry accompanied by instrumental music and singing were heard to come from Wattwiller; and that many lights were in evidence in the town. Also that search lights played frequently from Wattwiller over country to north and west of north west of town.

4. Calls for artillery were given by signal from G. C.'s on front line, and relayed by observation posts and verified by telephone. The calls met with prompt response, but the enemy fire continued apparently in full force.

5. Enemy did not enter our trenches at G.C.'s.

6. Very little fire was executed by the men of our G.C.'s. The Trench Mortar Officer reports that he fired 43 shells from 4 pieces.

The St. Etienne Machine Guns responded to Barrage Signals and fired in all 1500 rounds. (In ammunition report of this morning this was erroneously described as Hotchkiss ammunition.) All but one of the St. Etienne Guns that were fired gave trouble by jamming. Three guns were not fired. In some instances the St. Etienne Gun Crews, after meeting with jams, threw grenades into wire in front of their positions, the fog as stated interfering with vision.

7. Losses were as follows:—

Killed: 1st Lieut. Elmer E. Bucher, Company C, 369th U. S. Infantry. 1 Private, Company B, and 1 Private, Company C.

Wounded: 1 Private, Company A, 6 Privates, Company B and 1 Private, Company C.

Missing: 1 Private, Company B.

It is believed that the missing man will be found killed and buried in extreme right post of G.C. No. 9 which cannot be searched until dark, owing to enemy observation.

Three other men named as missing in early reports have been found dead or wounded.

It is not believed that the missing man is a prisoner in view of all circumstances noted.

8. The men, as a whole behaved well and took cover under competent orders. Most of the casualties were caused by first rounds of fire.

1st Lieut. Bucher was responsible for two G.C.s No. 5 and 3, and was killed while attempting to pass under fire from one to the other. His death was caused by special devotion to duty and in my opinion, 1st Lieut. Bucher is deserving of commendation.

ARTHUR W. LITTLE<br>
Major, Commanding 1/369th U. S. Inf.

Colonel Gastinel showed great sympathy and interest in our losses and situation. He expressed relief by telephone when, shortly after dark, upon the evening of October 28th, I was able to report that the dead body of the man missing from Company "B" had been found, buried under the débris of *Groupe de Combat* No. 9.

The next day I received the following note:

Le Colonel Hatton Cdt 1' I.D. 161 *ier* asks M. Le Colonel Gastinel *Cdt le S/Secteur* to consent establishing a text of Citation *a l'Ordre de la Division* in behalf of *S/Lieutenant Bucher* of the 369th killed in action on the 28th of October.

Le COLONEL HATTON, *Adjoint au*<br>
General of Division Cdt. the Infantry of the 161 *ier* Division.

Transmitted to *M. le Commandant Little Cdt. le Quartier Collardelle* for execution. Kindly return the present note with the text of the Citation.

*Le Commandant du S/Secteur A*<br>
*P. O.* Le Capn *Adjoint Perrin.*

HEADQUARTERS COMPANY, CAPT. EDWARD J. FARRELL
UNGERSHEIM, DECEMBER 12, 1918

35590

THE CEREMONY OF DECORATION OF REGIMENTAL FLAGS AND COLORS, 161
DIV. (FRENCH), PLAINS OF MUNCHAUSEN, DEC. 13, 1918

In response, I prepared an appropriate citation, and some months later, the mother of Lieutenant Bucher received the posthumous decoration of her son.

Upon November 5th I was ordered to attend a school for Field Officers of the French Army, to study the principles of co-operation between Tanks and Infantry in open warfare. The school was to be held at the great French Tank center at Martigny les Bains.

The course of instruction lasted two days. It was interesting, and would have been beneficial to me if I had had to make a new offensive; but, fortunately, the signing of the armistice prevented that.

Upon returning through Langres, I found that I had more than half a day to wait for a train. I heard that about eight kilometers outside of Langres, was a Tank center of the American Army. I borrowed a side car, ran out to the camp, and found, to my delight, that the 326th Battalion of Tanks was stationed there.

I called upon the commanding officer, introduced myself, stated my business, and was invited to lunch. After lunch, the Colonel sent his adjutant with me to find the quarters of Company "C."

At the orderly room of Company "C" I inquired for Sergeant Little; and a minute later a smart little soldier bounced across the street, and snapped up before me into "salute."

He had merely been told that a strange officer wanted to see him. He commenced to speak, in formal report:

"Sir, Sergeant Little, Company 'C'——" and then his jaw dropped in astonishment; his eyes grew wide in more astonishment, and finally, he continued his speech, but in a very different tone from that in which it had been commenced, saying:

"Oh, Father! I'm so glad to see you. They told me you'd been killed."

I got 24 hours' leave for the boy; and together we went into town—for a party.

319

The first thing we did was to cable his mother—"Father and Son send greetings." Then we dined, and went to a theater. After that, we got a room at the Y. M. C. A. hotel, and went to bed and slept. At about three o'clock I was called. It was time for me to go for my train.

Winslow, my son, hadn't slept in a bed for many months. He had been tearing off a great sleep. I insisted upon his remaining there to sleep the night out; and by the time I was dressed, he was almost off again.

But I was happy as I left him to sleep on through his night; for I was confident that the war was over, that he would not again have to go under the fire of the enemy, and that when he awoke it would be to read of the signing of the armistice.

For this day was the 10th of November.

# THE ARMISTICE
## *November 11, 1918*

UPON the evening of November 10th, as I stepped out of the dining room of the Grand Hotel Tonneau d'Or, at Belfort, to look about for a table at which to have my coffee and cognac, I observed a United States Army Officer sitting alone, and just giving his order.

In accordance with the custom of the service, I stepped up to this officer and introduced myself. In return the officer told me that he was Colonel Howard of General Headquarters, Quartermaster Department (in the regular service a major of Coast Artillery), and traveling in search of the very regiment of which I had reported myself a member, in hopes of being able to provide for the payment of our men, a function, which had not been celebrated for a number of months.

Colonel Howard invited me to join him for coffee, and then inquired whether I was returning to my regiment or departing from it.

Upon learning that I was returning, Colonel Howard said that if I would guide him, he would be glad of my company as his traveling companion upon the morrow. He had a fine big touring car, but neither he nor his chauffeur had ever before been in that part of France.

We met for an early breakfast, and at a quarter past eight o'clock upon the morning of November 11th, we made our start.

The Armistice was, of course, to go into effect at eleven o'clock. All the Valley was *en fete;* and the civilian inhabitants of the Alsatian towns turned out in their gay native costumes.

321

Each town mustered at least one band, and in each town through which we passed some kind of public celebration of thanksgiving was being conducted.

At our Regimental Headquarters I found Colonel Hayward in happy and expansive mood.

He said: "The day Christ was born was the greatest day in the history of the World; and this day is the second greatest day."

Colonel Hayward also told me with a happy expression of pride that he had been informed by General Lebouc that our regiment was to be decorated as an organization, for our part in the offensive battle of the Meuse-Argonne.

Captain Fox, the Regimental Supply Officer, fixed me up with a side car, and at about four o'clock, I reached my P.C. at the *Quartier Secteur Collardelle,* to resume command of my battalion.

I was given a cordial reception. Captain Bates assured me that he had changed his mind about a battalion commander in sector having an easy job. My Joe started purring over me, and wanting me to put on my slippers and wrapper, and to make myself comfortable. The adjutant brought me a fine lot of mail from home, putting me up to date with October 15th.

MacClinton came over to say "how do" and to tell me that he too, while I had been away, had gone to school. He had been sent to Amarin, for a lecture on Chemical Warfare. The school was for French line officers. Like me, MacClinton had been almost the only American present. Also, like me, he had found himself somewhat handicapped in getting full benefit of the lecture (which had been carried on in rapidly spoken French) on account of his lack of knowledge of the language.

I asked him how much of the lecture he had been able to understand.

"Just two words," MacClinton answered, "just two words— *gaz* and *secteur.*"

All my callers stayed for supper.

322

As we were taking our seats, my little French aide rushed in, apologetic for being late, and slightly out of breath. Under either arm he carried a bottle of Champagne, which he solemnly deposited in front of my plate—with his compliments.

Not a drop was wasted.

The war was over!

We were happy and thankful. In the front line trenches our spirit of thankfulness did not take the form of wild orgy, of which, some weeks later, we were to read in the stories of how New York and Paris took the news.

But I doubt if the hearts of any of the wildest revellers were more deeply stirred with emotion than were those of our little group of officers who sat with me that night upon my mountain top, with the stars of our canopy very near and very beautiful— watching the display of firework being set off from the trenches of the enemy, and listening to their cheers. Yes—the Germans in the front line trenches—they were happy too.

A few days after this "second greatest day in the history of the world," we received an official note which tells its own story, and which I quote in full as follows:

HEADQUARTERS 369TH INFANTRY U. S. A.
AMERICAN EXPEDITIONARY FORCES
FRANCE, 21ST NOVEMBER, 1918
Blodlesheim

Document
21-11-3
Bulletin

1. The following is published and will be read to the command.

The Commander in Chief
of the Allied Armies
General Staff              Allies G.H.Q., Nov. 12/18.
1st Section
No. 5.961

OFFICERS, NON-COMMISSIONED OFFICERS
AND PRIVATES

After having boldly stopped the enemy, you have attacked them for months with indefatigable faith and energy, giving them no rest.

You have won the greatest battle in History and saved the most sacred cause, the liberty of the world.

Be proud of it.

With immortal glory you have adorned your flags.

Posterity will be indebted to you with gratitude.

> The Marshal of France
> Commander in Chief of the Allied Armies
> FOCH.

> By order of COLONEL HAYWARD
> T. A. RYAN
> 1st Lieutenant 369th Infantry
> Acting Adjutant.

*Distribution*
Battn. Hdqrs.
Companies
Supply
Medical
Militia Police
Hdqrs.
Personnel

# THE FIRST TO THE RHINE

*November 12–December 10, 1918*

NO soooner had the fighting stopped, than the Germans, both military and civilian, wanted to establish social relations.

Large parties and small parties would approach our lines and beg to be received as guests. Strict orders had been promulgated not to permit visiting; but it was a difficult order to enforce. For the first couple of days, until the Germans were made to understand, the possibility of a clash of arms over this order was a cause of a grave anxiety to us who were responsible for its enforcement. Upon a number of occasions, we had to send our platoons with fixed bayonets, and have our men, with rifles held at "Port Arms" (but ready to shift instantly into "Charge," if necessary) shove back the intruders, somewhat after the fashion in which our policemen push back a street crowd—good naturedly, but with persistence.

In spite of all precautions, there were a number of instances in which the rules were violated. Germans did visit our lines and fraternize with our men; and our men returned the visits. I believe the French soldiers were even greater offenders in this regulation than were our men. Happily, however, no clashes occurred; and the order of suspension of firing was not violated.

There was another class of visitors, which grew larger, day by day. This class had to be not only received but taken care of, and kept track of. This class was made up of released prisoners of war, refugees, and interned citizens.

The Germans seemed to be glad to be relieved of the care of

these unhappy people. They sent them across No Man's Land in a steady stream—men and women, soldiers or civilians—there was no order nor organization of their coming. There was one universal condition of their arrival, however, they were all hungry, and they were almost all insufficiently clad.

We could do nothing for them in the way of clothing; but we usually managed to get them up something to eat while they were being held at our mobilization stations, until the company would grow to be large enough to warrant a properly conducted tour to the rear. These people were officially tagged before leaving the German lines, and passed along on the way to their homes, with forwarding visas stamped upon the tags.

At four-thirty upon the morning of November 17th the 1st Battalion evacuated the *Secteur Collardelle,* by going over its trenches to the front. We had not often evacuated our lines in that direction, and we had never before done so without meeting with a reception by firearms.

We had been working like beavers for several days to clear the sector for evacuation. We had sent to the rear more than fifty truck loads of sector material, including a large amount of ammunition. The moving job was completed at about one o'clock in the morning. Reveille came at 2:30 and a hearty breakfast was served at 3 o'clock. The hour and a half between breakfast and the zero hour for going forward was no more than was needed. To find one's way through dense mountain woods in the dark is no easy matter.

I took station at the point of rendezvous well before the zero hour; and shivered and waited. One of the liaison men suggested making a fire. So we could—the war was over—we could have lights! The fire was made, and we waited in a little more comfort.

By the appointed hour, all units had filed by and been checked out, all except one platoon. I waited for a quarter of an hour, or so, and then had our fire stamped out, and moved to the head of our waiting column. We couldn't afford to lose any more time. We had to connect with the Regimental Column at a point

326

some six kilometers away at 7:30, and to get there, we had to travel through a country which had been the enemy's country, through which we had been able to make no reconnaissance. We had our maps, but our maps gave no information as to the possibility of closed ways, and the necessity for detours.

The lost platoon was a source of embarrassment to me, but not of anxiety. The war was over. I should probably be laughed at a bit by Colonel Hayward; but that would be all. In good time, the lost platoon would come home, after the fashion in which Mary's little lambs had reached home—all safe, and wagging their tails behind them—the only person due to suffer being myself, who really couldn't help it much more than Mary had been able to help having her dreadful dream.

And so it turned out.

About twelve and a half hours later the platoon came in. They had gotten lost, first in the mountains, and later upon the roads of our march towards the Rhine. They had been walking practically all the time during the entire twelve hours. They had nothing to eat but the sandwiches which each man had been ordered to carry for lunch. They were a tired little company.

The lieutenant reported to me, and then threw himself down on a bank by the side of the road, flat on his back.

When he came to, I asked him how he came to get himself lost in the woods. He couldn't understand. Didn't he have his sector map? Oh yes.

He was a new officer, that is, new to us. I asked him what his business had been in civil life.

"I'm an official guide to the tourist department of the Union Pacific Railroad," he answered; "and my specialty is personally conducted tours through the Yellowstone Park."

To this day, I've never been quite able to make up my mind whether that chap was guying me or not. At any rate, I invited him to dinner.

Colonel Hayward was assured of his laugh.

We went forward from our sector, across No Man's Land,

through the deserted German trenches, to the town of Wattwiller. From Wattwiller we turned south, and marched through Uffholtz. From Uffholtz we continued south to the large town, Cernay. We marched through Cernay to the Southwestern City line, and there, we waited for the regiment.

At a few minutes before eight o'clock the regiment, less our battalion, came swinging along—the 1st Battalion moved into column behind the band—the bugles sounded *"Forward"*—and the last phase of the march of our colored volunteers, *from the Harlem to the Rhine,* had been inaugurated.

We marched through Cernay, through a number of small towns to Wittelsheim, a distance of no more than six kilometers. At Wittelsheim the 1st and 2nd Battalions dropped out of the column, to billet for the night. The Headquarters units and the 3rd Battalion kept on for from eight to 10 kilometers more, to be billeted, respectively, at Pulversheim and Schoenen-Steinbach.

All of the towns that we went through upon that first day of *"The March to the Rhine"* were evacuated towns. There had not been much destruction by artillery fire, however. The houses of Wittelsheim were for the most part standing and in sound condition. It was obvious that they had been used for the billeting of German troops; but there were no marked signs of looting. Many of the doors were unlocked. There was a large casino with two assembly floors of area sufficient to provide sleeping quarters for several hundred of our 1500 or more men. We found unlocked barns with enough hay loft space to accommodate the balance. It so happened that the house which I chose for my quarters had electric lights in good working order. Electricity always was a mystery to me. I couldn't figure out where the current for my lights came from. There was certainly no power plant in operation in Wittelsheim, and Wittelsheim seemed to be miles and miles from anywhere. But anyway—we used the lights.

Our baggage train and kitchens caught up with us early in the afternoon. We had a comfortable night.

Reveille call was at 4 o'clock upon the morning of Nov. 18th. A hearty breakfast was served at 4:15. At 5 o'clock assembly sounded, and, a few minutes later, we were on the march.

We reached Pulversheim shortly before 7:45, the hour set for the regimental rendezvous at that point.

From Pulversheim we marched, in regimental formation, some six kilometers, to Ensisheim. Upon the outskirts of Ensisheim, we were held for a time during the mobilization of the 161st Division, for review by its General.

Ensisheim was not an evacuated city. Upon the contrary, it was an active, bustling town. The activities of the city for the day of November 18th were centered in a purpose to give to the entering Army of the Allies a rousing reception. They made a good job of it.

Every house had its display of flags. Across the streets, great banners were hung. Pictures of President Wilson appeared in hundreds of windows. Girls and young women in the gay costumes of native Alsatian dress, threw flowers into the streets to make a carpet for soldiers to walk upon; and wherever the troops were at rest and the discipline of the moment permitted, these young women bestowed kisses upon the men in uniform.

In many windows, and from streamers and street banners were displayed signs of welcome:

*"Vive la Republique!"*
*"Greetings to our Deliverers."*
*"God Bless President Wilson!"*

and many other expressions of grateful emotion.

The Division paraded through the city, and, before a stand erected in front of a church in the center of a large plaza, passed in review before its General.

It was my first formal review before a French officer. I was interested to note the contrast of manner of General LeBouc, in receiving the salutes of the officers filing past, as compared with that of most officers of our own country under similar circumstances.

The French General, in acknowledging a salute would smile cordially; and, if he happened to be personally acquainted with the officer who was passing, he would call to him a greeting. Thus, as the 1st Battalion passed, General LeBouc shouted: "Ah— Little—I am glad to see you—you are looking very well—it is a beautiful day!" And, to a number of our company or platoon commanders, he called out compliments upon the fine marching of the men.

Upon leaving Ensisheim, the organizations of the Divisions separated to proceed to their several points of assignment.

Our regiment hiked along, some fifteen or sixteen kilometers eastward, to Blodelsheim. There, the Colonel and all Head-quarters units dropped out to take station. The 2nd Battalion remained in Blodelsheim, too.

The 1st and 3rd Battalions turned to the north, and con-tinued the march for another three kilometers, to Fessenheim. At Fessenheim, L'Esperance dropped out of the column, with his 3rd Battalion to take station.

The 1st Battalion continued to the north to Balgau and to Nambsheim, two and four kilometers distant from Fessenheim, respectively. In Balgau I established our headquarters, and held the troops of Companies "B," and "D," and Machine Gun. To Nambsheim I sent Company "C" under Captain MacClinton.

I was awakened upon the morning of November 19th by my orderly, who informed me that a great line of civilians was forming outside of my house, to take their turn in speaking with the commander of the troops.

"What do they want?" I inquired.

"Passes, Sir," was the answer.

I hurried to get dressed, and sent for Lieutenant Carl E. Anderson, who could speak German.

We opened an office in the building that served the town as "City Hall," and we turned the line of civilians into that building.

How the Germans must have ridden those citizens! The permissions which they sought were, for the most part, for matters of the most ordinary kinds of civilian rights.

Some desired permission to drive their cows back and forth from pasture to milking stables. Some desired to go to market in Blodelsheim. Some desired to visit the cemetery, a kilometer away, to place flowers upon the graves of their dear ones. And so it went—a steady stream of timid pleas from the lips of people who had become accustomed to the government of tyrants.

Just before noon I received a call from the Acting Regimental Adjutant, 1st Lieutenant Timothy A. Ryan.

Ryan had been sent to inform me officially of my duty to take over the government of the two towns; and that I was to consider myself (in addition to my other duties) as Governor, Mayor, Justice, Police Commissioner, Burgomaster, or any other thing that might appeal to me.

"But for God's sake," Ryan continued, "get out some kind of a proclamation to make these people understand that we are not going to abuse them. They go around in our town like a lot of whipped curs. I suppose you are having the same experience. The Colonel says one of the most important things that you can possibly do during the next few days, is to make these people sense the contrast between our government and that of the Kaiser. In other words, stay clear of the bearing of the Irish policeman who brought his club down upon the head of an unoffending citizen, saying, "I do not bate because I hate you, but because I have au-t'or-i-tee.""

Early upon the morning of November 20th, the town crier rang his bell, and, when the populace had assembled upon the principal square, in front of the church, my proclamation was read, as follows:—

To the Citizens of Balgau. Nov. 20th, 1918.

The occupation of this town by the troops of The United States Army is an occupation of friendliness to the people of Balgau and for their protection.

In order to avoid misunderstanding which might result in unpleasantness, the following explanations are made:

This territory having been evacuated by the German Army under certain stated conditions, mutually binding upon the armies of both parties to the war, it is the duty of the army of occupation to insure obedience to the conditions.

To this end Military Government is established in this town.

The present civil authorities and ordinances and regulations are confirmed. Until further notice they will be respected and obeyed under approval of the Military Government.

All new appointments or ordinances or regulations made by the civil authorities will be submitted to the Military Government, and approval obtained before being put into operation.

The following regulations are published for the information and guidance of all concerned, to take effect at once.

The sale or gift of wines, liquors, beers or any form of spirituous liquors to the enlisted soldiers of this garrison (colored soldiers) is forbidden.

All males who are or who have been soldiers of any army will register their names and any other personal information which may be required with the Military Officer on duty for this purpose at the house of the Burgomaster between the hours of 9 and 11 in the morning and between the hours of 2 and 4 in the afternoon.

Any such persons not registered by four o'clock upon the day of November twenty-first will be subject to arrest.

Passes will be given to the citizens so registered who may be entitled to them.

Every morning between the hours of 9 and 11 a Military Officer will sit at the office of the Burgomaster for the purpose of hearing complaints of all kinds; and with the object of finding relief for any and all citizens in connection with matters coming properly before government for consideration.

All violations of the regulations of the Military Government are punishable under the Military Law of the Government of the United States.

ARTHUR W. LITTLE
Major 369th U. S. Infantry
Commanding Officer, Balgau.

This proclamation was subsequently translated into German and into French, and copies in all three languages were posted in the windows of public buildings.

We took it as a compliment to America that, within a few days after our arrival, the people of our towns dug up their buried silverware from their gardens, and, in one case of my personal knowledge, openly tore up the boards of the kitchen floor and brought into the open, a sack of flour and a nice store of dry groceries.

At 10:30 upon the morning of November 20th, I returned to my quarters from two hours of riding and observation of the company drills of the units of the battalion.

An order had just come in—an order marked *"Urgent."*

Blodelsheim<br>20th November, 1918.

To:

C. O. 1st Battalion

Orders from Army to push outposts to Rhine.

Occupy Nambsheim by a patrol and cover Rhine approaches.

Also cover with patrols the Rhine approaches south of Nambsheim. Immediate execution.

Report execution to this Office by telephone and follow by written report and sketch this afternoon.

By order of COLONEL HAYWARD<br>T. A. RYAN<br>1st Lieutenant 369th Infantry<br>Acting Adjutant.

I sent an orderly, quickly, to recall my horse. At the same time I sent an order to Captain MacClinton to hold up the dismissal of his company from drill, and to pick his most reliable men for patrols, and see that they were given their dinner without delay. Then, he was to await me at Nambsheim, mounted, and ready to accompany me upon reconnaissance. Next, an order was sent to my machine gun officers, to report immediately, mounted, and ready for reconnaissance.

333

We cut out dinner.

MacClinton was waiting for us as we entered Nambsheim. Directions were given for his patrols to follow us along the road to the river. I talked as we rode, and explained to the officers accompanying me the work to be done.

We had, as I believed, a good chance of gaining the distinction of being first to The Rhine. The day which had been set for moving forward to The Rhine had been November 21st. General Lebouc, in compliment to his American regiment, was giving us a bit of an inside track. I hoped that Colonel Hayward was carrying along the good work, and giving the 1st Battalion an inside track.

As we rode forward through the woods of approach to the river we met a civilian party of laborers. We stopped to make inquiries as to the best of the several ways opening before us. The civilians answered politely, but they shook their heads in warning. At the end of the road which we were following was a cable ferry. The evacuating troops of the German Army were using that ferry; and they had not yet all crossed the river. The civilians seemed to fear a clash of arms, if we should run into the retiring Germans. I did not. I didn't believe that the Germans were any more anxious to fight than we were, that morning. Those words, "IMMEDIATE EXECUTION," in my order, covered me. We pressed on. A few minutes later we came out of the woods into the open. The wonderful swift running water of The Rhine was flowing past us to our left. Upon the opposite bank, a squad of gray uniformed soldiers were clambering out of a flat-bottomed scow attached to a steel cable, stretched from shore to shore.

We dismounted, and shook hands all 'round in congratulation.

I must have been quite excited. I made a little speech, and boasted that I felt as if neither DeSoto, nor Drake, nor Frobisher, nor even Columbus had anything on me.

Then we went about the duty of establishing our posts.

A few hours later I rode to Blodelsheim, and handed my report and map to Colonel Hayward in person.

The Colonel was very happy. We sat and talked of the wonderful events of the day.

The Colonel said: "Little, when I got to the Rhine this morning I was so excited that I guess I acted a little bit crazy. At any rate, I made the officers who accompanied me dismount, and I made them a speech, claiming the waters of the Rhine for our arms. Then I climbed down the bank and I scooped up some of the water in my hands; and I drank it as I breathed a prayer of thanksgiving.

"And I said to those officers who were with me, Little, I said to them in a kind of boastful way, that I felt as if neither DeSoto, nor Drake nor Frobisher, nor even Columbus had anything on me."

I was startled—with a newly born but horrible suspicion; but I tried to speak calmly, as I asked:—

"What time did you get to the Rhine, Colonel?"

"About 10:30 this morning," came the answer. "As soon as I got my orders from higher up I called for my horse and beat it. I left word with Ryan to send your orders right along, but I didn't wait to review them."

So the Colonel had been drinking his water of The Rhine at the very minute that I had been reading the order which I had hoped was giving to me a chance for a nice little distinction of sentimental conceit—which all goes to show the advantages of being a colonel as compared with those having to do with the rank of major.

The period of the occupation of the towns of Blodelsheim, Fessenheim, Balgau, and Nambsheim, and of the West bank of The Rhine along the area of those towns, by the 369th Infantry, passed uneventfully. We remained about three weeks, when, upon December 9th, we received the welcome orders to start immediately for the west, to prepare to leave the French Army, as the first step towards going home.

In closing this chapter I deem it appropriate to quote a letter of November 22nd addressed to Colonel Hayward by our beloved Division Commander, the General Lebouc.

22 November, 1918.

Le Colonel Hayward
Cdt. le 369e Regt. d'Infie, U. S.

My dear Colonel:

I am greatly pleased with your thoughtful attention. You have collected the water of the Rhine in your hand and you have placed the "Black Watch" along the river.

It is ours from now on, but no Frenchman ignores that it is to the Americans that we owe this conquest. Therefore, you will permit me not to accept the personal compliments you paid, except with the following reserve. I shall never forget that the opportunity has been given me, in the course of this war, to have under my command an American regiment which, with little previous training, has fought with extreme bravery, and which since the last combat has applied itself to such regular and steady work that as far as attitude and military discipline are concerned, this American Regiment can compare with any of my French Regiments.

Therefore, it is to yourself, Colonel, to Lt. Colonel Pickering and to your battalion commanders that must be addressed all congratulations. And it is for this reason that I make it a point to reward officially the 369th R.I.U.S. with a collective citation in the orders of my Division.

When the citation is approved, I shall have great joy in decorating your flag and in kissing you in front of your Regiment. And that day we shall not only drink water from the Rhine, we shall drink Champagne, and it will be a beautiful day for your General Commanding the Division.

Believe, my dear Colonel, in my sentiments of affectionate comradeship.

LEBOUC.

336

# THE CROIX DE GUERRE
# PINNED TO OUR COLORS

*December 13, 1918*

FIFTEEN or sixteen kilometers northeast, as the crow flies, from the city of Mulhouse, and sandwiched in between the great Forest of the Harth on the south and the Forest of Rothleible on the north, lay the Plains of Munchausen—a great parade ground made by nature.

In the early afternoon of the 13th of December, 1918, upon this parade ground, the troops of a Division of the Army of France were formed in hollow square, or rectangle, the sides of which measured almost a thousand yards, and the ends, five hundred.

All branches of the service were represented in that assembly, and all sub-divisional classes and departments of the three primary branches of military establishments—artillery, cavalry and infantry. The troops faced in—towards the center of the hollow square.

The day was one of mildness despite the season of the year; and, upon the fixed bayonets of the infantry and the burnished metal of the cavalry and artillery equipment, the sun shone brightly.

For some time after the organizations had taken their positions, the troops stood at ease. Presently, a flourish of a whole corps of trumpets was sounded, and promptly, the soldiers, by sharp commands, were brought to attention.

A long ways off, to the west, a group of horsemen could be

337

seen—moving, and rapidly coming nearer. Soon, they came near enough to admit of a recognition of colors.

In the dozen or more figures who rode at the gallop, stretched out to the rear of the leading figure, there were all the bright colors of military uniforms that go to mark the distinction of service. Amongst these followers of the leader there appeared to be no great desire for the maintenance of any particular formation. The irregularity of the order in which they rode, and the flying skirts of overcoats of many colors, contributed to the dash of the picture.

The leader of the group, however, soon drew the focus of all eyes, and held it. When one's eyes had once settled upon the leader, the followers were no longer interesting as principals in the scene. They were merely a part of the setting, just as the troops of the great hollow square were a part of the setting.

The leader wore the crimson riding breeches and the horizon blue greatcoat of a General of France. The formal high-crowned cap of red, with golden bands of oak leaves covered his head. The horse of the General was of a color of cream white, and, as he galloped over the field, the skirts of the rider's coat flew back to expose the startling contrast of color made by an enormous crimson shabrack (or horse housing, or saddle cloth, as the layman might call it).

The leader of that group of dashing horsemen was the General Lebouc, Commanding the 161st Infantry Division of France.

The troops, formed in hollow square, were the troops of that division, fresh from triumphs of the fields of battle.

At the right of the line upon the north side of the square, were the colored soldiers of the 369th U. S. Infantry, a regiment which had won distinction upon a number of planes, and a unit of General Lebouc's command in which he loved to express his pride.

There was no skeleton line of officers standing in front of the soldiers of the ranks to interfere with the clear view of the General as he passed down the line, in inspection. The company officers were posted in order of rank upon the right of the company lines. The regimental commander and the battalion commanders, mounted, were in post in their relative order of rank upon the right of the regiment.

General Lebouc entered the hollow square from the southwestern corner, turned in to the left, and rode (still at the gallop) along the front of the organizations stationed at the western end. As he rode, he waved his hand in salutation, and called out his compliments of greeting.

Then he turned to the right. The General Lebouc had come to the right of his American regiment of volunteers.

"*Ah—Mes Amies,*" he shouted, and he smiled into our faces as he dashed by, "*mes cheres amies—Hayward, Pickering, Little, L'Esperance, Clark—Je suis bien content! C'est une belle journeé.*"

When the General had completed the circuit, he rode to the center of the field and dismounted.

That was the signal for all other officers to dismount.

Then the order was passed for the colors of all organizations which had been designated to be decorated to be brought to the front and center. From the center of our regiment, Colonel Hayward stepped out, bearing the national colors of the 369th Infantry. Two other officers stepped with him. On the left of the trio marched Lieutenant Colonel Pickering, bearing the regimental colors. In the center marched Major Little (the author). These three field officers, and two others, had been named in the Regimental Citation. These three were to receive the kiss of their General. The other two officers named could not experience that honor. One, still lay wounded in the hospital. The other slept the long sleep of eternity, on the slopes of Bellevue Signal.

General Lebouc decorated the colors of the several organizations, which had been called to the front and center in order, from right to left.

When it came to be our turn, he read as follows:

Sous le Commandement du Colonel Hayward qui, bien que

339

blessé, a tenu à conduire son régiment au combat, du Lieutenant Colonel Pickering, admirable de sang-froid et de courage, du Commandant Cobb (tué), du Commandant Spencer (grièvement blessé), du Commandant Little, véritable entraineur d'hommes, le 369ᵉ R.I.U.S. qui lors des attaques de Septembre 1918, voyait le feu pour la première fois, s'est emparé de puissantes organisations ennemies, énergiquement défendues et a enlevé de haute lutte le village de Sechault, a fait des prisonniers, ramené 6 canons et un grand nombre de mitrailleuses.

### Translation

"Under command of Colonel Hayward, who, though injured, insisted on leading his regiment in the battle, of Lieutenant Colonel Pickering, admirably cool and brave, of Major Cobb (killed), of Major Spencer (grievously wounded), of Major Little, a true leader of men, the 369th R.I.U.S. engaging in an offensive for the first time in the drive of September, 1918, stormed powerful enemy positions energetically defended, took, after heavy fighting, the town of Sechault, captured prisoners and brought back six cannons and a great number of machine guns."

Then he pinned to each of our colors at the peak, the *Croix de Guerre*. After that, he pinned upon the breast of each officer of the citation who was present, the *Croix de Guerre;* and then, very solemnly, he kissed us, each in turn, first upon the right cheek, and then upon the left.

When the presentations were over, the troops moved to the eastern end of the field, and took formation to march in review.

I have never seen such a review. The infantry regiments formed and marched past in regimental line of battalion phalanxes. Each of our battalions was formed in a solid rectangular mass of 800 men. There were 30 paces of interval between the battalions. Line officers were formed as the front rank of the phalanx of their respective battalions. The major of each battalion rode alone, 5 paces in front of its center. The colonel rode 30 paces in front of the major of the center battalion.

I believe the mounted organizations were even more impressive than the infantry as they passed in review at the trot. And when the artillery rumbled by, the earth of the Plains of Munchausen fairly trembled.

Then we hiked back to our billeting towns, fifteen or seventeen kilometers distant. We had hiked once over the road in the morning; and we had marched two or three kilometers in the course of the ceremonies. Long before we reached our home towns darkness had descended upon us. We were a very tired lot of men when the day's work was complete; but I heard of no grumblings over the fatigue.

Our men had tried to make history of honor to their race; and their efforts had been recognized.

As was intimated by promise near the close of the preceding chapter, our regiment had moved from its posts upon the Rhine, and from the towns which it had garrisoned—Blodelsheim, Fessenheim, Balgau and Nambsheim—early upon the morning of December 10th. We had hiked westward, all but the 1st Battalion to be billeted at Ungersheim; the 1st Battalion to keep on for a couple of kilometers still farther to the west, to be stationed at Feldkirch. Our battalion had in all had something over 30 kilometers to do for its day's march, the 3rd Battalion had had about 4 kilometers less to do, and the balance of the regiment had had about 4 kilometers less than that. A good long hike—but nobody had cared. The weather had been fine, and each pace had carried us 30 inches nearer home.

As the 1st Battalion towns were farthest to the north, we, naturally, had commenced the march. As we had passed through the towns to the south of us, the other units of the regiment had fallen into column. At the western boundary of Blodelsheim, the Band had taken post in front of our battalion, the Colonel and his staff had ridden to the head of the column, and with a united regiment, the pendulum had started upon its returning swing, this time, from—"The Rhine—*to*—The Harlem."

December 14th found us back in our billeting towns, resting.

On the 14th and 15th, the Signal Corps camera men from G.H.Q., Amer. E. F. had taken a lot of pictures of the regiment—movies and stills. Upon the 14th, I had received by courier from the General Lebouc, his photograph with complimentary inscription, which I take pride in publishing as a part of my story with the Fifteenth.

Upon the morning of the 16th, an aide of the General called upon me at my house in Feldkirch, presented the compliments of his chief, and said that at 4 o'clock, if convenient to the Commandant Little, the Commanding General of the 161st Division would take to himself the pleasure of paying a call upon the Commandant Little to say his official and personal farewell.

There was quite a flurry in the house of *Monsieur l'Abbe Zurbach, curé a Feldkirch,* in whose very comfortable residence I had established my living quarters. The flurry was of the kind that an anxious debutante in a small town experiences when she learns that the social leader of the town has announced that she will attend the girl's "coming out" reception.

We had a great house-cleaning, and Granville Malachi made sandwiches and cakes. We sent scouting officers through to the surrounding towns, and scared up seven or eight bottles of champagne.

At a quarter to four all of the Battalion Officers had assembled in my dining room, *Monsieur l'Abbe Zurbach* having most considerately insisted upon its being looked upon as mine, during the period of our establishment at Feldkirch.

The non-commissioned staff, in best bib and tucker, was assembled outside of the front door.

To the right of the front door the Company of The Guard was held in line, with the bugler of each company pressed into service for the great occasion, formed upon the right of The Guard.

At four o'clock, exactly, the buglers sounded two flourishes and the rifles of The Guard Company rang, in obedience to the order *"Present ARMS!"*

Cookson jumped to the door of the limousine as the car stopped at my door.

An instant later, and to General Lebouc were being presented in order of rank the officers of the 1st Battalion, 369th U. S. Infantry, for some time and until that day a unit of the 161st Infantry Division, of the Army of France.

The short speeches were quickly over. The General assured us of his official respect and of his personal affection. We believed him. He had proven up. The toast—"France and America, Allies and Friends!"—was drunk in bumpers. Then, for a second time, the General shook hands, all around.

Most of the older officers accompanied me to the door, as I put our distinguished visitor into his car. There was another ringing of rifle straps, and another flourish of bugles—and, if I may be permitted to resort to a colloquialism, the General Lebouc was off, in a cloud of dust!

The company commanders and I strolled back into the dining room—our minds filled with a horrible suspicion. The suspicion was justified. That young scamp, Webb, had organized the youngsters, and during the brief period of our doing of the honors at the door, an after party had been pulled off.

Not a cake left. Not a drop of champagne was remaining, either in bottles or in glasses!

But, as several times before, I have remarked—nobody cared. We were going home.

# XLVI

# HOMEWARD BOUND

*December 17, 1918–February 12, 1919*

IT seemed to us, in our eagerness to get home, that we were as long in making the trip, after we had started, as we had been in getting to France.

In a sense, we had started for home when, upon December 10th, we had left our posts on The Rhine, to hike back to Ungersheim and Feldkirch. When we continued our march, however, after being formally released by the French command, we felt that we were, sure enough, on the way. And we commenced that continuation of our march the day after the General Lebouc had honored us by personally presenting his parting compliments.

Our orders were to move by battalions, and hike to various towns for billeting, in one-night stands.

The 1st Battalion left Feldkirch at 8 o'clock upon the morning of December 18th with the day's objective, Roderen, a march of about 22 kilometers in a southwesterly direction.

December 18th was a bad day as to weather. We had rain, sleet, and snow—all day and all night—progressively in the order named. The thermometer performed appropriately, and conformed to the antics of its half brother, the barometer. By the time we arrived at Roderen, we were a forlorn crowd—wet, and cold, and stiff.

A few kilometers out from Roderen a messenger reported to me with a note. The note was from 1st Lieutenant Webb, who had preceded the battalion with a small detail to act as billeting officer. Webb reported that Roderen was filled up with a whole regiment of Moroccan troops, that the Moroccans had neither orders nor inclination to move, and that the town major had assured him (Webb) that he could do nothing for us. So, Webb continued in his report, he was riding north to Thann, to try to find accommodations there; and he suggested that I turn into the Thur Valley to save the possible retracing of our steps, as he was confident that we should be able to find shelter in one of the towns thereabouts.

No, my orders were specific. They must be obeyed. The 1st Battalion continued its march to Roderen.

I gave my horse to an officer, however, and the adjutant's horse to a reliable man to serve as orderly for the officer, and despatched them to Regimental Headquarters, to make oral report of the situation. I told the officer to push forward with all possible speed, to procure new orders for us, and to borrow the Colonel's car in returning to me, in order to endeavor to make whatever march might have to be made to a new objective, before dark.

We didn't succeed in beating the darkness. The officer returned just about as darkness descended, with orders to go to Bourbach-la-Haut for the night.

Bourbach-la-Haut was about five or six kilometers to the west from Roderen. Also, it was well named. As we climbed in the dark, the steep, snow and slush-covered primitive mountain road, to Bourbach-la-Haut, we felt as if we were dragging our way over the Himalayas.

A number of the men gave out. Most of the wagon teams gave out. Two men, with feet out of business, rode my horse. Other men rode the horses of other mounted officers. We, all who were strong, helped to carry the rifles and packs of those who were weak. Teams were doubled and tripled on the heavy wagons, and, supplemented by many hands on the wheel spokes, one vehicle at a time gained the plateau upon which was situated the village of Bourbach-la-Haut.

When we were all up, new troubles confronted us. The billeting space of that village was equal to about one half of our strength. After making a personal inspection, accompanied by my most reliable officers, I still had more than 300 men unprovided for. And the snow storm was still raging. I could see but one solution.

I called upon the priest, and asked him to offer our men the shelter of the church. He refused.

Then I ordered the men to go into the church, to keep away from the chancel, to be particular to disarrange nothing, and to make no disorder of any kind, to spread their blankets on the benches and on the floor, and to sleep.

Then the priest came to me in great excitement and indignation of protest, and asked me to order the men out. And I refused.

I am a Christian, and I am a religious man. I am not familiar with the laws of the Catholic Church. I assume that that priest, in acting as he did, was obeying the laws; but I am confident that if it had been practicable to appeal to a higher authority of the church, permission would have been granted me to shelter, in the house of the Lord, those children of the Lord, from further exposure of that night of storm. Whether or not my surmise is correct, and whether or not I am ever forgiven by the officers of the church for what that priest termed my sacrilege, I am confident that God smiled upon my decision.

The weather cleared during the night. Upon December 19th we hiked to Petite Fontaine, a comparatively easy march of about fifteen or sixteen kilometers.

Upon December 20th we resumed our march as a battalion, travelling in a southwesterly direction, about fifteen kilometers, to the outskirts of the city of Belfort. There the regiment was mobilized in marching formation; and, as a regiment, we paraded through Belfort.

After marching through Belfort, once more divided into separated battalions, we proceeded to billeting towns for station. Regimental Headquarters was established at Banvillars.

346

The 1st Battalion was quartered in the villages, Urceray, Buc, and Argiesans.

The 2nd Battalion, Captain John Holley Clark, Commanding, was quartered at Dorans.

The 3rd Battalion, under the newly made Major David A. L'Esperance, was quartered at Bavillers.

These villages were suburbs of Belfort, at distances ranging from five to eight kilometers.

We had a lot of rain and snow and rough weather in general during the period of our occupancy of those towns suburban to Belfort.

On Christmas Day, we all made an effort at hilarity. Many had received boxes from home. A Red Cross station at Belfort supplied gifts of various kinds for the men. We delved into the credit of our company funds, and purchased at the markets of Belfort a lot of the kinds of food commonly associated in our minds with Christmas dinners. And all hands shouted "Merry Christmas," back and forth, and cracked our faces into smiles.

At about three o'clock in the afternoon, just after we had gone through that regular Christmas dinner function of letting out the belt three holes, came the sounds of martial music. In an instant our banquet table was deserted. Down the rickety stairs we rushed, out through the shed into the open, and there in our barnyard, facing us, standing in the crescent of "concert formation," and playing my favorite march of Aix-les-Bains. *Our Director*—was "Europe and His Band."

We had a happy hour—all of the men of our town and the civilian population, too, crowded into that barnyard, to listen to the best music of the American Army, to dance and to sway to the rhythm of the jazz—to listen, big-eyed, to Noble Sissle, as he sang his *Joan of Arc*.

Then the Drum Major, Sergeant Gillard Thompson, the veteran of the 9th Cavalry whom General Walsh (a captain of that crack colored regiment of the regular army, of many years

347

before) had recognized and greeted at St. Nazaire, stepped out to make a speech.

Sergeant Thompson's speech was in the form of a letter addressed to me, and signed upon behalf of all the members of the band. It was a letter couched in extravagant terms of affection—of flattery, I dare say—but it touched my heart and made me happy. Of such weakness are men made! I'm not publishing the letter—it's too personal—but I'm saving it for my sons to have, after I'm gone.

Upon December 31st the regiment commenced once more to move toward home. Upon that day the 3rd Battalion hiked eight or nine kilometers to Marvillars, and entrained for Le Mans, upon the outskirts of which city had been established a great American "Forwarding Camp."

Upon January 1st the 2nd Battalion followed the 3rd Battalion.

The 1st Battalion spent its New Years Day at Urceray, Buc and Argiesans—in the good old-fashioned custom of making and receiving calls, and in tendering to all, well wishes for the coming year.

Upon January 2nd, the 1st Battalion hiked from six to eight kilometers to Hericourt, and entrained for Les Mans.

We arrived at Les Mans at about 3 o'clock upon the morning of January 4th; and, just as daylight came, we joined the regiment at the camp some three or four kilometers outside of the city.

The 369th, once more, was an American regiment in an American camp.

Our stop of a week or so at Les Mans was a good deal of a bore; and we were uncomfortable, physically. We were not particularly unhappy, though. The physical discomfort was, for the most part, caused by rain and mud (for which no reasonable person could blame the Commanding General) and by crowded quarters.

The general atmosphere of the camp at Les Mans was one

of cheerfulness, and there was evidenced none of the program of brutal morale baiting which we were to experience a few days later, when we moved to Brest.

Our chief activities at Les Mans were delousing, re-equipping, and the preparation of embarkation lists. We all got to be very tired, but that was all a part of the game. There were no kicks. We had done our bit. We were going home. We were happy.

There was one activity of our stop at Les Mans which aroused indignation in some of us, and amusement in others.

A couple of days after our arrival, we were ordered to attend lectures upon the subject of the Fort Sill Musketry Course. The lectures were followed by practical work in the field—in sighting exercises, trigger squeeze, positions for firing, standing, kneeling or prone, and target designation.

It may be recalled that our regiment had spent many hours of study of this subject during the months of September, October, November and December, 1917, that most of the officers and many of the men had passed creditable examinations upon the subject, and that, in an experience of almost nine months in front line positions, we had found no part of the course whatsoever to have been useful to us in our work.

In all our period of service in France, until this time at Les Mans, when we were preparing to go home to be mustered out of the military service to return to civil life, we had had no instructor from the American Army visit us.

We had been under fire 191 days.

The young officer who was assigned to instruct us in the musketry course was an officer whom some of our officers were said to have known at the army schools in France as a fellow student—an officer who had not, at the time of his acquaintance with our officers at school, had any practical experience in warfare, and who had not subsequently had any.

Upon January 9th came the splendid news that Brest was waiting for us.

Upon January 10th we departed from Le Mans.

Upon the evening of January 11th we arrived at Brest.

The happiness of our men during the journey to Brest was a beautiful thing to behold—beautiful when considered from the viewpoint of the cause of the happiness.

Here were about four thousand men of the colored race, a race which had suffered wrongs of humanity for centuries; a race which had been classed by some almost as one of the lower animal kingdoms, not quite as human beings; a race still suffering, and bound to suffer for a long time still to come, from prejudices in the hearts of white men, the cumulative prejudices of hundreds of years.

And these men, in full appreciation of the worldly handicaps enumerated above, were going home as heroes!

They had achieved the impossible!

Recruited as fighting men, in ridicule; trained and mustered into Federal service, in more ridicule; sent to France as a safe political solution of a volcanic political problem; loaned to the French Army as another easy way out—these men had carried on.

In patience and in fortitude these men had served. Their triumphs of battle had been great; but their triumphs of orderliness, of cleanliness, of personal and civic decency, had been greater.

France had wept over them—wept the tears of gratitude and love. France had sung and danced and cried to their music. France had given its first war medal for an American private to one of their number. France had given to them the collective citation which gave to their beloved regiment the honor of flying the *Croix de Guerre* streamers at the peak of its colors. France had kissed these colored soldiers—kissed them with reverence and in honor, first upon the right cheek and then upon the left.

And now, they were going home—home to the plaudits and cheers of their fellow countrymen, their fellow townsmen—home to the arms of their loved ones. They had helped not only to win the war, but they had helped, too, in the longdrawn struggle still to be, for the betterment of conditions for their race.

SERGEANT COX, OUR COLOR BEARER, MAY 5, 1918

ONE OF OUR BOYS AT UNGERSHEIM (NEAR THE RHINE)

All the way from Le Mans to Brest, conjectures were made as to whether we should go aboard ship that night or wait until morning. Those boys all hoped we might wait until morning. Of course everybody would want to see us; and, of course, everybody would want to hear the band; and, of course, the Commanding General of Brest would want us to pass in review before him; and, of course, a dozen other things—the ebullitions of the hearts of happy soldiers justly proud of their record.

As our trains pulled in to Brest four thousand pairs of feet were dancing in spirit, four thousand hearts were singing.

And then—within a few minutes after we had detrained, a private of my battalion, confused in his sense of direction upon returning to his company from a latrine, had his head split open by a blow from the club of an "M.P."! Why? Because he had dared to interrupt the "M.P." while in conversation with another, to inquire as to his way.

A crowd gathered, a crowd that might well have meant something serious for the "M.P.s" of Brest. Captain MacClinton got the news—how I don't know, but that man had a genius for being in the thick of things. He rushed to the scene of trouble, worked his way into the center of the crowd and asserted his authority. The crowd dispersed. Our men went back to their company areas, and then, up spoke a captain of the Military Police, with insolence to MacClinton. I hate to think of what might have occurred if the thing had gone on a minute or so longer. Old Mac's Scotch was up. I arrived, and demanded an explanation of what had occurred, and information as to what was to be done with our man who had just been carried away. The Captain of "M.P.s" turned upon me with his insolence, and I ordered him to stand at attention to his superior officer.

He stood at attention with bad grace, and growled something about my not being his superior officer, because, as "M.P.," he represented the Major General Commanding.

I held him at attention, and informed him that as a Major of the United States Army I represented the President, as commanding officer of the troops just detrained I had my duty of responsibility, and that I proposed to exercise it.

The Captain of "M.P.s" became more respectful then, and, in the course of his explanations, he let slip a line to the effect that they had been warned that our "Niggers" were feeling their oats a bit and that instructions had been given to "take it out of them quickly, just as soon as they arrived, so as not to have any trouble later on."

The next morning our man, with head bandaged, was brought back to us with the oral message that it had been decided to prefer no charges against him. Pretty smart! If that man had been placed on trial, the whole story would have come out, under oath. "Brest" was already under the fire of journalistic attack; but most of the stories had to be published with the qualification: "It is said by an officer whose name, for obvious reasons, cannot be exposed."

Soon after a late supper had been served, the regiment marched out to Camp Pontanezen. The hour was well on towards midnight.

At the top of a long hill we halted to rest. Two mounted "M.P.s" passed me as I stood at the head of the column. They were going towards Brest. They offered no salute; but it was fairly dark, and, at the moment, I gave no great thought to the matter. Presently, they returned. One of the "M.P.s" demanded:—"Who is the Commanding Officer of this outfit?"

"I am. My name is Major Little, and this is the 369th Infantry."

"All right," said the "M.P.," "I want you to go right down to the center of your column and stop that disturbance."

"I am Major Little of the 369th Infantry," again I informed the "M.P."

"All right, I say," answered the "M.P.," "I tell you I want you to go right down to the center of your column and stop that disturbance. There's a lot of your 'niggers' yelling at us as we pass, 'Who won the war?'"

"Are you clear that you are addressing Major Little of the 369th Infantry?" I inquired.

"Yes—you told us that three times!"

"Then dismount, and stand at attention, and address me, if you have anything to say to me, as I presume you must, at one time, have been taught to address an officer."

"Aw—I don't have to—see."

"Do you mean to say that your officer of the guard has instructed you that you do not have to?"

"Yes."

"Very well—then, of course, I have no direct authority. I shall report your case through the proper channels."

"Well now—are you going down there to stop that rumpus?"

"There is no rumpus," I answered. "Our men are well disciplined, and all of the companies are under command of their own officers. I gave the order to halt and to rest. The men have a right to speak. If you don't like the call 'Who won the war,' your best course of action is to make believe you don't hear it. We've travelled all the way down from the front lines—hundreds of miles. At every stop, wherever troops of other branches have been at the railroad stations, our men have called out 'who won the war' and then, in good nature, they've answered their own call saying: 'The Bakers,' or 'The Q.M.'s' or 'The Stevedores,' or 'The Red Cross' or 'The R.T.O.'s or 'The MPs'— or, in fact any branch of the S.O.S. that happened to be represented on the platform of the station. Along the way of hundreds of miles our men have exchanged those greetings with other men, and always in good nature on both sides. We've virtually laughed our way through France. You people in this town are the first people to act as if you didn't like our men. You two men are the first men in the whole army who have been unwilling to accept as a joke the call 'Who won the war.' Now, I advise you to go along about your business. I'm running this regiment, just now."

353

"This will get you three months!" The spokesman of the "M.P." couple gave his parting shot, as the pair rode on down the road.

I wondered what the man meant. Were they giving line majors three months imprisonment in Brest for correcting privates on M.P. duty, for lack of disciplinary manners?

We were soon to be made to understand.

We arrived at Brest January 11th. We embarked from Brest for home, January 31st. During that period of three weeks, no day passed (and but few hours) during which we failed to get some notice of petty fault-finding coupled with a threat of disciplinary action against the entire organization by placing its name at the bottom of the list for embarkation.

A number of our men gave themselves the pleasure of writing articles or stories of their service, and I was favored with copies of a number of such literary efforts. One of these works, written in the form of a diary, and entitled:

With the Fighting 15th New York Infantry

In France and Germany

1917 ———————— 1918 ———————— 1919

"The Black Rattlers"

handles the Brest experience in language which I quote, as follows:

Jan. 11/19 (train) Brest, Finnistere. Hiked to Embarkation Camp supposedly for a brief stay. Deloused and detailed night and day and it seems as if we at last had struck something worse than the Germans and many were taken sick as a result of the conditions under which we were compelled to live and work. The word "attention" comes into its own at this camp, being very strictly enforced by the front-dodging M.P.'s, the pampered pets of the war—Feb. 1/19.

It would not be fair to bid farewell to Brest without paying our respects to the magnificent efforts of the workers of the Red Cross, the Y. M. C. A., the Knights of Columbus, and the

Salvation Army, to make the lives of the men who had hoped to be heroes a little less unendurable. They did everything that they were supposed to do, and did it indefatigably and well— everything that they could do, for the physical and spiritual and mental welfare of men and officers.

At last, came the day for which we had worked and waited. Embarkation orders came as follows:—

Headquarters, Headquarters Company and 1st Battalion, S.S. Stockholm, January 31, 1919.

Second Battalion and Supply Company, S.S. Regina, February 1, 1919.

3rd Battalion and Regimental Machine Gun Company, S.S. Le France, February 1, 1919.

Upon the afternoon of January 31st, I led the troops for our embarkation of that day from Camp Pontanezen to and through the city of Brest, down to the docks where tenders waited to carry us out to the steamer. We marched in silence. Every man had been warned and every man had taken his warning seriously.

We might have been off upon a mission similar to that of the immortalized "Burial of Sir John Moore":

"Not a drum was heard—
"Not a funeral note."

As we marched upon the docks, my son waved to me in greeting. He had been at Brest with his organization all the time that I had been there.

As our last tender was ready to shove off, the Chief of Staff of the base who stood talking with me, said "Major, I didn't notice before, but you've got your band with you, haven't you?"

"Yes sir," I answered.

"Can they play?"

"Yes sir."

"Well, why don't you give us a tune as you leave?"

"I'm sure it would be very welcome to us, sir," I answered;

"but I'm not taking any chances of losing our sailing place. If you so direct, sir, I will give the order."

"Yes, yes, by all means, let us have some music!"

"Mr. Europe," I addressed the leader, "you may play!"

And so our men, once more with the music that they loved so well stirring their hearts, bade farewell to France.

That Chief of Staff was a human being.

The return voyages of the 369th were uneventful.

The 3rd Battalion passed us on the way, and landed in New York upon February 9th. The other units of our colored regiment landed upon February 12th, Lincoln's Birthday.

Our families met us down the bay on police boats and the excursion steamers of citizens' committees.

The scenes of joy and excitement, of the bursting of pent up emotions, I cannot describe; but we all appreciated that welcome home.

Mayor Hylan and his Committee of Citizens were helping to make our men forget Major General Helmick and his "M. P." bullies. One of the days so long waited for had come.

Our men slept, as they were carried on Long Island Railroad cars to Camp Upton at Yaphank—and as they slept, they dreamed that they were heroes.

# XLVII

# OUR GREAT PARADE

*February 17th, 1919*

UPON February 17th, 1919, Colonel Hayward saw his dream come true.

It may be recalled that during the early summer of 1917, the 15th New York Infantry had suffered a number of disappointments which appeared to some almost in the light of slights.

For example: When the "Rainbow Division" was announced, with the 69th New York Infantry (which had not been included in the 27th Division) as one of the elements, Colonel Hayward had endeavored to get our regiment put in with the Rainbows, too— only to be informed, with a laugh, that black was not one of the colors of the rainbow. And when the 27th Division had staged a farewell parade, as the boys left New York to go into training at Spartanburg, once more the Fifteenth was left out of the day's program.

Our regiment had not been accorded the thrill of a going-away parade; and, within our ranks, there had been disappointment. Colonel Hayward had promised, in what to some had seemed to be a spirit of bitter recklessness, that we should have a parade when we should come home.

That promise had been worked to the limit within our regiment. The welcome home parade was a matter of daily discussion. After the armistice had been declared, the parade came to be a medium of disciplinary exactment. I believe there were nowhere in the whole army any better behaved soldiers than our soldiers. Our men had averaged well in deportment all

357

through the war; but there were, of course, scapegraces in every company, just as in most families there are "black sheep." It was to the scapegraces that we addressed the threat of penalty of a deprivation of the privilege of parading with the regiment up Fifth Avenue, when the citizens of New York should turn out to welcome us home.

That threatened penalty had to be inflicted in but very few cases. In the majority of cases, the men just made up their minds not to miss that parade—and, accordingly, they carried on without delinquencies.

In the Spring of 1917, when the active recruiting effort was on, a parade had been attempted through the streets of Harlem, with a view to stirring the citizens to enthusiasm and prompting the youth of the colored race to enlist.

Someone had taken a photograph of that parade.

It was a dreadful picture to record. A couple of hundred men or less were shown in a stringy column of irregularity, which some way had named, "Column of Bunches," and some other wag had added: "And not much of that."

That photograph had been shown to Colonel Hayward with a laugh and sneer.

The Colonel had taken a good, long look at that photograph. At first there had been red spots of anger in his cheeks. Then the cheeks had gone pale; and presently his eyes had closed. When Colonel Hayward had opened his eyes again the photograph upon which they had focussed was still there before them, but as the eyes had rested upon the picture the second time, a new light and expression had come over the face of the man.

Then the boyish looking colonel had spoken: "Do you know," he had said, to the officers who had been his companions, "Do you know, a kind of vision has come to me out of that picture— a dream, I suppose you might call it. And those poor little bunches of undisciplined looking soldiers have taken on a new and magnificent dignity. I'm looking a long ways ahead now, and I'm not sure whether I'm in the picture or not, but the men are there—only their numbers have increased twenty-fold. And the poor, dribbling column of bunches has become a splendid machine-like column of military strength. The spectators on the sidewalks have changed in appearance, too. There are more of them, and they seem to be greatly excited. Some are waving their hats, and apparently shouting. And some are crying, too. Some are smiling. But the ones who laugh, seem to be laughing with a different quality of laughter than the ones in this picture here today.

"Do you know," the Colonel mused on, "I'm having a kind of silly dream about that column of bunches. This visionary picture that I see shows the war to be ended, and these men marching home. And it's obvious that they've done well, too, and that their home-coming is one of triumph. I doubt if I ever shall forget that dream. I wonder if it can come true."

And within two years, upon February 17th, 1919, Colonel Hayward's dream did come true. The 15th New York Infantry, known in France as the 369th United States Infantry, marched up 5th Avenue to receive the plaudits of a million grateful citizens of New York, and then marched on for the full length of the Lenox Avenue Boulevard, through Harlem, to turn a quarter of a million of men, women, and children of the colored race wild with a frenzy of pride and joy and love.

We left Camp Upton at daybreak, ran by special trains into Long Island City, crossed the river upon ferry boats, marched through 35th Street to Madison Avenue, and down Madison Avenue until the head of the column rested upon 23rd Street. Thus far the parade had not started. The marching was by way of mobilization, by battalions, and in column of squads.

Upon Madison Avenue, as we extended north from 23rd Street, we formed phalanx by company. In the phalanx formation we marched with equalized companies of 16 squads each, 4 platoons of 4 squads each, in close line without interval—a solid mass of men about 35 feet square. The sergeants marched 2 paces in front of their platoons. Lieutenants marched on a line

3 paces in front of sergeants. The Captain marched 5 paces in front of the line of lieutenants. It was, I believe, the first time New York had witnessed such a formation for parade—a formation which we had learned from the French.

At about eleven o'clock in the morning word came that the city officials had passed up 5th Avenue on the way to the reviewing stand at 60th Street, and Colonel Hayward, for the last time gave to his regiment of colored volunteers, the order—*"Forward MARCH!"*

We marched west through 23rd Street, along the southern border of Madison Square Park, to 5th Avenue. At 5th Avenue we turned to the north. We were the first of the home-coming troops to march under the Victory Arch at 25th Street. We continued straight on to the north until we reached 110th Street. There we turned west to Lenox Avenue, and at Lenox Avenue we turned north again and paraded to 145th Street. At 145th Street we turned east to Lexington Avenue, where we boarded subway trains for downtown. At 33rd Street we detrained, and marched into the 71st Regiment Armory. There the citizens' committee had prepared a fine lunch (chicken, of course)—and an entertainment for all hands.

For the first time in the history of the regiment, the 15th New York Infantry as a whole, had a roof over its head.

I doubt if any of us shall ever again be privileged to share in such thrills of varying emotions as were ours upon that 17th of February, 1919, thanks to the whole-heartedness of the citizens of New York.

New Yorkers are sometimes jeered at as a bustling, hustling people so intent upon the pursuit and worship of the almighty dollar as to be lacking in spirits of hospitality, civic pride, and even patriotism. It is no part of my purpose, or present duty, to enter upon debate in refutation of such a slander.

New York's severest critics, however, could have found no fault with either the quantity or the quality of the red-blood which ruled the passions of its people that day upon which they welcomed home the 15th Heavy Foot.

I marched at the head of the 1st Battalion—about 60 paces (150 feet) behind Jim Europe's Band of sixty pieces of brass and reed, and a field music section of thirty trumpets and drums.

During the entire progress of that seven mile march, I scarcely heard ten consecutive bars of music. So great were the roars of cheers, the applause, and the shouts of personal greetings!

The multitude of fellow citizens who greeted us that day—the tens of thousands who cheered, the women who wept—the men who cried "God bless you, boys!"—all were united to drown the music of Jim Europe's Band. They did not give us their welcome because ours was a regiment of colored soldiers—they did not give us their welcome in spite of ours being a regiment of colored soldiers. They greeted us that day from hearts filled with gratitude and with pride and with love, *because ours was a regiment of men, who had done the work of men.*

Upon the 17th of February, 1919, New York City knew no color line.

When we arrived at the Harlem districts, Colonel Hayward halted the regiment and ordered the formation changed.

That French phalanx formation of solid masses was impressive, and the parade in that formation was a great success down in that part of New York where the greetings were, for the most part, impersonal.

Up through the avenues of Harlem, however, such a formation would have been a cruelty. So far as might be possible, the face and figure of each soldier boy must be made to stand out, for his loved ones to see and to recognize.

We continued the march in platoon front, with good deep distances between front and rear ranks. And the music of Jim Europe's Band was—"Here comes my daddy now!"

And the new open formation proved itself as great a success

361

for the home districts of the colored men as had the phalanx for Fifth Avenue.

Mothers, and wives, and sisters, and sweethearts recognized their boys and their men; and they rushed right out through the ranks to embrace them. For the final mile or more of our parade about every fourth soldier of the ranks had a girl upon his arm —and we marched through Harlem singing and laughing.

It may not have been good military business, but it was great human business. And a nation of great, honest, human emotion is a great nation.

# XLVIII

# MUSTERED OUT

*February 28, 1919*

THE days following that of our great parade were trying days.

It is harder to get out of the U. S. Army than to get in. There are many examinations to be taken, accounts of many kinds to be squared, each man's service record to be perfected and signed up by each officer concerned. There are final payrolls and final pay vouchers to be made out and checked. There are lectures upon a number of subjects, to be attended, and farewell speeches to be listened to. Finally, there are discharges to be made out for each man, and signed.

Our western and southern replacement men and officers were sent off in groups to the camps nearest their homes for discharge. That lessened the number of men to be handled for complete discharge at Camp Upton, but it also cut down the number of officers remaining to do the work.

And, of course, no man had any further interest in the service.

As I have said, the days from February 18th to February 28th were trying days.

Three days after the big parade, Henry Johnson came back.

A good many chapters ago, representing a lapse of nine and a half months, I told the story of *The Battle of Henry Johnson;* and we left the little hero in the hospital.

Three months later, Johnson rejoined the regiment. He was a physical wreck; but he pleaded so hard in the French hospital against being sent to an American base for discharge, that he succeeded in remaining in the service. One of Johnson's feet had

had most of the bones removed, so that he had to walk in a manner that might be described as "slap-foot." And in one of his legs he had a silver tube in place of the shin bone. Besides these disabilities, he had a number of other wounds.

We all felt a deep affection and sense of admiration and gratitude for Johnson, in consideration of the splendid advertising that had come to our regiment through his exploit of May 13th.

When he came back to the regiment, it was realized that he could not be expected to do regular line duty; so special duties were picked for him.

Colonel Hayward expressed the affectionate feeling of many of us when he said, in reference to Henry Johnson, that he thought the least we could do for him, after all he had done for us, was to treat him as the old 7th Cavalry had treated Custer's horse—let him nibble grass around Headquarters, and when company came call him in and show him off.

So Henry Johnson was made a sergeant, and he became one of the great pets of the regiment.

Some people used to think that he was a bit spoiled; but to me he was always a sweet, unassuming boy, ready and eager to do whatever he could do with his infirmities.

I do not mean by this that Henry was lacking in full appreciation of his own greatness. While democratic in his bearing, just as the late Colonel Roosevelt was democratic, still he never forgot that he wore the purple. And he never let anyone else forget it.

One day, after our regiment had reached The Rhine, an officer, newly joined, noticed Sergeant Johnson strolling along an avenue of Blodelsheim, with a *Croix de Guerre*, carrying a palm, pinned to his overseas cap.

The officer, of course, had heard of Johnson but he had never seen him. Although many citations favoring our men had been sent forward, there had been up to that time, only three medals actually presented. Of course Johnson's was one of the three. Some of our men had shown a tendency to purchase medals, and to wear them without authority, which tendency we were striving to repress with sternness.

The new officer, spying Johnson, with medal worn jauntily upon the cap, felt that he had a duty to perform. So he proceeded to action:

"Halt, Sergeant! What is that thing you've got on your hat? And where did you get that *Croix de Guerre*, anyway?"

Sergeant Johnson halted. He cast a withering glance at the lieutenant; but with perfect execution, snapped into salute. "Sir," he said, "Ah guess yoo doan know who Ah am!"

"No, I don't," snapped back the lieutenant. "Who the hell are you?"

"SIR," answered the sergeant with such frigid civility as to verge right up to the border of the field of scorn—"SIR, AH'M HENRY JOHNSON!"

After the rendering of which knockout, the former little red cap executed about face, marched away, and left the lieutenant flat.

When the regiment had arrived in New York, the reporters made much of Johnson. They photographed him and they interviewed him. Johnson, always with an eye to the dramatic, told a new story of his fight to each new group of reporters. But it all went. In those days of excitement Sergeant Henry Johnson was not the only member of the regiment who yielded to the temptation to tell a good story.

When the day came for our parade, Johnson had been carried along in the rear of the regiment in an automobile, as scores of others of our wounded had been carried.

Johnson's car, however, had been laden with flowers, and the little fellow himself was fairly garlanded with wreaths and ropes of roses. He stood in his car throughout the parade, and received the plaudits of a multitude, with dignity.

When the regiment boarded the Long Island Railroad trains upon the evening of February 17th, to return to Camp Upton, Sergeant Henry Johnson was A.W.O.L.

And then, three days after the big parade, Henry Johnson came back.

He was brought to me for instructions as to discipline. In response to my questioning, he told me that after the parade he had been taken in charge by a group of gentlemen, who had taken him successively to a number of 5th Avenue clubs and hotels, where he had been entertained with food and drink, and rewarded with money. He explained that he didn't see how he could refuse the hospitality of these gentlemen without reflecting upon the standard of politeness of the regiment, as many of the gentlemen had spoken of some of the officers of the regiment as friends of intimacy. And so he had stayed on and on, and finally it had become necessary for him to rest. As corroborative proof of his story, the Sergeant showed me a bundle of money which he said amounted to more than six hundred dollars. My guess was a lot more.

Of course, Johnson was forgiven.

# "AH'M ER GOIN' BACK TER MAH REG'LAR JOB"

*Feb. 28, 1918*

THE last day of February had come. The long, tedious detail of mustering a regiment out of the service had worked its way to completion. All the men had gone—all, I believe, but my orderly Joe, who was waiting to do me my last service, before he should report to the hospital, as a resident for treatment to clear up some eye trouble from gassing.

It was past eleven o'clock of the forenoon, and I sat at my desk in the little cabin which had served as my office for the preceding two weeks. There were a few more papers to clear, and then I too would be leaving for home. My bit was done.

A knock sounded at my door.

"Come in!" I called.

The door swung open, and there, with hand at salute, stood Henry Johnson.

"What is it, Sergeant?" I inquired.

"Suh, Major Suh," the little homicidal king murmured, "Ah've ben discharged fum der U. S. Army. Ah'm er goin' home. Ah'm er goin' back ter mah reg'lar job, and Ah've cum ter say good-bye."

For once the little hero wasn't grinning.

I knew that the men had all been put on the 10:15 train for New York; and I understood that Johnson must have contrived to get off again, to tramp over to my cabin. That meant a walk of a good mile, at least, on his poor, crippled feet; and another mile to get back again for an afternoon train.

367

My heart was touched. As I looked into his eyes, I saw something that seemed to put a lump in my throat.

My eyes searched through the windows of my little office and, as far as I could see in three directions, I saw—barracks, and nothing else. Not a soldier in sight! As I gazed, a cloud that a few seconds before had dimmed the bright sunshine, sailed away. The sunshine once more had come back; the future was pictured in optimism and hope.

Like a flash the wonderful cinema of my two years with the 15th Heavy Foot passed before me. I realized that this great little first class fighting man, Henry Johnson, the colored porter of the Albany railroad station, was teaching me a lesson of peace, even as he had taught hundreds of his comrades a lesson of combat.

The work for which we had volunteered was over. The emergency which had made militarism the duty of good citizenship had passed.

It was time to say good-bye, I was to see my beloved soldier boys no more.

I rose, and walked over to where the former Sergeant Johnson stood at attention. My eyes were moist, as were his. My lips a-quiver.

"Good-bye, Henry," I said, as I wrung his hand. "Good-bye, Henry, don't forget me."

"Furgit yer! Suh Major, Sur," answered Henry Johnson— his eyes opening wider and wider. "Furgit yer! Suh? Why, Suh Major Sur, yer made a man of me!"

The End.

# APPENDIX

## ARGONNE-VIENNE-LA-VILLE

16 DIVISION

May 16, 1918

ORDER NO. 697

General Gallais Cd$^t$ of the 16:DI cites to the order
of the Division the soldiers of the 369$^{th}$ R.I.U.S.

1st: Johnson, Henry, No. 103348, soldier in the said command: doing double
night sentry duty, was attacked by a group of a dozen Germans and put
one out of the fight by gunshot and seriously wounded two with a knife.
In spite of having received three wounds by revolver shots and grenades
at the start of the action, went to the help of his wounded comrade who
was being carried away by the enemy and continued the strife until the
rout of the Germans. Gave a magnificent example of courage and energy.

2nd: Roberts, Needham, No. 103369, soldier in the said command: Doing
double night sentry duty was attacked and seriously wounded in the leg
by a group of Germans; continued the strife by throwing grenades, in
spite of having fallen to the ground, until the enemy was put to rout.
Good and brave soldier.

The General requested that the citation for soldier Johnson be changed to
the citation of the Order of the Army.

2A Chief of Etat Major
Boye
General Cdt. of the 16th D
GALLAIS.

369

# APPENDIX

LE GÉNÉRAL GOURAUD
MEMBRE DU CONSEIL SUPÉRIEUR DE LA GUERRE
GOUVERNEUR MILITAIRE DE PARIS

Le 19 Decembre 1925

Mon cher Général et ami,

Vous rappelez vous avoir rédigé vos ordres pour la glorieuse journée du 26 Septembre 1918 devant le P.C. d'un chef de battaillon français nommé Lefèvre, qui commandait alors un groupe du 421 d'Artillerie lourde?

Il m'a apporté l'autre jour les photographies ~~que voics et~~ que je suis heureux de vous faire parvenir, *souspli sipare* pensant qu'elles rappelleraient à vos braves soldats un beau jour de bataille, et que vous voudrez peut-être les placer dans votre Armory.

Les tranchées que ces photographies représentent, sont les tranchées à l'est de Minaucourt où votre régiment bivouaqua dans la nuit du 25 au 26.

Les photographies 1 et 2 représentent vos soldats s'équipant avant de quitter la tranchée où ils ont passé la nuit.

La photographie 3 : ils se rendent au lieu de rassemblement pour rejoindre les troupes d'attaque engagées depuis 5 h 25.

Les photographies 4 & 5 représentent un groupe d'officiers attendant l'heure du depart devant le P.C. du Commandant Lefèvre. Le Commandant du Bataillon (qui, d'après les souvenirs du commandant Lefèvre, doit être vousmême) assis devant le P.C. vient de recevoir l'ordre de porter son bataillon en avant, et rédige ses ordres d'attaque.

La photographie 6 représente un groupe de soldats au repos, en attendant l'heure du départ.

Je profite de cette excellente occasion, mon cher Général, pour vous envoyer mes voeux, ainsi qu'au General Hayward et à tous vos officiers, pour Noël et la Nouvelle Année.

Croyez-moi votre bien dévoué.

Monsieur le General Arthur LITTLE,
   Cdt le 365 Regiment d'Infanterie,
     NEW YORK CITY

# APPENDIX

GENERAL GOURAUD

Member of the Supreme Council of War

MILITARY GOVERNOR OF PARIS

19 December 1923

My dear General and Friend:—

Do you recall drafting your orders for the glorious day of September 26, 1918, before the P.C. of a French chief of battalion named Lefevre, who then commanded a group of the 421st, Heavy Artillery?

He brought to me the other day the photographs which it gives me pleasure to forward to you under separate cover, thinking that they will recall to your brave soldiers a magnificent day of battle and that perhaps you would like to place them in your armory.

The trenches that these photographs represent are those to the East of Minaucourt where your regiment bivouacked on the night of the 25th to 26th. Photographs 1 and 2 show your soldiers equipping themselves before leaving the trench where they passed the night. In photograph 3 they are going to assembly point to join the attacking troops that have been engaged in the battle since 5.25 o'clock.

Photographs 4 and 5 show a group of officers awaiting the march hour before the P.C. of Commandant Lefevre. The commandant of the battalion (who, according to Commandant Lefevre's recollection, must be yourself) has just received the order to take his battalion to the front and is drawing his orders for the attack. Photograph 6 shows a group of soldiers at rest, awaiting the hour of departure.

I am availing myself of this excellent opportunity, my dear General, to send you my best wishes, and also to General Hayward and all your officers, for Christmas and the New Year.

Believe me your devoted

(signed)     GOURAUD

To General Arthur Little
Commanding the 369th Regiment of Infantry
New York City.

371

# APPENDIX

## THE ROSTER OF OFFICERS

WHO SERVED IN THE

369TH UNITED STATES INFANTRY

(15TH NEW YORK INFANTRY, N. G.)

Between July 15, 1917, and March 1, 1919

### COLONEL
William Hayward (5-7-8)

### LIEUTENANT COLONEL
Woodell A. Pickering (5-6-7)

### MAJORS
Edwin W. Dayton (5)
Arthur W. Little (5-7-8)
David A. L'Esperance, Jr. (5-7)
Monson Morris
Lorillard Spencer (5-6-7)

### MEDICAL DEPARTMENT
Major G. Franklin Sheils, M.C. (4-7-8)
Major Edward L. Whittemore, M.C. (7)
1st Lieut. John C. Bradner, M.C. (7)
1st Lieut. James C. Graham, M.C.
1st Lieut. Ernest J. Hoover, M.C.
1st Lieut. Verner Kennedy, M.C.
1st Lieut. Willis H. Keenan, M.C. (6-7)
1st Lieut. George W. McSweeney, M.C.
1st Lieut. Carlton T. Harris, D.C.
1st Lieut. Nils H. Larsen, D.C. (7)

### CHAPLAINS
1st Lieut. William H. Brooks (3)
1st Lieut. Benjamin C. Robeson
1st Lieut. Thomas W. Wallace

### CAPTAINS
Aaron T. Bates (7)
Frederick W. Cobb (1-6-7)
Louis B. Candler (7)
C. H. Ranulf Compton (5)
John H. Clark, Jr. (5-7)
Robert G. Evans
Hamilton Fish, Jr. (7-8)
Charles W. Fillmore (7)
Robert F. Ferguson, Jr. (7)

Edwin R. D. Fox (7)
Edward J. Farrell (7-8)
George F. Hinton
Seth B. MacClinton (7-8)
Comerford McLaughlin (6-7)
Napoleon B. Marshall
John O. Outwater (7)
Julian F. Scott
Lewis E. Shaw (7)
Samuel Shethar (6-7)
Arthur E. Wenige
James D. White (7)
Eric S. Winston
Edward A. Walton (6-7)

### 1ST LIEUTENANTS
Horace R. S. Allen
Otto A. Arnston (7)
Carl E. Anderson
M. S. Acree
Oscar H. Baker (7)
George R. Brown
Edward B. Burke
Wilmot Berry
Elmer C. Bucher (1-7)
Harry L. Blake
Harold H. Benedict
John W. Castles (6-7)
John H. Connor (7)
Francis Y. Cowle
George S. Delafield
John C. Dunlap
Charles S. Dean (1-6-7)
James R. Europe (3)
Chester A. Easum
Charles F. Frothingham, Jr.
Conrad M. Fox (7)
Harry Grant
G. M. Grant
Raymond G. Grams (7)

(1) Killed in action. (2) Died in service. (3) Deceased since war. (4) Medal of Honor.
(5) *Légion d'Honneur.* (6) Distinguished Service Cross. (7) *Croix de Guerre.*
(8) U. S. Citation for Gallantry.

# APPENDIX

James B. Gillen
Douglas L. Hilliker
Michael J. Hourigan
Gorman R. Jones (7)
Marshall L. Johnson (7)
Don L. Kooker
Whitney Kernochan
Eugene B. Kinnaird
Hyman King
Harold M. Landon (6-7)
George C. Lacy
Walter R. Lockhart (7)
Hugh A. Page (7)
Thomas P. Pontius
Richardson Pratt (7)
Ralph M. Rowland (7)
William A. Raymond
Frank D. Roberts
George S. Robb (4-5-7)
James K. Ramsay
Durant Rice (7)
George F. Seibel (1)
Frank W. Stewart
Eugene V. Seidle (7)
William R. Sattler, Jr.
Hoyt Sherman (7)
John S. Stevens
Roy E. Spock
Herbert W. Schabacher
Charles R. Voorhees
Donald H. Vaughan (7)
W. L. Vogel
Roger Whittlesey (7)
Hayward H. Webb
William O. Waters
Frank B. Wakeman

## 2ND LIEUTENANTS

Generous C. Armstrong
Reeves B. Burke
Leo M. Cassell
John A. Cleeve
Emmett Cochran
Paul M. Clendennen (1-7)
Leon J. Cadore
Roscoe R. De Armond (7)
Joseph R. Earl
Eugene C. Ewing
Kenneth R. Elliott
Joseph S. Guppy
Stephen H. Horie (7)
Ernest H. Holden (1-7)
Perry J. Hawkins
J. B. Hendrix
Robert G. Hundley
Eugene E. Joseph
Frank D. Kent

Roger Koops
Edwin C. King (7)
William F. Leland (1-7)
Wickliffe B. Lewis
Forman B. Longshore (2)
Ernest A. McNish (1)
Edward J. Morey (7)
Herbert W. Maloney
William A. Miller
Harry S. Miner
John S. McKensie (1)
George H. Mellon (7)
Walter R. Murphy (2)
Charles R. McLain
Joseph T. Mogford
Philip J. McKee
H. S. Mohlman
James A. Noe
Elbert A. Nostrand (7)
Wayland Osgood
Oliver H. Parish (7)
Timothy A. Ryan
John Richards
Levi C. Roakes
Demus L. Reid
Charles S. Ristine
Herbert J. Slingo
Clyde C. Sims
John A. Stahl
Cecil B. Simpson
George F. Stowell (7)
Albert W. Scholles
H. J. Sargent (1-7)
John B. Tierney
Alfred Tyson
Joseph D. Thoma
George B. Thackston
John J. Tighe
Frank B. Thompson (7)
Albert F. Underwood
Mat. H. Walterman
Abner J. Wessburg
Thomas McWilliams
Basil M. Wooley (1)
Arch D. Worsham (1-7)

As a matter of record, the following
officers served as

## REGIMENTAL ADJUTANT

Capt. John H. Clark, Jr.
Capt. Arthur W. Little
Capt. Seth B. MacClinton (acting)
Capt. George F. Hinton
1st Lieut. Roger Whittlesey (acting)
1st Lieut. Harold M. Landon (acting)
Capt. Robert F. Ferguson, Jr.

(1) Killed in action. (2) Died in service. (3) Deceased since war. (4) Medal of Honor.
(5) *Légion d'Honneur*. (6) Distinguished Service Cross. (7) *Croix de Guerre.*
(8) U. S. Citation for Gallantry.

# APPENDIX A

Extract of *Instruction Upon Field* Organization

The *front* is the whole of the line of fight.

It is divided into *Secteurs*—

The *Secteur* is a zone limited in width and depth which is defended by a great unity (Army corps, Division, Brigade).

It is divided in, at least two *sous secteurs*—

The sous secteurs generally defended by a regiment is divided in *Centres de Resistance*—

The *Centre de resistance* (C.R.) is composed of several *Points d'Appui* under command of the same chief, generally a Major, the Garrison of a C.R. being generally a battalion—

The *Point d'Appui* (P.A.) which garrison is generally a company is composed of several *Groupe de Combat* under the same chief (Captain).

The *Groupe de Combat* (G.C.) is composed of a certain number of specialists (*fusil mitrailleur* (F.M.), *grenadiers-voltigeurs* (G.V.), *grenadiers* V.B. (G.R.V.B.), eventually *mitrailleurs*, fighting together under the same chief (of section or half section). The ordinary garrison of a G.C. is a section—

This scheme gives an idea of the constitution of a *secteur du front.*—

Communications on the front are ditches called *Parallèles* and *boyau* (bowels).

*Parallèle* is a ditch generally parallel to the front—

*Boyau* is a ditch generally perpendicular to the front—

*Parallèles* and *boyaux* may be used as fighting places on more or less long-length.

The part of the ditch so organized is called *tranchée*—

The part of the ditch made for circulation is called *sape*—

*Parallèls* and *boyaux* are then made of *tranchées* and *sapes*: the profile *tranchée* predominating in the *parallèles* and the profile *sape* in the *boyaux*—

The whole of the organizations occupied by the defense troops is called premier position—(first position).

A second position is established at 6 or 8 kilometers in the rear of the first one—

A defensive organization is always composed of at least two positions, but between the first and second one there may be other positions called *position intermédiaire*—

In every zone of action (in a waiting situation or in an offensive or defensive fight).

One calls parties actives the parts where are concentrated the troops, and *intervalles* the parts lesser occupied or even unoccupied. These intervals (inside a G.C.—a P.A. or a C.R.) must be surveyed and fiered at with efficiency—

An organized position is composed of several parallels from the front to the rear—

1st. The parallel of survey (if the petit postes instead of being alone are connected.

2d. The main parallel.

3d. The parallel of *doublement* (at 30 or 40 metres) behind the main line.

4th. The parallel of support (150 or 200 m behind)

5th. The parallel of the *Reduits*—

Between these two last ones there may be some intermediate, doubled by parallels of support.

The *Bretelles* (Braces) are *boyaux* organized as the parallel and cutting them obliquely so to be able to act laterally.

When digging a trench, the workmen are employed all along the out line, it is called: *travail en ligne.*

When one begins by one end, or by both, it is called *Travail par le haut*—

### Organization of a Fighting Group

The G.C. (Group de combat or fighting group) is the elementary cell in all defensive organization—

It required always an automatic arm (F.M.—fusil mitrailleur—or mitrailleuses) protected by a variable number of specialists (grenadiers, a main, grenadiers V.B., voltigeurs).

The mission of a G.C. is the one given to the automatic arm.

Each place on which are sheltered and fighting the specialists of the group is one of the element of G.C.

The automatic arm and specialists not being able to do their duty unless they are protected from the fire until the moment they have to act, *l'abri* (shelter) is the main element of a G.C. organization—.

The G.C. possesses an observatory or watchers post and all must, if possible, be connected by underground galleries.

The G.C. is near a boyau or a parallel in order to communicate with the other parts of the organization—

The principle is that the elements of a G.C. must be disposed in order to post at intervals the men by groups of specialists in the way of length and depth—

The principle of posting the men at intervals in the way of length and depth is the base of organization of a P.C. a G.C. etc.

For that reason fighting places have been established in the field for communicating, and hide the shelters, the entrances of galleries leading to the fighting places in the field, etc.

Colonel de Villiers had, very thoughtfully, prepared this paper for me, and Captain de Beaumont had translated it into English.

# APPENDIX B

GENERAL CONDUCT OF MELZICOURT CENTER OF RESISTANCE, INCLUDING

SECRET

PRINCIPLES OF PLANS OF DEFENSE.

1. This plan is somewhat complicated, owing to the fact that it is undergoing a complete reorganization. The form of organization as it existed upon our arrival at this post is represented upon the small sectional map, upon which I have marked in lead pencil "Old Plan". In greater part, this so-called Old plan is the ruling plan of today. In one or two instances, however, notably Machine Gun positions, the Old Plan has commenced to give way to the New Plan. Obviously the Battalion Commander should check up from his report of work day by day, the changes as they are effected and mark off, group by group, position by position upon the Old Plan as fast as it gives place to the corresponding position upon the New Plan, so that by a combination reading of the two maps he can instantly know which positions are actively in organization and force. Upon a typewritten sheet appended to the so-called "Old Plan" will be found the explanation of the map, showing the number of men by sections and half sections assigned to each post. Appended to this same sheaf of papers is a pen and ink analysis drawn by Lieuy Drubay, in English, showing briefly the duties of the several organizations and groups of the Battalion in connection with this old defense.

2. Upon the large map, I have marked in lead pencil in the upper left hand corner, the words "New Plan". This new plan map shows the projected new positions as described in detail in these typewritten sheets, numbered in lead pencil in the upper right hand corner consecutively 1 to 14. These sheets are written in French and I rave not had time since their receipt late last night to have them translated, but I have been over them in French and there would seem to be no difficulty in the relieving C.O. to accomplish their translation piece by piece in time to keep up with the work of reorganization as it progresses.

3. As I understand the general plan of defense of the positions under the Old Plan, it was the advanced posts of the posts upon the line of observation were to lock themselves into their posts in case of attack or raid, and stay there, putting up the best defense possible, but practically abandoning all hope of escape, either from death or from capture. In case of a raid or attack, the enemy, of course, would lay a barrage right along the line of the front observation trenches and the garrison of these trenches would be forced into the *Abris*, unless they wanted to take a chance of being killed by the shelling. The raiding party would then enter the trench, the barrage would be temporarily lifted and they would come to the door of the *Abri* and threaten the soldiers hiding therein with a grenade, unless they came out and went away as prisoners. During the delay of all this action, the scheme was for the line of resistance to become manned with the groups planned for its defense, and a counter attack organized from the reserve company made with a view to trying to keep the enemy from getting away before their barrage could drop in and cover their retreat. This was the general plan of the 131st Regiment Territorial, which we originally relieved. Lieut. Drubay of an active regiment who has been with me constantly as an assistant, told me that in the active fighting regiments, this plan of quietly waiting for death or capture was being abandoned, and that the soldiers in such a position of advanced posts were following the practice of jumping out as soon as they recognized the fact that they were going to be raided, going over the top, so to speak, in front of their own trenches, finding shelter in shell holes in front or boyaux if possible, and taking their change of letting the barrage pass over them and play upon the empty trench. When that maneuver was successful, the defending group found themselves in the position of being able to give battle to the attacking group upon equal terms as the barrage would be in front of both parties and, of course, could not be brought back for the defense of the attacking party while they were mixed up with the defending party. I pass this on as general information, but it would not be used under our new plan as outlined by Colonel Belhumeur, as you will recognize from what is to follow.

4. Colonel Belhíumeur's general plan of defense instructs us to order our Chiefs of Platoons in the line of observation, as soon as it becomes obvious that a general attack upon their position is to be made, to abandon the line of observation, locking it with wire doors as they come back and retreat as fast as possible through the boyeaux to the line of resistance. Upon arrival at the line of resistance, they will go into the line as combat groups in positions already arranged for them in connection with the plan of defense, and the entire resistance to the enemy will be made from this line of resistance, thus obviously strengthened in men by the accession of the combat groups

from the line of observation. Before leaving the line of observation, the Chiefs of Platoons should give their regular signals for Machine Gun barrage and the Battalion Commander will in turn be notified of the situation and he will, by telephone through the Regimental Commander, request regular Artillery barrage to defend the general situation. Theoretically the situation would then result in the Germans finding themselves in an undefended front line observation trench, with our Artillery playing upon them from the rear, and our Machine Guns going with crossing and flanking fire between the observation line and the line of resistance, to prevent the enemy advance upon the line of resistance.

5. This theory of defence in a case of a general attack, as described in the above, must not be confused with the plan of defense in case of a mere raid upon a small portion of the line. In the event of such a raid, the combat group should if possible move back out of danger of the barrage, into the boyeaux to the rear or to the shell holes in front, as already described, in preconcerted plan, and as soon as the barrage lifts so as to give them a free and fair fight with the enemy, they should immediately make a counter attack under the command of their officer or non-commissioned officer at that post, according to prearranged plan and drilling, and prevent if possible the enemy getting away with prisoners or advantages of any kind.

6. It must, of course, be understood that at the very first suspicion of either attack or raid, the entire battalion must be on the alert and every man sent to his post, so as to be ready. As soon as some of the important features of reorganization of the line of resistance and line of redoubt posts are made, the battalion should be drilled over and over again in having the different groups take their positions and rehearse exactly what they have to do in those positions, the non-commissioned officers and officers in charge, should be quizzed from the positions when taken, as to what their duties are to be and then having demonstrated their familiarity with their duties, they should instruct, time after time, the men of their command as to their part. As I understand the situation, the instructions contained in our Manual of Chief of Platoon calling for immediate counter attack after being driven out of a position, have now been done away with by command of General Petain. With the exception of the counter attack in the case of a raid upon a small combat group or section of combat groups, counter attacks are not to be made except by express directions through Regimental Commanders. Battalion Commander will, in the event of a fight, report promptly to Regimental Commander the progress and situation, but he will not order a counter attack until he gets orders from higher up.

7. In all of these plans of resistance, it will be seen that there are two platoons placed at the disposal of the Battalion Commander, and not disposed of regularly in any of the three lines for regular defense. The object of this is that these fresh troops without duties be held ready for instant use by the Battalion Commander for reinforcement or for protection of an especially threatened group.

8. Too much stress cannot be laid upon the importance of the signal familiarity. The meaning of rocket signals should be a matter of daily drill upon the part of combat groups and machine Gun Teams. At recent inspections made by the C.O. 1st Battalion, a number of combat groups were found, in which the men seemed to have been informed as to the use of rockets, but they were not supplied with matches. The 1st Battalion followed the plan in this connection of considering a box of matches part of the ammunition property to be turned over to the relieving group, making the non-commissioned officer of each group responsible.

9. This is in brief, the plan of defense, but the plan should be studied in detail, as appended, in the language of Lieut. Colonel Belhumeur.

## WORK

10. The work should be divided into two classes, first; work of renovation and upkeep, second; work of construction. The first class should be handled by the reserve platoon of the company covering each *Point d'Appui*, and it should consist of daily clearing up and draining of the boyeaux and trenches, repairing of treads in "Duckboards", keeping covered all products of defecation and refuse. The second class of work, that of construction, should be performed by the company in reserve, plus the details of Sappers and Bombers assigned to duty from Head-quarters Company, also the reserve platoon of the line companies which may be spared from the work of the first class.

11. Too much stress cannot be laid upon the actual need of haste in this construction work. The position as at present organized, is not a strong position and in case of a determined attack, an effective resistance could not be made. The position as projected would be a strong position, and no effort should be spared to attain the projected organization as soon as possible. This sector has been quiet so long, that it would seem as if upon the general laws of average, it might become active within a reasonably short space of time. In building or organizing these combat groups at the positions located by Colonel Belhumeur, the general specifications of the Manual of the Chief of Platoon should be followed.

## PATROLS AND AMBUSCADES

12. Colonel Belhumeur has given oral instructions that each company in *Point d'Appui* send out each night a patrol or ambuscade for purposes primarily of exercise or drill, but of course seeking such information and prisoners as may be taken without undue exposure of the men. It is doubtful if at this sector and if at this period of operations, results commensurate with the

# APPENDIX

evil effects of having prisoners taken from this command can be obtained by patrolling parties of extraordinary daring. Over ambitious young officers must therefore be controlled in connection with their undoubted instincts of personal bravery and ambition to seek personal distinction for daring service. This tour of duty of this regiment is primarily for training purposes, to help to win the War, not to win the *"Croix de Guerre"* solely. In this connection it should be noted that our patrols have demonstrated fairly well that *Pont Pardon* is usually occupied by an enemy guard at night. Our patrols have been fired upon from that situation. An important feature of patrol work is the interior patrol which Colonel Belhumeur has ordered orally for each night and each morning. The night interior patrol consists of a squad which must go through at a different hour each night boyaux and trenches of each *Point d'Appui* seeking lurking enemies. The morning interior patrol consists of two or three men and perform the same service in daylight. The reason for this interior patrol is that the enemy has recently taken advantage of the thick woods in which we are located to sneaking over at night and hiding themselves in boyeaux and trenches. The week before we arrived here, a sneaking enemy patrol of this kind walked off with two French soldiers in broad daylight.

## COMMAND OF COMBAT GROUPS

13. The French custom has been to leave combat groups in charge of non-commissioned officers and under the mere supervision of commissioned officers. The 1st Battalion established the practice of having an officer always in the front line trenches—in active command, through liaison, with all the the combat groups in that line.

## UNIFORMS AND ARMS

14. It is a general order that all officers and soldiers outside of the immediate vicinity of their own quarters must be uniformed in steel helmet and gas masque and armed with rifle or revolver according to their status.

## LIAISON

15. Liaison is, of course, of fundamental importance in order to maintain anything like team work. The Battalion Commander must have at instant hand, a runner for each of his companies, for each of his neighbors (right and left Battalion Headquarters), and for Regimental Headquarters. Where Regimental Headquarters is at a distance, as in this case, the runners should be relayed at a half way point. At the Battalion Office or bureau all night should be the Sergeant Major and the Sergeant Interpreter ready to receive and show to the Battalion Commander, at any hour, all communications. Company Commanders should carry out the same scheme of liaison with their platoon organization.

16. Telephones are not used, except in great emergency for quick action. Telephones should not be used in the English language, but in French and for any message of any military importance, telephone messages should be given in secret code numbers.

## REPORTS

17. First is the inventory of property, ammunition and supplies. This inventory is made by companies and consolidated by Battalions and signed in triplicate, executed by the Commanding Officer (incoming). One copy retained by the incoming officer, one copy left with the relieved officer and one copy transmitted to higher headquarters.

## OBSERVERS REPORT

18. At 6:00 P. M. each evening, there must be filed at French Regimental Headquarters, the Observer Sergeant's consolidated report made from the notes contained in the Observer's books during each day. It will be borne in mind that there are two observers for each company on duty through the entire daylight period and the Sergeant Observer acts as an inspector of this service, making frequent rounds and examining the books of these observers.

## TELEPHONIC REPORTS

19. At 7 o'clock in the morning, at 4 o'clock in the afternoon, and at 7:30 at night, a telephonic report from Battalion Headquarters must be made to Regimental Headquarters in code, stating briefly the situation of the quarter sector. If nothing unusual has transpired or is transpiring, "all is well," is all that is required. It must be borne in mind, however, that if anything important transpires between these hours of report, prompt advice must be given. Practically, therefore, these stated-hour reports are merely a check up of the proper working of the wire.

## WRITTEN REPORTS

20. At 8:00 o'clock each morning, there must be filed at the French Regimental Headquarters, the written report, consolidated from the Battalion of the condition of the Quarter Sector of the preceding day. The form which must be followed in this report is appended. With this morning report of condition of the preceding day must go forward also the report of patrols and ambuscades of the preceding night. As the work of consolidation is sometimes con-

# APPENDIX

siderable on these reports, it is well for company commanders to be required to have their reports in at Battalion Headquarters at least 2 hours before the time at which Battalion report is required to be made at Regimental Headquarters.

## ADVICE OF PATROL PARTIES

21. Reports in the form of advice of patrol parties must be sent by way of timely warning to neighboring battalions upon right and left, and to neighboring companies within the Battalion' own Quarter Sector, giving briefly the hours and location of patrols and ambuscades to be sent out, in order to protect these parties from the fire of our own guards in advanced posts. In turn similar warnings are received from our neighbors and such warnings must be communicatd promptly to the company commander and through them to their combat groups, who may be concerned in the conditions reported.

## GUARDS

22. Fire guards, gas guards, and aeroplane guards are needed in each headquarters, and to cover each group of *Abris*. Upon an alarm of an enemy aeroplane, all men must take cover and remain out of sight. Upon an alarm of gas, the alarm must be repeated by making all the noise possible by Klaxon horns, by beating upon empty shells hanging about on trees, and in every way, determined effort must be made to have every man awake as promptly as possible and have his masque adjusted. In case of fire alarm, of course, the usual plan of fire fighting will, so far as practicable be put into operation. Our soldiers apparently suffer from great temptation to go hunting through the woods. We have made considerable progress towards the discouragement of this practice of roaming promiscuously and firing rifles, either at marks, at birds or at wild boars. No officer has yet seen a wild boar, but every man in the regiment has seen a lot of them. The French regulations for disciplinary control in the face of the enemy, accord great discretionary powers to Commanding Officers and the Commanding Officers of the 1st Battalion have exercised these powers, for the protection of the post, and of the lives of men endangered by the recklessness of the thoughtless truants who display to the enemy observers by the most obvious signs of unmilitary deportment, the fact that green and inexperienced troops are occupying the sector.

## RATIONS

23. Our system of drawing rations has changed frequently. At present we are receiving supplies from Regimental Supply Department, each evening at 6 P.M. at No. 44. There the company details assemble and receive their proportions under direction of one of the Mess Sergeants, acting for that period each day as Battalion Mess Sergeant. All details sent out should be supplied with rations (cooked or uncooked) to cover the period of absence.

Received with above:—
"Old Plan" and Map (3 sheets)
"New Plan" and Map (15 sheets)
Inventory of Munitions (1 sheet)
Inventory of Material (1 sheet)
Key to Rocket Signals (1 sheet)
Works— (1 sheet)
Patrol Report Model (Eng. and French)
Consol. Report of Activities (Eng. and French)
Report on Observations (Eng. and French)
Secret Code No. 172
Passwords May 1 to 15

W. B. CHANDLER.

# APPENDIX C

While the contents of that pamphlet may have been familiar in 1918 it is probable no one recalls it today. For the information of my readers those contents are here fully reproduced.

We are glad, now that we see the facts with no veil of false pretense about them, to fight thus for the ultimate peace of the world and for the liberation of its peoples, the German people included; for the rights of nations, great and small, and the privilege of men everywhere to choose their way of life and of obedience. The world must be made safe for democracy. Its peace must be planted upon the tested foundation of political liberty.

We have no selfish ends to serve. We desire no conquest, no dominion. We seek no indemnities for ourselves, no material compensation for the sacrifices we shall freely make. We are but one of the champions of the rights of mankind. We shall be satisfied when those rights have been made as secure as the faith and the freedom of nations can make them.

WOODROW WILSON.

Americans all, whose fame is no more to be hemmed in by State lines than their talents and patriotism were capable of being circumscribed within the same narrow limits. . . . When my eyes shall be turned to behold for the last time the sun in heaven, may I not see him, shining on the broken and dishonored fragments of a once glorious Union; on States dissevered, discordant, belligerent; on a land rent with civil feuds, or drenched, it may be, in fraternal blood! Let their last feeble and lingering glance rather behold the gorgeous ensign of the Republic, now known and honored throughout the earth, still full high advanced in arms and trophies streaming in their original lustre, not a stripe erased or polluted, not a single star obscured, bearing for its motto no such miserable interrogatory as "What is all this worth?" nor for those other words of delusion and folly, "Liberty first and Union afterward"; but everywhere, spread all over in characters of living light, blazing on all its ample folds, as they float over the sea and over the land, and in every wind under the whole heavens, that other sentiment dear to every true American heart,—Liberty and Union now and forever, one and inseparable.

DANIEL WEBSTER.

"Reply to Hayne," January 26, 1830.

## THE AMERICAN FLAG

Thy stars have lit the welkin dome,
    And all thy hues were born in heaven.
And fixed as yonder orb divine,
    That saw thy bannered blaze unfurled,
Shall thy proud stars resplendent shine,
    The guard and glory of the world.
Forever float that standard sheet,
    Where breathes the foe but falls before us!
With Freedom's soil beneath our feet,
    And Freedom's banner streaming o'er us!

JOSEPH RODMAN DRAKE.

"Be then your counsels, as your subject, great,
A World their sphere, and time's long reign their date,
Each party-view, each private good, disclaim,
Each petty maxim, each colonial aim;
Let all Columbia's weal your views expand,
A mighty system rule a mighty land."

TIMOTHY DWIGHT, 1787.

What a history our land has had! From Eric the Red, that Norseman Viking who stepped on the shore of Greenland nearly two thousand years ago and whose fighting sons became somewhat familiar with the New England rocks, to Christopher Columbus, five hundred years later, winning through difficulties, storms, and mutinies; from the Santa Maria, the Nina and the Pinta sailing on and on into the sea of the west, to Hudson and his *Half-moon* entering, after another century, the placid bay of New York and coasting along by Jersey: from the dreamer of the North-west passage to the Pilgrim Fathers and the *Mayflower:* from Miles Standish and John Endicott and Roger Williams to George Washington, and on to Abraham Lincoln, and still on to Woodrow Wilson. It is a story of pioneering always, of ventures into the unexplored, of turning the world's eyes and mind to new things, bigger, and better.

379

# APPENDIX

Our slogan, for long, was Independence. But the note Timothy Dwight sounded a hundred and thirty years ago is being rung anew today by our great President, not Independence but Dependence. It is as true of the world as Lincoln perceived it to be of the States, it cannot exist half-free and half-slave—"whether one member suffer, all the members suffer with it." The ideas of the Central Powers, or the ideas of the Allies must become universal, for we are all dependent on each other for life, liberty, and the pursuit of happiness. The Independence Bell has rendered a good service, but it is cracked. We are now forging a new one in the furnace of Europe that will sound forth with sweeter and more pervading tones, tones that will be welcomed by the smallest and weakest of nations as well as by the great and strong, the bell of Dependence, destined to

"Ring in the valiant man and free,
The larger heart, the kindlier hand;
Ring out the darkness of the land,
Ring in the Christ that is to be."

ROBERT FREEMAN.

General Pershing's appearance in Paris at the head of American troops, July 4th of last year, had the same tremendous significance for France that General Lafayette's presence with French troops at Yorktown had for the United States at the close of the Revolutionary War. The great Republic of the West had come to France to pay a debt of long standing. With gratitude in their hearts the Parisians thronged the streets, tens of thousands of them, and cheered the marching soldiers from the land of the free and the home of the brave. Suddenly the American troops were halted beneath the shadow of a heroic statue that stands in the Tuileries Gardens. While the troops stood at attention General Pershing rode forward, draped the statue with the "Stars and Stripes," saluted, and said:—

"Lafayette, we are here!"

This dramatic incident and this speech will live in history connecting and relating the struggles for freedom of the peoples of two continents, struggles now apparently at the climax, that have lasted more than a century.

When General Sherman was making his campaign for Atlanta, Georgia, during our Civil War, General Corse was engaged in a desperate struggle at Altoona Pass, and Sherman was moving to his relief. Hoping to encourage him, Sherman signalled across the mountain tops that message that has become famous throughout the world:—

"Hold the fort, I am coming!"

When we declared war against Germany, April 6th last year, we sent the same message to France. And France, brave, bleeding France, answered in the same spirit that Corse showed in his answer to Sherman:—

"I am shot through the jaw and have lost a leg, but I can whip all hell yet!"
And France held the fort against our coming!

H. C. EVANS, Iowa.

It was only a little river, almost a brook it called the Yser. One could talk from one side to the other without raising one's voice, and the birds could fly over it with one sweep of their wings. And on the two banks there were millions of men, the one turned toward the other, eye to eye. But the distance that separated them was greater than that of the stars in the sky; it was the distance which separates right from injustice. The ocean is so vast that the sea-gulls do not dare to cross it. During seven days and seven nights the great steamships of America, going at full speed, drive through the deep waters, before the lighthouses of France come into view; but from one side to the other hearts are touching.

Essay by ODETTE GASTINEL,
Little French Schoolgirl.

"Thou, too, sail on, O Ship of State!
Sail on, O Union, strong and great!
Humanity with all its fears,
With all its hopes of future years,
Is hanging breathless on thy fate!
\*      \*      \*      \*      \*
Fear not each sudden sound and shock,
'Tis of the wave and not the rock;
'Tis but the flapping of the sail,
And not a rent made by the gale!
In spite of rock and tempest's roar,
In spite of false lights on the shore,
Sail on, nor fear to breast the sea!
Our hearts, our hopes, are all with thee,
Our hearts, our hopes, our prayers, our tears,
Our faith triumphant o'er our fears,
Are all with thee,—are all with thee."

LONGFELLOW.

# APPENDIX

## AN AMERICAN CREED

I believe in my country.

I believe in the principles of freedom upon which it is founded and in the ideals toward which it is striving.

I believe that, as my homeland, it is worthy of my love and my protection.

I believe that, since those who established it and those who have thus far upheld it, did sacrifice much for its welfare; I, too, should be willing to sacrifice greatly that it may survive among nations.

I believe that we as a nation should strive for ever to hold peaceful relationships with all the peoples of the earth and that we should, therefore, avoid all acts that savor of discourtesy, selfishness, or tyranny towards our fellowmen.

I believe that it is my duty so to live that I shall never cast the shadow of disgrace upon my country, but that my every word and deed shall reflect honor upon it and its institutions.

I believe that I should be willing to serve it in times of peace with whatever talents I may possess, and this too without expecting therefrom any profit whatsoever save that my country's gain is my personal pride and its prosperity my ardent desire.

I believe that I should be willing to serve it in times of war, because its loss is my loss and its destruction my greatest earthly misfortune.

I therefore vow that, for my country's sake, I shall endeavor to live nobly, act justly toward all men, and nations, strive to reflect its glory and righteousness in all my doings, and, if need be, sacrifice my all, even to my life, in defense of my homeland.

So help me God this vow to keep!

CARL HOLLIDAY.

## IN FLANDERS FIELDS

In Flanders fields the poppies grow
Between the crosses; row on row,
That mark our place; while in the sky
The larks, still bravely singing, fly
Unheard amid the guns,
We are the dead? Short days ago,
We lived, felt dawn, saw sunsets glow,
Loved and were loved, and now we lie
In Flanders fields.

Take up our quarrel with the foe.
To you from falling hands we throw
The torch. Be yours to bear it high.
If ye break faith with us who die,
We shall not sleep, though poppies blow
In Flanders fields.

Whether I am on the winning or losing side is not the point with me: it is being on the side where my sympathies lie that matters, and I am ready to see it through to the end. Success in life means doing that thing than which nothing else conceivable seems more noble or satisfying or remunerative.

Had I the choice I would be nowhere else in the world than where I am. Even had I the chance to be liberated, I would not take it. Do not be sorrowful then. It is the shirkers and slackers alone in this war who are to be lamented.

To me the matter of supreme importance is not to be on the winning side, but on the side where my sympathies lie. Feeling no greater dignity possible for a man than that of one who makes himself the instrument of Destiny in these tremendous moments, I naturally ranged myself on the side to which I owed the greatest obligation.

The essence of success is in rigorously obeying one's best impulses and following those paths which conscience absolutely approves and than which imagination can conceive none more desirable. Given my nature, I could not have done otherwise than I am doing now, and anything that I may do after the war is over, if I survive, will be less, too. I have always had the passion to play the biggest part within my reach and it is really in a sense the supreme success to be allowed to play this.

(From the letters of Allan Seeger, the young American poet, killed July 4, 1916, fighting with the Foreign Legion at Belloy-en-Santerre.)

# APPENDIX

## EAST AND WEST

Men look to the East for the dawning things,
   For the light of a rising sun.
But they look to the West, the crimson West,
   For the things that are done.

For out of the East they have always come—
   The cradle that saw the birth
Of all the heart-warm hopes of men,
   And all the hopes of earth.

There in the East arose a Christ,
   There in the East there gleamed
The dearest dream, the clearest dream,
   That ever a prophet dreamed.

And into the waiting West they go
   With the dream-child of the East,
And find the hopes we hoped of old
   A hundredfold increased.

For there in the East we dreamed the dream
   Of the things we hoped to do,
And here in the West, the crimson West,
   The dreams of the East come true.

---

"Oh make Thou us, through centuries long,
In peace secure, in justice strong;
Around our gift of freedom draw
The safeguards of Thy righteous law;
And, cast in some diviner mould,
Let the new cycle shame the old."

WHITTIER,
Centennial Hymn.